The New Regionalism
in Asia and the Pacific

Issues in World Politics Series

James N. Rosenau and *William C. Potter,* consulting editors

Other Publications in the Series

The New Regionalism in Asia and the Pacific

by

Norman D. Palmer
University of Pennsylvania

Lexington Books
D.C. Heath and Company/Lexington, Massachusetts/Toronto

Library of Congress Cataloging-in-Publication Data

Palmer, Norman Dunbar.
    The new regionalism in Asia and the Pacific / by Norman D. Palmer.
        p.   cm.
    Includes bibliographical references (p.   ) and index.
    ISBN 0–669–20971–6 (casebound : alk. paper).—ISBN 0–669–20972–4 (paperbound :
alk. paper)
    1. Asia—Foreign relations.   2. Pacific Area—Foreign relations.   3. Regionalism
(International organization)   I. Title.
JX1569.P35   1991
327'.095—dc20   90–13203
                                                                                 CIP

Published simultaneously in Canada
Printed in the United States of America
Casebound International Standard Book Number: 0–669–20971–6
Paperbound International Standard Book Number: 0–669–20972–4
Library of Congress Catalog Card Number: 90–13203

The paper used in this publication meets the minimum requirements of American National
Standard for Information Sciences—Permanence of Paper for Printed Library Materials, ANSI
Z39.48–1984. ∞™

Year and number of this printing:

91 92 93 94 95 8 7 6 5 4 3 2 1

Contents

Series Editors' Foreword

As world affairs become ever more complex and dynamic, so have those in the field of international studies become increasingly innovative. There is no alternative. New approaches, methods, findings, and theories are needed just to keep up with the changing foci and concerns of international relations. The Issues in World Politics series, of which this volume is but one entry, is designed for serious students who are open to rethinking basic premises and pondering new insights.

Each volume in the series addresses a major dimension, problem, or dynamic of the expanding field of international studies. Each of them is also innovative in both content and method, thereby providing an opportunity to stay abreast of the changes in world politics and the changing modes of comprehension. At the same time, the series is not intended to advance a particular theoretical, methodological, or value perspective. Rather, its unity derives from the readiness of all its contributors to think afresh and creatively about the subject domain with which they are concerned.

James N. Rosenau
William C. Potter

Preface

The proliferation and growing impact of what I have called the *new regionalism* are among the most significant aspects of the rapidly changing international scene. This new regionalism deserves greater attention and more sophisticated analysis than it has yet received, even by students and practitioners of international affairs. Unlike the "old regionalism" of the 1950s and 1960s, it is a worldwide phenomenon. It is leading to an upsurge of regional cooperation in Western Europe, the center of the old regionalism; but this upsurge, mainly evidenced by the movement of the countries of the European Community to form a single market by the end of 1992, must now be considered within the larger framework of the new possibilities for regional cooperation in all of Europe. This seemed to be out of the question in the foreseeable future before the advent of Mikhail Gorbachev in the Soviet Union and the collapse of the Communist systems in most of the countries of Eastern Europe.

Two other centers of the new regionalism are North America, especially since the conclusion of the U.S.–Canada free trade agreement (with the possibility of expansion to include Mexico in the near future) and Asia and the Pacific, with major participation by Japan, China, South Korea, and Taiwan in East Asia and the member states of the Association of Southeast Asian Nations (ASEAN), the South Asian Association for Regional Cooperation (SAARC), and the South Pacific Forum (SPF).

Although more attention is being given to Europe and North America, the development of the new regionalism in Asia and the Pacific may be of equal, if not greater, longtime significance. This is the theme and focus of the present study. It could be argued, as I do, that Asia and the Pacific provide the most exciting and most dynamic laboratory for both theoretical and practical study of the new regionalism.

International regionalism is a subject in which I have long been interested. My interest in Asia and the Pacific is also of long standing. It has grown with the unfolding course of world events and with my frequent visits, periods of residence, and personal contacts and associations in the Asia–

Pacific region. During my most recent visits to Asian countries I have been particularly impressed with the rapid development of the new regionalism in that part of the world and its great significance for both the regional and the international future.

Since I cannot adequately acknowledge my indebtedness to the many individuals, organizations, and institutions that have given me invaluable assistance in this study, I shall confine my acknowledgments to a few persons who have provided me with special guidance and/or up-to-date information on various aspects of my overall undertaking: to John McBride, Executive Officer of the International Secretariat of the Pacific Trade and Development Conference (PAFTAD), for information on PAFTAD; to R. Sean Randolph, International Director General of the Pacific Basin Economic Council (PBEC), for information on PBEC; to Mark Borthwick, Executive Director of the United States National Committee for Pacific Economic Cooperation, for information on the Pacific Economic Cooperation Conference (PECC); to S. D. Muni of the School of International Studies of the Jawaharlal Nehru University, New Delhi, a longtime friend, for information on the South Asian Association for Regional Cooperation (SAARC); to Lee Hahn-been, an internationally known Korean scholar, administrator, and political leader, for insights regarding the evolution and future prospects for Asia–Pacific regional cooperation, which he shared with me on several occasions during my two-month visit in South Korea in April–June 1989; to James N. Rosenau, coeditor of the series in which this volume appears; and to Paul O'Connell, senior editor, Lyri Merrill, production editor, Andrew Lewis, copy editor, Stephen Dragin, director of marketing, and Molly Paige, marketing manager of Lexington Books.

The new regionalism will increasingly appear on the international agenda in the 1990s—and after. So too will Asia and the Pacific, now emerging as a major world region of equal importance to any other. This major world phenomenon, and this major world region, cannot be neglected by anyone who is trying to understand the "new realities" that are shaping our changing and bewildering world.

Acknowledgments

For permission to use material from the following publications I am indebted to the following: the United Nations Institute for Training and Research (UNITAR) for the organization chart of ASEAN and the list, "ASEAN: Non-Governmental Organizations," in Jun Nishikara's *ASEAN and the United Nations System* (1983); the Regents of the University of California for Peter Drysdale's "The Proposal for an Organization for Pacific Trade and Development," *Asian Survey* 23, no. 12 (December 1983); the Pacific Trade and Development Conference for Peter Drysdale's *The Pacific Trade and Development Conference: A Brief History* (1984); the Pacific Basin Economic Council, R. Sean Randolph, International Director General for M. Mark Earle, Jr. and Eric A. Trigg's "Pacific Economic Cooperation and an Overview of the Canberra Process," PBEC Papers 1985; the Weltform Verlag for S. D. Muni's "South Asian Association for Regional Cooperation: Evolution and Prospects," *Internationales Asienforum* 18, no. 3/4 (1987); the Union of International Associations, Brussels, for a portion of table 3 in volume 2 of *Yearbook of International Organizations 1988/89* (1988); the United States National Committee for Pacific Economic Cooperation, Mark Borthwick, Executive Director for the organization chart of the Pacific Economic Cooperation Conference (PECC); and R. Sean Randolph, International Director General, Pacific Basin Economic Council for the letter to Norman D. Palmer, dtd. 25 July 1989, and the organization chart of the PBEC.

1
Regionalism in International Relations: Old and New

I n the 1950s and 1960s a great deal of attention was given to international regionalism, both in theory and in practice.[1] From the theoretical perspective these decades mark the transition from the years when champions of *federalism* on a regional or global scale flourished to an era when concepts of integration, usually on a less ambitious and more realistic level, provided the basis and incentive for productive research. From the practical perspective the period witnessed the emergence of regional networks and institutions in Western Europe that were perhaps the most far-reaching examples of regional cooperation and institutionalization that had ever been translated into working reality. They seemed to bridge the great divide between federalism and functionalism and to add important political dimensions to the newly created functional institutions.

Integration was the word commonly used to characterize the new and more successful regional experiments.[2] While it fell far short of the aspirations of the federalists and was used in so many ways that it almost lost any terminological precision, *integration* did serve as a term that, perhaps more than any other, seemed to be most appropriate for the new forms of regional institutionalization and for their conceptual and political underpinnings. These new institutions came closer than any previous forms to breaking the sacred barrier of national sovereignty; but it soon became apparent that, like less successful efforts of the past, they were primarily instruments of the nation-state system. It remains to be seen whether they will also be forerunners of a higher level of effective authority.

From the Old Regionalism to the New

By the late 1960s and 1970s nationalism seemed to experience a surprising revival; and at the same time interdependence became so pervasive that it could not be ignored. A very different fate befell regionalism. The years of theoretical and practical growth were succeeded by the "locust years" of disappointment and partial rejection.[3] This was the transition period between the old regionalism and the new.

The late 1970s and 1980s witnessed a remarkable revival of regionalism. This was characterized by a new period of growth of West European regional institutions, especially the specialized organizations that now form the European Community, still a less truly integrated community than some of the founding fathers of the member organizations envisioned. This community is moving toward its next great breakthrough when, in 1992, it becomes a single market and the largest and most powerful trading entity in the world. Its progress toward greater political as well as economic integration must now be viewed in the light of the major changes that have occurred in the Soviet Union and in Eastern and Central Europe, consequent upon the changes initiated by Mikhail Gorbachev under the rubric of *glasnost* and *perestroika*.

These changes, which began when Gorbachev came to power in 1985, led in 1989 to the collapse of communism and communist regimes throughout most of Eastern Europe and to a weakening of the communist monopoly of power in the Soviet Union. They also led to the steps toward German reunification that finally became possible with the removal of the barriers that had long divided the two Germanies (symbolized by the breaking down of the Berlin Wall on November 9). This new situation, full of hope and uncertainties, opens up the possibility of a new relationship between Eastern and Western Europe, and of new patterns of regional cooperation in Eastern as well as Western Europe and indeed on an all-European scale.

Of equal importance, the new regionalism was a more truly worldwide phenomenon. It had more linkages with both nationalism and transnationalism, and it developed in more of the world's regions than any previously organized forms of cooperation. Moreover, this new regionalism was more outward- than inward-turning and its external links seemed to strengthen it, rather than undermine its regional effectiveness. Indeed, its transregional dimensions seemed to be one of its most distinctive characteristics. In 1979 Donald Lampert observed that

> we seem to be living in a world of transregional rather than regional systems. Those regimes which . . . do meet empirical criteria for constituting meaningful regional systems are those most significant for transregional patterns of linkage and interdependence. This is not to say that the study of regional politics is unimportant, far from it. It is to suggest strongly that the ways we conceptualize the place of regions in interdependent world politics should be cast in a new light.[4]

A decade previously, when the revival of regionalism in its new and more widespread forms was less clearly perceived, Louis Cantori and Steven L. Spiegel wrote, "[B]y not considering the importance of regional international relations within regions, those scholars who are preoccupied with the state took too restricted a view, while those who concerned themselves with the international system as a whole had too broad a perspective."[5]

In the light of more recent thinking and developments, one might advance some minor qualifications to these perceptive statements. Lampert's observations could be interpreted as suggesting that transregional systems have become more important than regional. Transregional systems hardly exist in fact; but there are important transregional links, including a large number of international regimes, joining in varying degrees regional with both national and international systems. These are major dimensions of the new regionalism. On the whole, they help to make regional institutions and other forms of regional cooperative programs a more meaningful and conspicuous part of the overall international system. Obviously, however, all of the three levels of the larger system have many conflictual as well as cooperative dimensions.

Cantori and Spiegel made an important contribution during the "locust years" of regionalism by calling attention to the neglect of "regional international relations"; but their addition of the words "within regions" suggests too narrow an approach to the emerging new regionalism, which embraces linkages between as well as within regions, and with both a revived nationalism and a growing transnationalism.

It is interesting to note that all three of these central phenomena are experiencing simultaneous growth and that, while they have many contradictory and conflicting aspects, they now show more promise than ever before of developing close and cooperative overlapping associations. It can be argued that these overlappings and these interlinkages strengthen rather than weaken each of these trends, and that, on the whole, they make for greater cooperation and offer greater hope for a more organized and peaceful world order. It can be further argued that each of these phenomena is greatly influenced by the other two and that none of them dominates the others. If this argument is valid, it is particularly significant in the case of regionalism; for elevating this phenomenon to a position of virtual parity in importance and influence to nationalism and transnationalism is indeed a challenging departure. It gives added significance to Lampert's prescient reminder that "the ways we conceptualize the place of region in interdependent world politics should be cast in a new light."[6] And it underscores the implications of the statement of Cantori and Spiegel that attention to regionalism may provide the wider view that nationalism lacks and at the same time may be more realistic and practical than the more nebulous and visionary globalist perspective.

It is possible that the new regionalism may serve an even larger purpose, namely as a mediator between a nationalism that is often too virulent as well as too inward looking and a transnationalism that is often too inchoate and too impractical. This role is still an underdeveloped one. It has been suggested from time to time—as early as 1968 Joseph S. Nye, Jr., noted that regionalism has been called "a halfway house between the nation-state and a world that is not willing to become one"[7]; but it has never been given full conceptualization, and it is just beginning to receive widespread recognition.

Through a growing number of associations and institutions, ranging from highly specialized to nearly all-regional comprehensive groupings, several world regions are already functioning in this mediatory way, still quite tentatively and with limited but hopeful results. These regions are also finding that such associational links enable them to exert a greater influence in global as well as regional affairs. These points were stressed by Richard Solomon, then director of the Policy Planning Staff in the U.S. Department of State and currently assistant secretary of state for Asian and Pacific Affairs, in a remarkable address in Los Angeles in March 1988:

> More and more countries are discovering that there is a premium to be gained from cooperation rather than unilateral action. Regional and functional groupings are gaining in stature, and international organizations . . . are playing ever greater roles. And regional associations now provide vehicles for a number of countries to exercise broadened influence in global affairs. . . . These organizations . . . serve to minimize conflict among members and provide a mechanism for resolving differences. . . . In the final analysis, these efforts reflect both a high level of regional integration and perhaps an even higher degree of participation in arrangements that transcend the region. . . . [They] may also reflect an understanding in the region that the future is being cast in global terms.[8]

These observations are particularly relevant to a study of regionalism in Asia and the Pacific. The examples of the broader role and influence that Solomon singled out for special mention were two major organizations in this region, the Association for Southeast Asian Nations (ASEAN) and the South Pacific Forum (SPF).

In both the old regionalism and the new, as defined in this study, attention has been focused on the role of regional organizations—mainly on the evolution of the organizations of the European Community in the first phase and on a worldwide burgeoning of regional organizations in the second. These organizations, whether governmental or nongovernmental, comprehensive or specialized, can be political, security, economic, social, medical, technical, or professional in nature. Even in the first phase they were more numerous than is generally recognized. While they were particularly conspicuous in Western Europe, scores of them existed in other parts of the world; but the focus of attention, in theoretical studies as well as in practical development, was on the West European region. In the later phase the number of regional organizations and other formal regional associations or arrangements increased manyfold, to the extent that organized regionalism became a universal phenomenon.

It should be borne in mind, however, that regionalism embraces far more developments and trends than the formation of regional institutions. There can be extensive regionalism without comprehensive regional organizations, although fully developed regionalism is always characterized by extensive contacts and linkages within regions, and increasingly also between regions. In East Asia, for example, which has no comprehensive regional organization, regionalism is developing at a reasonably rapid rate, still without much formal institutionalization, except in certain business, professional, and technical fields.

Regionalism in East Asia is also an example of another significant trend in international regionalism, namely a tendency of nations within a given region, in many instances, to opt for participation in interregional and international associations, in addition to and sometimes in preference to associations within the region. Japan seems to be in this stage of regionalism at the present time. It has growing contacts with its less powerful neighbors in East Asia, but as a global economic power it is also developing important contacts, mostly of an economic nature with important political aspects and implications, with other regions or subregions in Asia and the Pacific, notably the ASEAN countries, and with the global economy and the international system generally.

During the period of the old regionalism, stimulated by the new types of regional organizations emerging in Western Europe, an extensive literature on regionalism, featuring conceptualization and theories, was produced. Two "high priests" of this theoretical development were Karl Deutsch and Ernst Haas. Deutsch made major contributions to the theories of political and security communities, both integrated and nonintegrated, amalgamated and nonamalgamated, and in general to theories of the process of community formation. He tested his theoretical propositions by a detailed study, often in collaboration with other scholars, of the burgeoning regionalism in Western Europe; and he developed rather novel and promising techniques of analysis, for example, the use of *transaction flows,* to study these phenomena.[9] Haas helped to bridge the conceptual gap between federalism and functionalism by elaborating the concept of *neofunctionalism,* although he later repudiated this concept along with most other concepts that were central to the development of theories of regionalism at the time.[10]

Both Deutsch and Haas emphasized the importance of the "spillover" effects of functionally based organizations such as the European Coal and Steel Community that made these organizations the basic institutions of evolving political and economic communities. In common with many others they rang the changes on the theme of integration, perhaps the most widely used term during the theoretical renaissance of the old regionalism years. Unfortunately, students of regionalism could never agree on a precise definition of the term, and instead, as has been pointed out, used it with different meanings, ranging from complete federation involving the virtual abolition of the sovereignty of the nation-state to looser forms of regional cooperation and association that fell far short of real political union.

It is interesting to note that the term *integration,* one of the main "buzz words" of the old regionalism, is much less frequently used in the era of the new regionalism, and that when it does appear it seldom if ever connotes the extreme forms of association, transcending national sovereignty, that the exponents of the old regionalism often (but not always) had in mind.

Regions and Subordinate State Systems

In this study, concerned primarily with the new regionalism, some of the terms that enriched the vocabulary of regional studies in the years of the old regionalism, such as neofunctionalism and integration, will be used sparingly. But terms such as "region," "subregion," and "regionalism" (meaning international regionalism, not regionalism within a nation-state) will be used frequently. Usage of the first two terms may not be completely consistent, for if Asia and the Pacific are collectively described as a region, as they frequently are, then generally accepted geographical regions within this larger region must be considered to be subregions. These geographical divisions of Asia and the Pacific will usually be referred to as regions, and occasionally as subregions. Asia and the Pacific, constituting a large part of the land and sea area of the world, are too vast and diverse to be defined as a single region; yet they are often so described. Perforce, this loose use of the term "region" will often be encountered in these pages, along with the term *area,* which is more accurate but even less satisfactory.

Here the term *region* will be used primarily in a geographic sense, the most common and most conventional usage—and the most understandable. It should be remembered, however, that there are other definitions of international or world regions, and that these may be more appropriate for certain purposes. "Unfortunately," as Joseph S. Nye, Jr., has reminded us, " 'region' is an ambiguous term. . . . [M]any hours were wasted at the 1945 UN Conference in San Francisco trying to define it precisely." "There are," he insists, no 'absolute' or 'nationally determined' regions. Relevant geographical boundaries vary with different purposes. . . . [A] relevant region for security may not be one for economic integration."[11]

Regions may also be described in terms of levels of analysis as an increasingly important level between the nation-state and international institutions. They are also the geographic home for a variety of political, economic, social and cultural systems.

The concept of regional systems, or subsystems, is particularly useful for political analysis. This was developed quite extensively during the early phase of regionalism, especially in the form of state systems or subsystems.[12] After the seminal article by Leonard Binder, "The Middle East as a Subordinate International System," was published in 1958,[13] a spate of articles on this concept appeared in professional journals and books. Some of the best of these developed the concept quite significantly, and almost all applied it to specific international regions. Various terms were used to apply to essentially the same type of analysis: subordinate international systems, international subsystems, partial international systems, subordinate state systems, subordinate systems, regional systems, regional subsystems, state systems, systems of nations.[14] In general, all of these terms carried the same meaning and connotation, and often they were used synonymously and interchangeably.

Some scholars regard geographical identity as only one of several essential characteristics of a region. In 1967, for example, Bruce Russett listed five characteristics of a region. In addition to "geographical proximity," he listed "social and cultural homogeneity," "shared political attitudes and behavior," "political interdependence in the form of shared institutional membership," and "economic interdependence."[15] But one could argue that if a part of the world has identifiable "geographic proximity" and discernible boundaries, usually determined by geography and/or history, it may be called a region, even if it lacks the other four characteristics. In fact, some areas, such as South Asia, that are called regions lack "social and cultural homogeneity," while the political and economic interdependence of others, such as East Asia, links the nations of a region more closely with international than with regional institutions. The latter, in fact, may be quite underdeveloped.

As the concept of subordinate state systems was further developed and applied, some scholars in the late 1960s and early 1970s gave it new dimensions by examining it from a comparative perspective. Two influential contributions to this approach were *International Relations and the International System* (Chicago: Rand McNally, 1967), by Bruce Russett, and *The International Politics of Regions* (Englewood Cliffs, N.J.: Prentice-Hall, 1970), by Louis J. Cantori and Steven L. Spiegel. Cantori and Spiegel defined a "subordinate system," to use their term, as "two or more proximate and interacting states which have some common ethnic, linguistic, cultural, social and historic bonds, and whose sense of identity is sometimes increased by the actions and attitudes of states external to the system." They developed the thesis that each subordinate system had three subdivisions: a core sector, a peripheral sector, and an intrusive system. They defined an intrusive system as "the politically significant participation of external powers in the international relations of the subordinate system."[16]

This categorization has often been employed in regional analysis. It is a useful one, but there is usually considerable disagreement over the nations that belong in the first two categories—and sometimes in the third as well. This is particularly true for the first two categories in the case of East,

Southeast, and South Asia. There would probably be rather widespread agreement that the major intrusive powers in East Asia are the United States and the Soviet Union, although the Soviet Union, an Asian as well as a European power, occupying more territory in Asia than any other nation, might be classified in the core sector, if the basis of classification is political power, or in the peripheral sector, if the basis is geography. There would probably be almost general agreement that the intrusive powers in Southeast Asia are Japan, China, the United States, and the Soviet Union, and in South Asia the Soviet Union, China, and the United States.

This analysis calls attention to the importance of external actors in regional affairs, but it does not develop as well as students of the new regionalism have the extensive regional linkages on a broader and more cooperative basis, not only within the region but also with other regions and with the international system.

One of the few scholars who stressed this theory during the waning years of the old regionalism, Professor Karl Kaiser, observed in 1968:

> A gap seems to exist between present theory of international regional integration and political reality. The theory explains, generalizes about, and predicts regional integration on the basis of processes and factors internal to the region under consideration. . . . "External factors" . . . appear relevant to internal development of regional subsystems, including integration.[17]

The relative lack of this dimension in the work of theorists of regionalism in the 1950s and 1960s was later regarded as one of the reasons for what Ernst Haas in 1975 called "the obsolescence of regional theory."

Theories of Regional Integration: Their Rise and Decline

For students as well as practitioners of regionalism in the Western world, the 1950s and 1960s were an exciting time. Regional theory—or theories—developed more real content and sophistication than most of the earlier theories applied to regions, and even than the numerous proposals and blueprints for greater international integration on a regional or global basis, such as David Mitrany's *A Working Peace System* (Chicago: Quadrangle Books, 1961), Clarence Streit's *Union Now: A Proposal for a Federal Union of the Democracies of the North Atlantic* (New York: Harper & Brothers, 1939) and *Union Now with Britain* (New York: Harper & Brothers, 1941), and Grenville Clark and Louis B. Sohn's *World Peace Through World Law* (Cambridge, Mass.: Harvard University Press, 1958).

In Western Europe regional theorists as well as farseeing statesmen found their political laboratory.[18] Large numbers of important regional organizations were established in this region. The evolving institutions of the European Community—the Coal and Steel Community, the European Economic Community, and the European Atomic Community—seemed to represent a new kind of regional development, far more promising than almost anything that had existed earlier. The community idea seemed to be a real breakthrough, both in concept and in institutional form. It represented a higher and more sophisticated level of economic organization and cooperation and, more importantly, it was infused with a broader function and had broader objectives. It was manifested in a series of basically functional institutions, mainly of an economic nature, but its basic aims and character were more political than functional. The community idea did not really break the barrier of national sovereignty, although this was the aim of many of its main founders; but its institutional manifestations probably moved closer to truly supernational dimensions than any previous organizations in history had ever done.

In the halcyon days of the 1950s and 1960s many regional theorists saw in the emerging Economic Community the fulfilment before their eyes of the theories of regionalism that they had evolved; and many European and other Western statesmen saw in the new Community a major and promising new form of regional institutionalization, even though it did not develop into the political community that many of its founders and supporters regarded as essential. In this period, therefore, both theories of regionalism and concrete regional organizations flourished in Western Europe and to a lesser extent also in the North Atlantic Community, a less organized community linking the EC countries with the United States and Canada in a variety of transatlantic ties, of which NATO and the OECD were outstanding institutional examples. Elsewhere in the world regional institutionalization and relations were far less developed.

By the mid-1970s the strong movement toward regional organizations in Western Europe seemed to be slowing down, with little prospect that its ultimate goals would be realized.[19] The combination of "the obsolescence of regional theory" and the slowing down of regional institutionalization marked the end of the period of the old regionalism. The enthusiasm of this earlier phase gave way to widespread disillusionment. This disheartening trend was thus explained by Charles A. Duffy and Werner J. Feld in their examination of the question, "Whither regional integration theory?"

> Regional integration theory evolved into a cornucopia of explanations for the development of governmental institutions which seemed to go beyond the nation-state. But, as integration activities in Europe slowed with the emergence of De Gaulle and regional organizations based upon free trade

areas or common markets in Central and Latin America and East Africa
went into eclipse, the salience of regional integration theory seemed to
decline.[20]

The extent of this alleged decline was most dramatically proclaimed by
one of the "high priests" of neofunctionalism and other regional integration
concepts and theories, Ernst Haas, in an influential monograph published in
1975. His essential thesis was indicated by the title, *The Obsolescence of
Regional Integration Theory*. "In essence," he wrote, "I argue that the familiar regional integration theories are obsolete in Western Europe and ob-
solescent—though still useful—in the rest of the world." His disillusionment
regarding the evolution of Western Europe as a political community, as
predicted by regional integration theorists, was frankly professed: "Regional
integration in Western Europe has disappointed everybody—there is no federalism, the nation-state behaves as if it were both obstinate and obsolete,
and what once appeared to be a distinctly 'supranational' style now looks
more like a huge regional bureaucratic appendage to an intergovernmental
conference in permanent session."[21]

Another of Haas's central complaints was that regional integration theories had failed to take into account, or even recognize, "new interdependence patterns transcending the region." The region, he argued, was not the
primary forum for dealing with these new patterns, which were essentially
global and not regional in nature, and which called for global theories and
solutions. "Events in the world and conceptual developments in social science have conspired to suggest that the name of the game has changed, and
that more interesting themes ought to be explored. These themes—grossly
captured in the terms *interdependence* and *systems change*—can profit from
incorporation of aspects of the theory of regional integration," which is "ripe
for reconceptualization on a global scale"; but other and more relevant theories, including a reinterpretation of federalism and nationalism, should receive priority attention and development. It is essential to recognize, declared
Haas, "that the problems to which regional unification was thought to be a
solution are not in fact regional in scope. A major mistake made in the
context of European integration studies was the downplaying of the so-called
'externalization' factors. . . . Integration theories are becoming obsolete because they are not designed to address the most pressing and important
problems of the global agenda of policy and research."[22]

Haas's book may be said to have recorded the end of the period of the
old regionalism. But after only a few years of little progress in the development of regionalism, in theory or in practice, a revival of interest in regionalism and regional theories and of progress in the development of regional
institutions became the central if generally neglected feature of a new era.
One practical reason for this revival was the demonstration that regionalism

in Western Europe is by no means obsolete, that indeed it is experiencing an unprecedented period of growth, most dramatically illustrated by a remarkable revival of the European Community and agreement among its member nations to establish a single common market by the end of 1992. Even if it proves to be a disappointment to those of its supporters who recall the larger goals and visions of the founders of the European Community movement in the early 1950s, it will still be a major "leap forward." In much of the rest of the world regionalism has not stagnated, nor have regional theories moved from obsolescence to irrelevance, as Haas predicted.

Perhaps the main reason for the disillusionment of the students of the old regionalism is that they placed too much emphasis on *integration,* in theory and practice, to the neglect of less far-reaching but more realistic regional approaches. Perhaps they expected too much. Perhaps they were too easily discouraged by the failure of their well-developed theories to mesh with the limited, but significant, progress in regional institutionalization and development. By concentrating too heavily on integration, which was interpreted in many different ways, they gave inadequate attention to the conceptualization and encouragement of other forms of regional cooperation of less intensive but more realizable nature. For this reason, as Haas noted, they did not give adequate consideration to the "externalization factor," "a major mistake" in an era of the increasing impact of external events and forces on regional development.[23] Hence in theory as well as in practice the approach of regional theorists in the years of the old regionalism was at once too ambitious—as exemplified by the excessive emphasis on integration theories—and too limited—as indicated by their relative lack of consideration of the impact of growing global interdependence.

Haas and other regional theorists came to a belated awareness of the deficiencies in their theories for understanding the changing world; but their initial reaction was more one of disillusionment and resignation than of reconceptualization and renewed analytic vigor. One of Haas's criticisms of the theorization that he and his colleagues had developed was that "a clear choice among national, European, . . . and global forms of action was never made."[24] Actually such a "clear choice" should not, and indeed could not, have been made. One of the most important characteristics of the new regionalism is that regionalism is taking on new dimensions and is becoming more important at a time when the same observation can be made about both nationalism and interdependence.

It is not necessary or even desirable to choose one of these three major trends in the contemporary international system over the others. All three are of growing importance. They all have great potential for both cooperation and conflict. Linkages among them all are increasing in strength and significance, and these linkages strengthen rather than weaken all three trends. The interpretation that regionalism has become a factor of perhaps equal importance to those of nationalism and internationalism is a major new development in the study of the international system. So too is the potential for regionalism to play a significant mediatory role between the nation-state, which is showing a new vitality instead of proving to be obsolete, as Haas and many other theorists of the old regionalism predicted, and the interdependent international system, which is still inchoate and is moving in uncertain directions.

It is becoming apparent that a significant reconceptualization of regional theory—but not primarily of regional integration theory, unless developed in a different and more precise way—is already taking place. It is probably true, however, that the era of the new regionalism has not been as rich in theory as was the period of the old regionalism. Regional integration theory is certainly a less important part of international relations theory than it was a generation ago. Many, but not all, of the major concepts and theories of the earlier period are still being discussed, but usually from different perspectives, and greater emphasis is being placed on theoretical approaches that were present but not well developed in the earlier period, such as linkage, interdependence, dependency, systems, levels of analysis (as applied to regionalism), conflict resolution theory, and even theories of nationalism, power, community, and cooperation. But the regional theorists of the new era are still at an early stage of reconceptualization, adaptation, and innovation.

Regionalism and International Regimes

Well-developed, effectively functioning regional organizations are the most conspicuous concrete evidence of a high degree of regionalism; but regionalism may be well advanced even if it has not led to the establishment of major organizational forms. It may be evidenced primarily by an extensive pattern of cooperative political, diplomatic, commercial, and professional contacts, relations, and associations. It is important, in any balanced analysis of regionalism, to include this broader pattern of regional linkages and interactions, a pattern that should not be relegated to a residual miscellaneous category, as has sometimes been done by organizational and integration theorists.

Various well-established international-relations approaches, including issue areas and levels of analysis, can be helpful in giving this larger pattern of regionalism the attention it deserves. An especially helpful approach is the concept of *international regimes,* a concept that has received increasing attention in recent years. Possibly this concept may become as important in analyzing the new regionalism as that of integration was in analyzing the old.

In their perceptive analysis of "Theories of International Regimes," published in 1987, Stephan Haggard and Beth A. Simmons observed: "The subfield of international organizations, and particularly the study of regional integration, generated rich theoretical debates during the 1960s. Yet the field remained closely tied to the study of formal organizations, missing a range of state behavior that nonetheless appeared regulated or organized in a broader sense."[25] It is this "range of state behavior"—and nonstate behavior as well—that can be encompassed and clarified by the application of international-regime theory and analysis. As Robert O. Keohane and Joseph S. Nye, Jr. have pointed out, "The concept of international regimes has proven its value, identifying important phenomena to be explained and clustering them together. It has served as a label for identifying patterns of what John Ruggie called 'institutionalized collective behavior.' "[26]

A widely accepted definition, or definitional statement, is that of Stephen D. Krasner, who defined international regimes as "sets of implicit or explicit principles, norms, rules and decision-making procedures around which actors' expectations converge in a given area of international relations."[27] A similar and earlier definition was given by Bruce Russett and Harvey Starr, when they stated that an international regime "refers to the collection of formal and informal organizations, arrangements, rules, and patterns of behavior regarding some issue."[28] Both definitions call attention to the wide range of arrangements and patterns of behavior that are embraced under the concept of international regimes; and both indicate that the focus of such regimes is usually on some issue, or *issue area*. Both implicitly assume that regimes may be formal or informal and official or unofficial in nature. Russett includes a reference to "formal and informal organizations," which raises the question of the place of organizations in international regimes. One may conclude that such regimes may include organizational forms, but that they may, and usually do, take less institutionalized forms as well that may be at once more comprehensive and less structured than formal organizations. Generally, as suggested both by Krasner and Russett, they embrace a wide variety of arrangements relating to a wide variety of issue areas.

Much of the burgeoning literature on international regimes focuses on issue areas. Large numbers of issue areas have been identified in international-relations research, and the developing subfield of international regimes has given new prominence to the issue-area approach. Donald Puchala and Raymond Hopkins believe that "a regime exists in every substantive issue-area in international relations."[29] Since issue areas are almost limitless, and since several international regimes can be identified in many—perhaps all—of the issue areas, this means that international regimes must be considered as among the most pervasive patterns in the international system. This observation is generally valid even if one accepts the view of Haggard and Simmons, instead of that of Puchala and Hopkins, that "regimes emerge in some issue-areas and not in others."[30]

Many examples of significant research on international regimes in specific issue areas could be cited. Two broad issue areas—natural resources and the environment—are the focus of an important recent study by Oran R. Young.[31] Other scholars have been concerned with a large number of more limited issue areas within these two broad categories. The study of international regimes has been given concrete shape and application in such issue areas as international trade, monetary policy, oil, commodities, aviation, oceans, shipping, outer space, nuclear nonproliferation, human rights, Third World debt, and security.

Practically all of the studies of international regimes in all of these fields, and in many others, are relevant to a study of the new regionalism in Asia and the Pacific. They call attention to the broad dimensions of the new regionalism and suggest new theoretical and conceptual approaches to this subject. They provide concrete illustrations of the value and relevance of a study of international regimes when dealing with world regions. Linkages with international regimes, organizations, and forces are important and distinctive features of the new regionalism wherever it has achieved its fullest development, in Asia and the Pacific as well as in Western Europe and North America. In fact, just as the literature on international regimes has enriched the study of the new regionalism, so has the emergence of the new regionalism provided new opportunities and incentives for the development of both new theories and concrete case studies of international regimes.

The concept of international regimes provides a comprehensive framework for analyzing the wide and variegated pattern of regional and interregional as well as international interactions and linkages that occupy the vast area between normal political, diplomatic, commercial, and professional contacts, relations, and associations and formal and comprehensive regional, interregional, and international organizations. This conceptual framework can be used to ensure that the myriad interactions and linkages in regional and international society will not be overlooked. It helps to explain why regionalism is developing to a significant degree in some parts of the world—especially in East Asia—in spite of the absence of extensive regional institutionalization, and in spite of continuing and very serious barriers of an historic, cultural, ethnic, or political nature.

As Haggard and Simmons point out, "functional theories emphasize how the facilitating role of regimes helps them realize common interests"; but they also note that "regimes are also arenas for conflict and the exercise of power," and may "institutionalize inequalities."[32] This dual aspect of the impact of international regimes is often noted in the literature. On the whole, however, such regimes generally promote cooperation more often than conflict. This is particularly noteworthy when considering the important phenomenon of growing regional cooperation in the contemporary world.

As Keohane and Nye observe, we still have too little understanding of the impact of regimes, regime change, the relationship between regimes and "domestic structures," the "conditions under which cooperation is facilitated, and why governments seek to establish, and are willing to conform to the rules of regimes." In short, "our understanding of international regimes remains rudimentary."[33]

In 1984 Friedrich Kratochwil wrote that the concept of international regimes "cries out for conceptual development."[34] A year earlier Susan Strange expressed the view that it may turn out to be "yet one more woolly concept that is a fertile source of discussion simply because people mean different things when they use it."[35] Much progress in developing and applying the concept, both methodologically and substantively, has been made since this observation was written, but there is still a great deal of doubt about the nature and utility of the international-regimes approach, and about its place and significance in contemporary international-relations research. It seems to have some promising possibilities in the analysis of the new regionalism, and for that reason it is introduced in this study; but it is not given the central place that it may deserve because of the relatively underdeveloped state of this subfield of international relations.

The New Regionalism in an Era of Revived Nationalism and Interdependence

In the era of the old regionalism, movements toward regional association and institutionalization in Western Europe had more of a theoretical underpinning than they have at present. But, as Haas and other regional theorists eventually concluded, their theories of regionalism, featuring theories of regional integration, lacked predictive and explanatory power, and were increasingly out of line with the actual course of regional cooperation. From both a theoretical and practical perspective progress in regionalism in the current era has deviated even more sharply from the truly integrative approach. But regionalism, as a concept and as a practical reality, and regional organizations have proliferated as never before. The relative importance and influence of regionalism in the contemporary international scene is much greater than at any time in the past. "Today," as U.S. Secretary of State George Shultz observed in December 1987, "regional associations . . . are fast becoming an important and effective new milieu for political and economic interactions in the world. In this new environment the importance of regional community and functional groupings has been heightened. Regional, political, and religious blocs of nations . . . now provide platforms for a number of countries to exercise influence in global affairs."[36]

This is one of the most important dimensions of the new regionalism, which gives it a more significant and a more nearly universal role in world affairs than regionalism ever enjoyed in the era of the old regionalism. Those scholars who became disillusioned with the concepts of the old regionalism agree with current theorists on at least two points that have already been noted: "the problems to which regional unification was thought to be a solution are not in fact regional in scope," and "integration theories are becoming obsolete because they were not designed to address the most pressing and important problems on the global agenda."[37]

This *fin de siècle* mood may be understood because the earlier regional theorists placed so much emphasis on regional *integration* theories and tended to downplay the importance of less far-reaching steps toward regionalism and regional cooperation, even in the evolving institutions of the European Community. By setting their theoretical sights too high they neglected many other dimensions of regionalism, well short of true integration but of cumulative impact. Moreover, these integration theorists apparently failed to perceive that even though many of the great problems facing humankind were more global than regional in nature and demanded global solutions, these problems could be adequately dealt with, if at all, only on national and regional as well as global levels.

It now seems that the new regionalism is becoming increasingly important *vis-à-vis* both the nation-state and the network of global interdependence. Nation-states lack the capacity to meet many current needs, and often they find regional organizations and associations more responsive to their interests than the larger, more remote international organizations. This is particularly true for all but the major powers, and increasingly the major powers are finding regional cooperation more practical and satisfactory than resort to international agencies, at least in early stages of collective problem-solving endeavors.

Some observers have interpreted the new regionalism as so different from the old forms that it constitutes a relatively new phenomenon. This is a dubious thesis, but it does suggest the wider dimensions and significance of contemporary regionalism. It has not moved much farther along the integration route, and has indeed generally taken other routes; but the revival of the European Community, the rise of effective comprehensive regional organizations outside of Western Europe, the emergence of "trading blocs," the development of a mediatory role for regional organizations in the area of conflict resolution, the new linkages that they have formed with national and international institutions (with a consequent strengthening of regional organizations and of collective efforts at cooperation on all three levels), and many other trends all suggest that the new regionalism is more than just a revival of the old, and that it is becoming a significant new factor in international relations.

Examples of the promising aspects and significant achievements of the new regionalism can be found in virtually all parts of the world, even in regions such as Asia and the Pacific and Africa south of the Sahara where regional cooperation in the past has been severely limited and where the obstacles to such cooperation are particularly great.

Since this study is concerned with the new regionalism in Asia and the Pacific, a subject that is developed extensively in all the subsequent chapters, a large-scale example of the growing scope and importance of regional cooperation will be cited for another major world region, Latin America. In this area, regional cooperation has often been tried, but it has often led to breakdowns and disappointment. Periods of progress in cooperation have been followed by periods of intraregional estrangement and conflict. Writing in the mid-1980s, a student of Latin American affairs found much evidence of progress in regional cooperation:

> [N]ew regional efforts at political and economic cooperation outside the framework of existing institutions raised hopes for further progress in 1987. The newly-formed Group of "Rio de Janeiro," composed of the Contadora nations (Mexico, Panama, Venezuela, and Columbia) as well as other democracies (Brazil, Argentina, Uruguay, and Peru) began a new campaign supported by the heads of the United Nations and the Organization of American States (OAS), to diffuse the Central American crisis. In December, moreover, two of the region's largest economic powers, Brazil and Argentina, signed more than twenty agreements on a series of political and economic issues; these agreements were meant to be the first steps toward a Latin American common market, which possibly would be joined by Uruguay as well. Over the long term these measures toward closer cooperation among Latin America's leading democratic nations may be the most favorable sign of the region's emerging stability, development, and cooperation— factors critical to the solution of mutual problems facing the region.[38]

Since these words were written, trends toward regional cooperation in Latin America have been less apparent. Virtually all of the nations mentioned above have experienced political instability, economic slowdown, and social tension. What is obvious but has not been sufficiently emphasized is that there are still serious obstacles to regional institutionalization and cooperation in every part of the world, including even Western Europe. A reminder by Lester H. Brown, written at about the same time as Sally Shelton–Colby's optimistic words about growing Latin American cooperation, is quite timely: "[u]nderlying tensions will set strict bounds on what any regional organizations can do with respect to political and security co-operation in the future."[39]

Aside from specialized professional, scientific, and technical associations, which number in the hundreds, the most effective forms of regional institutionalization are those that emphasize economic cooperation. The many organizations of this type that exist throughout the world usually begin by excluding consideration of political or security matters, because these matters are too divisive and controversial; but in almost every case these organizations take on political dimensions, and in many instances security dimensions as well, even if they still manage to keep political and security issues off their formal agenda.

At the very least, comprehensive regional organizations of a primarily economic nature, such as the institutions of the European Community and the Association of Southeast Asian Nations (ASEAN), provide a venue for the exchange of views and tentative understandings among top-ranking officials of member countries. Sometimes these exchanges "in the corridors" prove to be more important and productive than the formal meetings of the regional organizations.

A major distinguishing feature of the new regionalism is the emergence of great "trading blocs" in two of the three major centers of economic power in the world—Western Europe, centered on the European Community, which is moving toward the formation of a common market in 1992, and North America, especially since the free trade agreement between the United States and Canada went into effect on January 1, 1989.[40] The West European and North American "trading blocs" are already taking operational form. This is not yet the case in East Asia, where obstacles to close regional economic collaboration are particularly formidable; but the outlines of such a "trading bloc" in this region are beginning to become clear. Japan would be the diffident, suspect, but inescapable leader, but the grouping would have to be pluralistic in character, with significant roles for South Korea, Taiwan, Hong Kong, and the People's Republic of China as well.

There has been much speculation about the effect of these emerging "trading blocs" on the entire world economy and about their overall impact on the international system. Some countries and observers are apprehensive lest these blocs become too powerful and protectionist despite assurances to the contrary. Trading blocs would lead to greater prosperity in the countries directly involved, and in the world economy generally; but they could also be more discriminatory than existing economic arrangements, which are already far too exclusionist.[41] However they evolve, they will be major features of the new regionalism, with important spillover effects worldwide.

Many lesser trading blocs may also emerge in various parts of the world—for example, in Eastern Europe, if present trends in that region continue; in Latin America, where more than one trading bloc may be formed; in the southwest Pacific and Oceania; in the Indian Ocean basin; and in Scandinavia. Conceivably, if the development of *glasnost* and *perestroika* persists, the Soviet Union, itself a vast trading bloc but with limited impact on the world economy, may become more outward looking, perhaps in a new and more cooperative association with the countries of Eastern Europe, and may be more closely integrated into the world economy. There are already many evidences that the Soviet Union wishes to move in this direction, as indicated by its more cooperative attitude toward international economic institutions and a desire to join some of the most important of them—for example, the Organization for Economic Cooperation and Development (OECD), the General Agreement on Tariffs and Trade (GATT), the World Bank, the International Monetary Fund, the Asian Development Bank, and even some unofficial market-oriented regional associations such as the Pacific Economic Cooperation Conference (PECC). Whether the Soviet Union will be accepted as a fully participating member of market-oriented regional and international economic organizations is still uncertain. That it seems interested in joining such "capitalist" organizations represents a revolutionary change in its external policies and orientation.

For both theorists and practitioners the old regionalism of the 1950s, 1960s, and early 1970s focused on Western Europe. This region, which may soon become the largest and most powerful "trading bloc" in the world, will also be a major center of the new regionalism. North America, having established a free trade area and now moving toward a single market, will be a more important participant in the new regionalism than in the old. The third most important area will be Asia and the Pacific, especially East and Southeast Asia, now the most dynamic regions, or subregions, in the world. In many respects this is the most exciting area for analysis in terms of new-regionalism theory.

The following chapters will concentrate on the evolution of the new regionalism in Asia and the Pacific, applying techniques of regional and comparative analysis and emphasizing the new interrelationships among nationalism, regionalism, and internationalism in this region. This will be a case study, or series of case studies, of a worldwide phenomenon that deserves more attention than it has thus far received.

2
Asia–Pacific Regionalism: An Overview

N owhere in the world are the signs of a growing new regionalism and of the new linkages among nationalism, regionalism, and internationalism more apparent than in Asia and the Pacific. Nowhere is there a better theater for studying the enhanced role of regionalism *vis-à-vis* the other two more obvious trends. A vast area where in the past regionalism has been particularly underdeveloped is now forming, in George Shultz's words, "a web of cooperative realities."[1] This is a development of great importance in contemporary international relations.

The Region and Its Subregions

First of all, we must acknowledge a major semantic problem. Can Asia and the Pacific be accurately described as a *region*? Is it not much too vast and too diffuse geographically, racially, culturally, and in many other respects to constitute a single region? It spans one-third of the earth's land and sea surface. Within this far-flung area live more than half of the people of the entire world. How can such a vast area be called a region? The answer has to be that it is not really a region, but a series of regions; but it is frequently called a region or an area or simply Asia and the Pacific—perhaps only to avoid repetition. In this study it will be characterized in all these ways, fully acknowledging the semantic license and recognizing the risk of confusion that this entails. In fact, to add to the confusion, the major parts will be described sometimes as *regions* and sometimes as *subregions*.

This problem of definition can neither be avoided nor resolved. Where are the outer boundaries of Asia and the Pacific? Much of the Soviet Far East may be included in East Asia, but what about the other parts of Soviet Asia, which altogether comprise nearly one-half of the entire Asian land mass? Large parts of the Western, Southwestern, Central, and South Pacific are included, but where in the Pacific Ocean do the outer boundaries lie? Should the Southeastern, Eastern, and Northern Pacific also be included? And what about the countries on the other side of the Pacific Rim, in North, Central, and South America, where at least one of the major actors in Asia and the Pacific, the United States, is located? By any definition Asia and the

Pacific include many nations bordering on the Indian Ocean. Should at least part of this Ocean be included in a working definition?

The semantic problem is virtually unresolvable, even if we confine it to questions of geography. It becomes even more difficult if we attempt to define Asia and the Pacific in political, economic, or cultural terms. Glenn D. Hook may be quite right when, in a discourse on "The Asia–Pacific Region," he concludes: " 'Asia–Pacific,' while embracing the geographical span of the appellations 'Asia' and 'Pacific', is more a political than a geographic concept, with a degree of fuzziness as to the region's boundaries."[2]

For the purposes of this study, not all of Asia and the Pacific will be the object of special analysis. It will not embrace large parts of the continent of Asia, including the entire Asia Middle East (Southwest Asia) and much of western Siberia; nor will it focus on regionalism and related developments in the eastern and northern parts of the Pacific Ocean. The focus will be confined to the four major regions (or subregions, if the entire area is considered as a region) of East Asia, Southeast Asia, South Asia, and the Southwest Pacific and Oceania.

All of these regions or subregions of Asia and the Pacific are experiencing what is here described as the new regionalism, in forms and to a degree that places the area in the spotlight of worldwide attention, just as Western Europe was in the spotlight when the old regionalism seemed to be an exciting development in regional cooperation and in international relations generally. All of the regions provide unexpectedly well stocked laboratories for a study of three of the most significant trends in the contemporary world: the simultaneous upsurge of manifestations of nationalism, sometimes in extreme and virulent forms, the growing interdependence of the global economy and other dimensions of internationalism, and a new burst of regional cooperation, both outward looking and inward turning. These trends are a significant feature of the most dynamic and most rapidly changing part of the world in the latter years of the twentieth century.

We shall study the nature and role of the "web of cooperative realities" in the entire Asia–Pacific region, with special attention to the "web" that is forming in each of the four regions or subregions, among these regions and the nations that are located in them, and between these regions and the external powers that are currently involved in them in major ways.

The forms of regionalism and regional interactions are many. Among the most numerous are various patterns of economic associations, alliance systems, professional and technical organizations, and international organizations that are especially active in Asia and the Pacific or that have members outside of this area as well as within it. Very few of these regional organizations are comprehensive in geographic scope; but there are three outstanding examples of such organizations, one in each of three of the four main regions or subregions of Asia and the Pacific. These are the Association of

Southeast Asian Nations (ASEAN), the South Asian Association for Regional Cooperation (SAARC), and the South Pacific Forum (SPF). All of these regional organizations will be examined more fully in subsequent chapters. So will a developing pattern of nearly all-regional economic associations, with particular emphasis on the Pacific Economic Cooperation Conference (PECC). Some special attention will also be given to three other nearly all-regional organizations, each with important external membership and participation—the Economic and Social Commission for Asia and the Pacific (ES-CAP), a regional commission of the United Nations; the Colombo Plan, which originated in 1950 as a Commonwealth-sponsored organization and was soon expanded to include most of the nations of Asia and the Pacific, and countries in Western Europe and North America as well; and the Asian Development Bank, a major regional bank with forty-seven member countries, most of which are in Asia and the Pacific, which helps to finance programs and projects of economic cooperation and development in the developing countries of the region.

The "web of cooperative realities" is by no means exclusively organizational in nature. Much of it is formed by a growing network of bilateral ties between governments of the region, and by growing contacts among private businesses, professional groups, and individuals in various countries.

These ties and contacts receive much less attention than the work of regional organizations, but they are much more extensive and perhaps, cumulatively, much more important. Of equal importance, and even less well known, is the impact on the Asia–Pacific region of various kinds of international regimes, which exist in many—perhaps all—of the issue areas that are of special concern to the region. The concept of international regimes can serve as an integrative and analytical factor in the construction of a comprehensive framework for analyzing the multitude of associations and linkages in Asia and the Pacific, especially if these regimes are considered, as they usually are, as intervening variables.

Even today some of the countries of these regions have more trade and financial dealings outside these regions, mainly with the United States and West European countries, than they have with each other. But regional and interregional trade and other economic contacts are now expanding rapidly. In recent years Japanese trade and investment have increased at a greater rate in East and Southeast Asia than in any other part of the world. This is an important dimension of the process of Asianization that, according to Robert Scalapino, "has been under way for several decades and has not yet reached its full momentum." "By Asianization," Scalapino has explained, "I mean a widening and deepening network of ties between and among Asian states of diverse political and cultural nature. Although this process has not eliminated the importance of peripheral powers, notably the United States and the USSR, to the region, it has introduced a major new, and partly independent dimension into the scene. Whether in conflict or in concert, the Asian states are creating or recreating relations between and among themselves, both hierarchial and equal. Interdependence within Asia as well as with external parties is growing."[3]

Political Systems: The Authoritarian Tradition

In Asia and the Pacific there are some unifying patterns, such as the Confucian tradition in most of East Asia and much of Southeast Asia, the bonds of Buddhism in its various manifestations in East and Southeast Asia, Sri Lanka, Nepal, and to a lesser extent in India, ethnic and other common ties among the peoples of Oceania, the experience and impact of many decades of foreign domination and control throughout most of the region, and certain common values and attitudes toward life; but there are also vast differences among the peoples, countries, and subregions.

In the past, the political systems of the nations in the area being considered were no less diverse than they are today, but in general they represented various forms of authoritarianism, both indigenous and imposed by foreign rulers. Old-fashioned territorial imperialism and control have largely disappeared, although their impact is still evident. Some of the current political patterns reflect the influence of what is often called *neocolonialism*, which can be political, economic, and/or cultural in nature. Certainly the authoritarian tradition persists.

More than three-fifths of the thirty-six countries in Asia and the Pacific, and all but five of the nations of East, Southeast, and South Asia, are rated as either partly free or not free in the 1990 version of the well-known—and much disputed—"Comparative Survey of Freedom," published by Freedom House in New York. The only countries in these three regions or subregions that are rated as free are Japan, South Korea, India, Thailand, and the Philippines, and of these all but Japan are at the lower end of the scale for free countries. In all of Asia and the Pacific only five of the thirty-six countries of the region—Australia, Japan, New Zealand, and the tiny Pacific Island nations of the Solomon Islands and Tuvalu—are given the highest rating on the freedom scale.[4]

These ratings are further reminders that authoritarianism is still the dominant political pattern in the entire region, and that more than traces of it can be found even in countries that are rated as free. Obviously the region is no stronghold of democracy, however this term is defined.

The Asia–Pacific region, therefore, is characterized not only by the relative absence of regionalism in the past, except as imposed and directed by foreign colonial powers, but also by a long and continuing tradition of authoritarianism, perhaps more marked in social, cultural, and religious fields than in political. This gives a different, and, one would assume, a more difficult dimension to the study of regionalism than in the Western world.

The Context of Asia–Pacific Regionalism

In analyzing the changing scene in Asia and the Pacific, one is struck with the many evidences, in most of the countries of the area, of a revival of nationalism in both constructive and destructive forms, while at the same time, as Scalapino pointed out, "interdependence within Asia as well as with external parties is growing."[5] While the nations of the area are becoming more involved in the world economy and in the international system generally, they are also experiencing a sharp upsurge of nationalism. This takes many forms, some helpful to nation building and to the achievement of a new and larger role and widespread recognition and a new international status, others of a disruptive and often more violent nature, which, to be sure, may be inescapable. But the Asia–Pacific countries are also, in Richard Solomon's words, "the pace-setters of a new internationalism that is reshaping our lives and the world order of the twenty-first century." In support of this statement Solomon called attention to the "economic dynamism" of the area, especially in East Asia, with Japan in the lead, the "popular pressures for more open politics," as illustrated in different ways in South Korea and China, and "the transition from a Pacific divided by the communist–capitalist confrontation into an era of diffusion of power among many nations." "The economic and political transformation of the Pacific countries," in Solomon's view, "has led to a unique outward-looking regionalism" that raises problems of linking the region to the global system.[6]

This transformation suggests one of the central questions regarding the new regionalism in Asia and the Pacific: Will it indeed prove to be a constructive "outward-looking regionalism" linked to the global system, as Solomon predicts, or an inward-turning regionalism, increasingly concerned with protectionism, political and cultural as well as economic, and with more extreme nationalist trends?

Most of the regionalism in Asia and the Pacific that is developing today may be characterized as examples of the new regionalism. It has emerged mostly since the late 1960s. It has brought into being the first comprehensive regional arrangements in the area, of which ASEAN, SAARC, and the South Pacific Forum are the leading official, institutionalized examples. It has developed wider interregional and even global connections and linkages. And it has made regionalism for the first time a factor equal in significance to the strong nationalistic behavior and outlook, on the one hand, and the growing global interdependence, on the other. It has given regionalism a new and more important place in the nationalism—regionalism—internationalism spectrum.

There had been, to be sure, numerous examples of the old regionalism in Asia and the Pacific. Some, like the Colombo Plan and the Economic Commission for Asia and the Far East (ECAFE, later renamed ESCAP), had members in all of the Asian regions and were quite comprehensive in scope, although their main work was in economic and social cooperation and development. Others, such as the Eastern Regional Organization for Public Administration (EROPA) and the Asian Association of Management Organizations (AAMO), were professional or business associations and therefore of a more limited nature. Two, the Southeast Asian Treaty Organization (SEATO) and the Asian and Pacific Council (ASPAC), were primarily security arrangements. Almost all of these had strong external participation. The Colombo Plan was initiated at a Commonwealth conference in the capital of Ceylon in 1950. ECAFE (now ESCAP) was a regional commission of the United Nations. EROPA and many other regional technical and professional associations relied heavily on foreign expertise.

SEATO, founded in 1954, was mainly the brainchild of John Foster Dulles, then U.S. secretary of state. He considered it especially important because it extended the American system of alliances against the Soviet Union to another vulnerable part of the Soviet—Chinese periphery. It was focused on Southeast Asia, as its name implies, but only two nations in this region, Thailand and the Philippines, and only one other Asian state, Pakistan, were members. ASCAP had an exclusively East Asia—Southeast Asia membership, with South Korea as the chief sponsor and Japan as the rather reluctant leading member; but it had a very short life, and it ceased to have much *raison d'etre* after the beginning of the change in relations between the United States and the People's Republic of China in the early 1970s.

The reasons for the generally abortive, limited, and in some cases externally initiated efforts at regional cooperation in Asia and the Pacific during the period of the old regionalism are quite clear. In fact, the surprise is not that such efforts were so limited in the past, but that they have proliferated so impressively in recent years. They have become, to an unprecedented degree, and for the first time in the Asia—Pacific region, an extensive "web of cooperative realities," to borrow again the description of former U.S. Secretary of State George Shultz.

One should not, however, exaggerate the nature, extent, or significance of the new regionalism in Asia and the Pacific. Like the old regionalism, the new and more extensive form is handicapped by the same obstacles that stood in the way of effective regional cooperation in former years. These include such obvious factors as the lack of any real sense of regional identity or of experience in regional cooperation. The peoples of substantial parts of the Asia—Pacific area have had minimal contacts with each other. They have been separated by great psychological as well as geographic distances. There are vast differences in cultures, religions, and ways of life, in levels of economic and political development, and in political and social systems.

During the long years of foreign domination, regionalism of a sort was instituted by Western colonial rulers, but this was obviously an externally imposed and superficial pattern. Even today regionalism is handicapped by the continued dependence of most of the nations of the entire Asia–Pacific area more on external than on regional sources of support, especially in economic and to a lesser extent in political and security fields.

Some of these obstacles are not as serious as they once were. Moreover, some major changes in both the global and regional environment have made real regional cooperation at many levels both more possible and more advantageous.

Externally, three of the major changes that have provided new opportunities and incentives for Asia–Pacific regionalism are growing interdependence, the technological revolutions that have brought the entire world into closer and more immediate and continuous touch than in any previous era, and the new, less contentious, and less dangerous relationships that are being forged between the United States and the Soviet Union and between the Soviet Union and China.

Interregionally, liberating and encouraging trends have increased. More extensive relations have been established among most of the nations of the entire Asia–Pacific area, to a limited extent including even North Korea and the Communist states of Indochina. A major stimulus has been the economic dynamism and progress of many of the nations of the region, especially of Japan and the "four little tigers" or "four little dragons" of Asia, South Korea, Taiwan, Hong Kong, and Singapore, often described as the newly industrializing countries (NICs) or, more accurately, as the newly industrializing economies (NIEs). These trends account in large part for the emergence of the Asia–Pacific area, and especially the subregions of East and Southeast Asia, as a major laboratory for studying the impact and significance of the worldwide phenomenon of the simultaneous upsurge of nationalism, regionalism, and internationalism.

The Changing Economic, Political, and Security Environment

At present the overall situation in Asia and the Pacific is quite fluid, with trends in both promising and alarming directions. It is especially difficult to predict how the new regionalism will develop in such a changing environment. On the whole the security environment seems to be more favorable than it has been for many years. The general relaxation of tensions between the United States and the Soviet Union, the increasing attention to economic issues in international relations, and the relative deemphasis of security issues have helped to create a better security environment throughout the world.

In Asia and the Pacific the security environment has improved because of these important changes in the world situation, and also because of important changes within the region, some of which are a partial consequence of the developments in the global situation. Among these have been the rapprochement between the Soviet Union and China, the improved climate resulting from the withdrawal of Soviet troops from Afghanistan and of Vietnamese forces from Cambodia. Another important development is the beginning of trade and other contacts between political entities that had refused to deal with each other in any peaceful way in the past, such as the Republic of China on Taiwan and the People's Republic of China, South Korea and both China and the Soviet Union, Japan and North Korea, and even to a limited extent North and South Korea and Vietnam and some ASEAN countries. More broadly, the apparent lessening of security threats in all of the Asia–Pacific region and the virtual breakdown of the once great divide between Communist and non-Communist states in East and Southeast Asia have created a fundamentally different and less threatening security environment in virtually the entire Asia–Pacific region.

The economic environment is in some respects even more favorable and more conducive to intra- and interregional cooperation and expanding economic contacts. The Asia–Pacific region, with Japan and the NICs leading the way, has become the most economically dynamic region in the world, with rates of growth higher than those of any other region. These growth rates are beginning to slow down, but they are still, relatively, quite high. All the countries that have achieved such an economic breakthrough have followed export-oriented and, with some limitations, free-market rather than ultra-restrictive policies. Inevitably this has meant that they have had to enlarge their contacts and outlook as well as their markets, and they have had to learn how to operate on regional and global levels.

Even the political environment has generally improved, especially because of growing regional and international political cooperation, the growing contacts between Communist and non-Communist countries and, as has been noted, between political entities that have long refused to deal in any cooperative way with each other.

But while the overall environment in Asia and the Pacific—strategic, economic, and even political—is unusually favorable, as compared with previous years, the improvement is a relative one, and old suspicions and animosities remain. Moreover, the apparent improvement in the overall environment is constantly in jeopardy because of continuing adverse developments and continuing evidence of underlying political instability in many of the countries of the region. Only the Southwest Pacific and Oceania would seem to be an exception to this generalization, and even this region is by no means free of problems. This is attested by the recent tensions in Fiji and New Caledonia, continuing problems of economic survival, and tensions with outside powers (e.g., with France on nuclear testing and colonial issues and between the United States and New Zealand over nuclear policies and alliance relationships). One is reminded almost daily by reports from China, South Korea, the Philippines, Vietnam, Burma, and elsewhere how fragile the existing political situation is in so many of the countries of Asia and the Pacific, and how uncertain the future political prospects really are. Certain quite alarming scenarios cannot be completely ruled out, although they are less likely than they seemed to be not long ago. "Detente II" between the United States and the Soviet Union could prove to be only a temporary lull in the "cold war." The end of the thirty-year rift between the PRC and the USSR may be followed either by a joint effort to exert dominance in East and Southeast Asia or by further tensions between the two communist giants. Either the Soviet or Chinese version of *glasnost* and *perestroika* may be succeeded by reversion to a harsher form of authoritarianism in either country or in both (as has already happened, at least temporarily, in China). The promised reductions in nuclear and conventional forces in Asia and elsewhere by the two superpowers may not be carried out in good faith. Soviet relations with Japan may remain stalemated and strained. The two Koreas may revert to their longstanding position of mutual hostility. The Cambodian question may not be resolved and any successor regime, especially if it includes the Khmer Rouge, may be more brutal than the existing regime. The gulf between Vietnam and the ASEAN countries may continue. If some or all of these dire possibilities (and many more that could be added) come to pass, the whole strategic environment in Asia and the Pacific—and elsewhere—will take a marked turn for the worse.

The economic environment, which in recent years has made possible the spectacular economic growth of many of the Asia–Pacific nations, especially in East and Southeast Asia, could also worsen. Economic progress in the region is being threatened by rising labor costs, by political and social unrest, by currency appreciation, by increasing competition among countries of the region and between these countries and other countries and trading blocs, by strong trends toward protectionism, especially in the United States, by unfair trading practices in almost every country in the world, and by increasing trade frictions and disputes that are making the professed dedication to open markets and free trade almost a mockery in actual practice. There is a real danger, in short, that the economic systems that existed during the years of the economic "miracle" in the Asia–Pacific region will break down under the impact of all of these adverse trends.

The developing new regionalism will obviously be affected by any major changes, for better or for worse, in the overall strategic, economic, and political environments; but if it develops along present lines, remains outward oriented, and gradually proves its worth as a mediatory force between nationalism and internationalism, it should be able to exert a positive influence in promoting regional and international cooperation as well as political stability and further democratization (along lines consistent with local conditions and needs), in the countries of the Asia–Pacific region.

Organizing the Asia–Pacific "Community": A Spate of Proposals

There have been all kinds of proposals for comprehensive cooperation and institutionalization in the Asia–Pacific area. Perhaps the best known are the Soviet demarche for "a system of collective security in Asia" and the "Pacific Community" idea. Others that are somewhat more specific and that have often been proposed are for Asia–Pacific organizations patterned after the Organization for Economic Cooperation and Development, the European Community (especially the European Economic Community), or the North Atlantic Treaty Organization.

The Soviet proposal, first advanced by Leonid Brezhnev in 1969 and often repeated, with some variation in detail and in degree of enthusiasm, since that time, received lip-service endorsement from a few Asian leaders, but was opposed by most, either publicly or by studied silence. No specific guidelines for creating "a system of collective security in Asia" were ever advanced by the Soviets. It was widely interpreted as one of the more ingenious elements of the Soviet "propaganda offensive" in Asia, the Soviet attempt to enlist Asian support against China at the height of the tensions caused by the Sino–Soviet split. In all probability the Soviets will not try to revive this proposal in any significant way, especially since they have now ended their rift with the other Communist giant.

The concept of a "Pacific Community" has been an underlying theme of many statements and proposals by official spokesmen of several Asian–Pacific countries, of many studies and proposals by academic scholars, especially Japanese, and of a large number of conferences and seminars in many countries of the region, and beyond. In the 1970s, in particular, there was much discussion of this theme, especially after it had been endorsed and expounded by some top Japanese leaders. But while it was an appealing theme for official speeches and conferences, it was too nebulous and subject to too many interpretations to provide the basis for concrete progress toward the avowed objective. In a sense, to be sure, a "Pacific Community" was being formed by the growing interactions among the countries of Asia and the Pacific; but in another and more realistic sense, the countries of the region were by no means ready to move immediately to take the steps necessary to create a real "community" or to give it institutional form. The concept of a "Pacific Community" was too vague, and in some respects too misleading. The Asia–Pacific region was far from becoming a real community, except in a symbolic sense.

There was, moreover, a great deal of uncertainty regarding the nature and membership of the proposed community. Who would be eligible for membership, and who would determine the criteria for admission? Would the Soviet Union, the People's Republic of China, and the smaller communist states of the Western Pacific be eligible? Would the community be mainly a "rich man's club," dominated by the United States and Japan, or would it be a genuinely participatory venture? What kind of institutionalization would be required? What would be its main objectives and focus?

The idea of a Pacific Community received little real support from most of the Communist countries of Asia and strong opposition from the Soviet Union, which mounted a powerful and continuous propaganda barrage against it. The Soviets alleged that the proposal was a thinly disguised scheme of Japan and the United States to link other Pacific Basin countries with them. Some of the Soviet spokesmen, however, took the line that the concept of Pacific Community was a good one, but that for a real community to develop in Asia and the Pacific a very different approach and a very different orientation were needed, and that no such community could be formed without Soviet participation and support.

Clearly, if only in a symbolic and aspirational sense, a "Pacific Community" is emerging; but a real "Pacific Community" is a long-term objective, not an immediate goal. Current emphasis is on more specific approaches, well short of real Asia–Pacific community, but for the first time offering a realistic prospect that concrete progress toward more coordinated Asia–Pacific cooperation can be made. The term "Pacific Community" is still current, but for various reasons terms such as "Asia–Pacific cooperation," or "Asia–Pacific economic cooperation", are more frequently employed.

Proposals for an Asian OECD are more specific than those for a Pacific Community, but they are even less adaptable to the current Asian scene. OECD came into existence as the long-term successor to the Organization for European Economic Cooperation (OEEC), which represented the European recipients of Marshall Plan aid from the United States. Its twenty-four member states are located mostly in Western Europe, but the United States, Canada, Japan, Australia, and New Zealand are also members. Thus there is already a kind of OECD extension into the Asia–Pacific area. But there is little prospect that a similar organization could be set up and function effectively in the Asia–Pacific, where most of the states are far less developed economically than most of the OECD countries and where there is no established pattern for the kind of sophisticated economic, financial, and developmental cooperation that OECD provides.

Prospects for the establishment of an Asia–Pacific Economic Community, along the lines of the European Economic Community, are equally remote. The EEC, the major institution of the overall European Community, is a highly organized entity that evolved very slowly after the first burst of enthusiasm following its creation. The conditions that account for its progress do not, by and large, exist in any of the regions of Asia and the Pacific, and certainly not in the area as a whole. Moreover, the conditions that prevented the EEC from developing more rapidly and in a more integrated, autonomous fashion abound in the Asia–Pacific area.

Even more farfetched is the proposal for an Asia–Pacific NATO. The experience with SEATO, a far less organized and effective security arrangement than NATO, should serve as a reminder that Asian countries are not interested in establishing a NATO-type institution in their region, and indeed would be apprehensive if such an institution was created. Including countries in an alliance relationship that are opposed to multilateral security arrangements, that do not share the same threat perceptions, and that are primarily concerned with internal security and with security against each other would be a novel but foredoomed experiment.

As the countries of Asia and the Pacific move toward greater regional cooperation, they can learn many lessons from a close examination of the experience in other regions, especially Western Europe. OECD, EEC, and NATO certainly merit special study, but they should not be regarded as prototypes. Regionalism in Asia and the Pacific evolved slowly and hesitantly for a quarter century or more after World War II, and then experienced a kind of takeoff. What is needed are approaches and organizations suitable for the special conditions and needs of the region and farsighted and influential leaders of regional cooperation movements, such as those Western Europe had in the early days of the European Community movement. Fortunately, a few such leaders have already emerged on the Asia–Pacific scene, and more will doubtless appear as the pressures of interdependence force nations to become increasingly involved in cooperation at regional and international levels.

Existing Regional Organizations: A Classification

In a comprehensive survey of regional organizations in Asia and the Pacific, Walt W. Rostow observed: "At first sight, the effective regional organization of Asia seems to be more absurd than inevitable."[7] This may be true of regionalism on an all–Asia–Pacific scale, but it does not apply to prospects for regional cooperation in any of the regions or subregions of the area. In fact, comprehensive regional organizations have already emerged in three of the four major subregions, and in all of the four a plethora of more specialized organizations, official and unofficial, exist. These organizations may be classified into three main categories: (1) all-regional organizations, (2) subregional comprehensive regional organizations, and (3) technical and professional regional organizations.

All-regional Organizations

While no comprehensive regional organization for the entire Asia–Pacific area has been formed, a few organizations based in the area extend their scope and activities throughout the region. The leading examples are the Economic and Social Council for Asia and the Pacific (ESCAP), a regional commission of the United Nations with headquarters in Bangkok, and the Colombo Plan, based in the capital of Sri Lanka, a Commonwealth-inspired organization which has extended its membership throughout the area and beyond. The Asian Development Bank, with headquarters in Manila, may also be listed here, although it has a more specific mandate than ESCAP or the Colombo Plan.

Several important private regional organizations for Asia–Pacific regional economic cooperation (with strong official links) are gradually extending their membership throughout all the subregions of Asia and the Pacific. Outstanding examples are the Pacific Basin Economic Council (PBEC), established in 1967 by leading businessmen from Japan, the United States, Canada, and New Zealand, and since expanded to include members from other Asia–Pacific countries; the Pacific Trade and Development Conference (PAFTAD), formed in 1969, "an informal private academic group of economists from various countries in the region"[8] (the core group representing Australia, Canada, ASEAN, and the United States); and especially the Pacific Economic Cooperation Conference, an expanding organization with national committees in every member country, including the People's Republic of China. The Soviet Union sent an observers' group to the annual PECC conference in 1986, held in Vancouver, and is seeking membership in the organization.

The admission of a major Communist country, China, and the possible admission of the Soviet Union, give PECC a truly all-regional flavor, and help to span the communist–non-communist divide, a division that has blocked all previous private efforts at comprehensive Asia–Pacific economic cooperation. It remains to be seen, however, whether even in the age of *glasnost* and *perestroika*, China and the Soviet Union will be willing or able to accommodate their policies to the market orientation of the PECC, or whether they will be cooperative or obstructionist members.

Possibly PBEC, PAFTAD, and PECC should be listed under a separate category of private organizations for Pacific economic cooperation. This is a category that is expanding in numbers and is becoming increasingly influential. Their essentially private nature is both a handicap and an advantage. Inevitably they must work to some extent with governments, and they lack the prestige and influence that governments enjoy.

A study of the membership of some of the national committees of PECC (even the Soviet Union has formed one, although it has not yet been admitted to full membership) shows the none-too-surprising fact that some of the member organizations and agencies on these committees have a distinct official or semiofficial status, the only kinds that are possible on the Chinese and Soviet committees. Academic scholars and officials (presumably in a private capacity) as well as businessmen regularly attend annual conferences of PECC. But PECC is essentially a private regional organization. It can take initiatives that governments, more cautious and more politically accountable institutions, may hesitate to undertake, or even strongly endorse.

It should be noted that all of these designated all-regional organizations, official and unofficial, have extra-regional dimensions. They either have members from outside the region (very influential members) or, in the case of ESCAP, are externally sponsored. They are listed as essentially Asia–Pacific organizations because all of them operate almost exclusively in the region.

Subregional Comprehensive Regional Organizations

The three most important comprehensive subregional organizations in Asia and the Pacific are to be found in Southeast Asia, South Asia, and the Southwest Pacific and Oceania. They are the Association of Southeast Asian Nations (ASEAN), the South Asia Association for Regional Cooperation (SAARC), and the South Pacific Forum (SPF). In many respects these are by far the most important regional organizations that exist anywhere in Asia and the Pacific; and ASEAN may perhaps be described as the most important truly regional, or subregional, organization that now exists anywhere in the world. All of these organizations will be discussed in some detail in subsequent chapters.

Technical and Professional Regional Organizations

There are scores of these organizations, in a wide variety of fields and specializations. Examples are the All-Asia Bar Association, the Asia–Pacific Broadcasting Union, the Asian Environmental Society, the Asian Oceanic Postal Union, the Asian Productivity Organization, the Asian–Pacific Parliamentarians Union, the Centre on Integral Rural Development for Asia and the Pacific, the Eastern Regional Organization for Public Administration, the Federation of Asian Womens' Associations, the Pacific Asia Trade Organization, the Pacific Science Association, the Pan-Pacific Community Association, and Asian associations (usually called confederations) in several popular sports.[9] All of these organizations or associations operate on an all-Asia–Pacific basis, although their focus may be on one of the four subregions. There are even larger numbers of associations, especially of a private nature, that have members in only one subregion, or at most two. Case studies of these all-regional and subregional associations would reveal the larger scope and dimensions of the new regionalism that is developing in Asia and the Pacific.

Other Regional Relationships

To this classification of regional organizations in Asia and the Pacific should be added other very different forms of regional relationships. One is the possible emergence of an East Asian, or perhaps an East–Southeast Asian economic group, or trading bloc, dominated by Japan and its powerful currency, the yen. There has been much speculation about this possibility in recent years. If it develops, it would be a significant new regional grouping, one that would at once make East Asia and Japan even more formidable international actors, and that at the same time would arouse serious apprehensions among virtually all of the other East and Southeast Asian states, including those that would be associated with this new grouping. This would be a development of great importance in the international economy. Its nature is indicated in an arresting article by John Yemma in the *Christian Science Monitor* in January 1989:

> [A]s global ideological competition wanes, a new phenomenon is arising: the trade bloc. North America, Western Europe, and East Asia are coalescing into regional zones, one dominated by the dollar, another by the mark, a third by the yen. These blocs promise more efficient markets within them, but they are already showing signs of conflict.[10]

After noting that the U.S.–Canada free trade agreement took effect on January 1, 1989, and that the twelve nations of the European Community are moving rapidly toward the creation of a single market in 1992, Yemma continued:

> As usual, the most dynamic performance continues to be in East Asia. Although a formal trade zone along the lines of the EC or U.S.–Canada is not yet developing in the eastern *[sic]* Pacific, the groundwork is being laid. The Japanese economy has shifted from strictly export orientation to domestic demand. Japan is absorbing more and more of the exports from South Korea, Taiwan, Hong Kong, Singapore, Malaysia, and China. The yen is becoming the dominant currency of the East Asian zone. But how much farther to go is an open question.[11]

Japan is the major source of foreign investment in South Korea, Indonesia, and Thailand, and is the second major source in China, Taiwan, the Philippines, and Malaysia. Its direct investments in Asia are now second only to its investments in the United States. Its trade with other Asian countries is growing rapidly, with a considerable surplus in its favor.

Whether such a bloc will develop by the inexorable pressures of economic forces, centering around Japan and the yen, remains to be seen. Certainly many foreign observers, such as Yemma, and many Asians see such a trend.

A larger Asian regional market would have some advantages, especially in competition with the single markets already established in North America and at a late stage of development in Western Europe. But many view this whole trend with great suspicion. Leaders of some East and Southeast Asian countries fear its political as well as economic consequences. A strong expression of doubt about Japan's real intentions was voiced by a Chinese writer in the *Beijing Review* in early 1989:

> Japan is now gung-ho about extending its force in the Asia–Pacific region through investments and trade. This is an attempt to form a so-called East Asian economic ring led by Japan. The circle is supposed to encompass Hong Kong, Taiwan, Singapore, South Korea and the members of the Association of Southeast Asian Nations (ASEAN). . . . Japan aims gradually to set up and lead an East Asian economic circle in preparation for further conquests in Australia, New Zealand and Latin America.[12]

Other forms of regionalism and regional relationships exist that involve the association of certain Asia–Pacific countries with extra-regional nations, organizations, and movements and that occasion a considerable amount of cooperation, and also of conflict, at national, regional, and international levels. Three conspicuous examples will be cited.

A leading example is the pattern of alliances and alliance systems that involve Asian–Pacific countries with external powers. Most of these are bilateral, such as the alliances of the United States with Japan, South Korea, the Philippines, and Thailand and of the Soviet Union with North Korea, Vietnam, and Mongolia. A few are multilateral, such as ANZUS (Australia, New Zealand, and the United States), now moribund because of the dispute between New Zealand and the United States over port visits by U.S. warships carrying nuclear weapons, and the Five Power Defense Pact among Australia, New Zealand, England, Malaysia and Singapore. Charges are often made that, instead of providing the nations of the region with security shields, these alliances heighten rather than lessen tensions in Asia and the Pacific and may involve the weaker Asia–Pacific members in superpower conflicts in or outside the Asia–Pacific region.

All of these alliances are still in place, in various stages of effectiveness and acceptance. Some others, of course, notably SEATO and the bilateral alliance between the United States and Taiwan, are now defunct.

There are no functioning military alliances with only Asia–Pacific members. Issues with security dimensions or implications are often brought up at meetings of Asia–Pacific organizations or by those leaders attending high-level meetings of these organizations, in informal meetings with each other, but these organizations are in no sense military alliances. The experience of ASEAN, SAARC, and to a lesser degree the South Pacific Forum, the three most important comprehensive regional organizations in Asia and the Pacific, has indicated that security issues cannot be avoided, although they can be kept off the formal agenda.

A second example is provided by the now-formalized *post-ministerial* meetings between the foreign ministers of the ASEAN countries, after their regular annual meetings, and their counterparts from their "dialogue partners," the countries with which ASEAN has the closest economic relations, namely Japan, the United States, Canada, Australia, New Zealand, and the European Community (one high official representing all twelve EC member states). This unique arrangement, described in some detail in chapter 4, has become perhaps the main regular forum for exchanging views on a wide variety of regional and global issues and areas of cooperation between the member countries of the most important regional organizations in Asia and the Pacific and the leading non-communist countries most deeply involved in Asia–Pacific affairs. It is an arrangement that is worthy of special study by all students of the new regionalism and indeed of international affairs generally. It may serve as a model for similar arrangements by other Asia–Pacific regional organizations, and also by regional groupings in other parts of the world. In fact, the practice has already been adopted by the South Pacific Forum, which engaged in its first post-ministerial meeting with major powers with special involvement in the Southwest Pacific and Oceania after its annual meeting in 1989.

A third example is the participation of Asia–Pacific nations in a large number of international regimes, many of which are based on agreements and linkages that are less institutionalized than regional organizations. In these regimes, which have both regional and international dimensions, the Asia–Pacific states are active and important participants. This applies to international regimes in such fields or issue areas as trade, monetary policy, oceans, and the environment.

Another general and comprehensive example of regional cooperation has to do with the increasingly consensual role that Asia–Pacific formal and informal groupings are playing in the large number of international organizations of which many, and sometimes most, of the states of the region are members and in the larger number of international conferences and other international programs and activities in which many of the countries of the region participate. Twenty-seven of the thirty-six nations in Asia and the Pacific (as defined in this study) are members of the United Nations. They are a central core of the Asia–Africa caucusing group in the UN, which often presents a fairly united front on many of the issues with which the UN, and especially its General Assembly, is concerned. Sixteen of the thirty-six member states are members of the Commonwealth of Nations, and their representatives often operate as a functioning pressure group at Commonwealth meetings. The same observation may be made of Asia–Pacific activity and behavior in the nonaligned movement, to which sixteen Asia–Pacific nations, including all of the South Asian states and six of the ten Southeast Asian states belong; in the General Agreement on Tariffs and Trade (GATT), with representatives of the states of the region taking a fairly united stand in opposition to some proposals advanced by the United States and other developed countries for broadening the scope of GATT regulations during the so-called Uruguay Round of negotiations; in the United Nations Conference on Trade and Development (UNCTAD), where these representatives generally present a united front in support of further concessions to less developed countries; and in a number of other international organizations and agencies.

Representatives of the Asia–Pacific countries often make collective approaches in areas of mutual interest and concern in the specialized agencies of the United Nations, notably the World Bank, the International Monetary Fund, the Food and Agriculture Organization, the World Health Organization, and the United Nations Educational, Scientific, and Cultural Organization. They usually operate with similar unity in the Economic and Social Council, the United Nations Childrens Fund, the United Nations Development Program, the United Nations Environmental Program, and many other organs, agencies, commissions, and programs in the United Nations system.

One of the most effective operations of any regional organization in the world was mounted by ASEAN countries in their concerted action, through this organization, on the Cambodian/Kampuchea issue. ASEAN representatives took the leading role in securing the repeated condemnation by members of the UN General Assembly of the Vietnamese occupation of Kampuchea and the Heng Samrin regime in Phnom Penh and continued recognition of the refugee resistance coalition—the so-called Kampuchean Democratic Coalition—as the legitimate incumbent of the Cambodia/Kampuchea seat in the UN General Assembly. In this effort ASEAN showed a remarkable degree of cohesion and effectiveness.

This is a role that the South Pacific Forum is also following, in a more limited way and on more limited issues, such as its continuing efforts to mobilize international support for the cessation of nuclear weapons testing and nuclear waste dumping by nuclear powers in the South Pacific and the successful efforts of the Forum in pressurizing the United States to conclude a more acceptable fisheries treaty with some of the Pacific island states. SAARC is also beginning to act on behalf of its members in international organizations and forums in pressing certain issues on which there is clear regional agreement. This a practice that the European Community has been following for some time but that is just beginning to become a common practice for the more recent and less integrated comprehensive regional organizations that have emerged in the Asia–Pacific area.

By working cooperatively through regional organizations, smaller and weaker nations can exert an influence on and play a role in international forums that would be impossible for these nations acting unilaterally. This is an important dimension of the new regionalism, and it seems to be developing among some Asia–Pacific countries. As Richard H. Solomon pointed out in an address before the Pacific Future Conference in Los Angeles in March 1988, "regional associations now provide vehicles for a number of countries to exercise broadened influence in global affairs. ASEAN and the South Pacific Forum are examples of this trend."[13] ASEAN, in fact, "is rapidly establishing itself as the focal point of interaction between Southeast Asia and the external world."[14]

Here we have concrete illustrations of the growing importance in this era of new regionalism of regional organizations as significant intermediary agencies between nation-states and international organizations, thus helping to some extent to provide a bridge of cooperation between the conflicting trends toward a revived nationalism and a growing and often bewilderingly complex internationalism.

All-Regional Institutionalization: Recent Initiatives

In the last three decades the question of organizing the "Pacific Community" through the establishment of an official all-regional organization has been much discussed—so far with only limited results. At first the proposals were nebulous, centering on the theme of developing a greater regional consciousness. There was widespread disagreement about the nature or even existence of the so-called "Pacific Community," and considerable resistance to any proposals to institutionalize it. This resistance was most evident in the Soviet Union, which branded the whole "Pacific Community" idea a thinly disguised effort by Japan and the United States to extend and institutionalize their imperialist condominium in the Asia–Pacific and in the ASEAN countries, which were apprehensive of the impact of larger all-regional institutionalization dominated by the major powers upon their own organization.

The opposition—or at least major resistance—of the Soviet Union and the ASEAN countries to an all-regional Asia–Pacific official organization has ebbed, but not completely disappeared, in recent years. The Soviet Union is now trying to develop a more positive and cooperative approach to all Asia–Pacific countries and has expressed an interest in joining a number of comprehensive Asia–Pacific organizations, such as the Asian Development Bank and the PECC. The ASEAN countries are still wary of involvement in an all-regional organization, but their growing confidence is reflected in their willingness to participate in deliberations leading to this objective. The United States also seems to be giving more positive support to this movement, although, unlike Japan, it is not willing to take the initiative. On the whole, it would probably be wise for both of the economic powerhouses of the Asia–Pacific area, Japan and the United States, to leave the initiative to smaller nations and to support any initiatives that they regard as moving in the right direction.

Two all-regional proposals were advanced in early 1989, one by a prominent American senator, the other by the prime minister of Australia. Both attracted widespread attention, the latter much more than the former.

On April 13, 1989, Senator Alan Cranston, chairman of the Subcommittee on Asian and Pacific Affairs of the Foreign Relations Committee of the United States Senate, introduced a bill in the Senate calling for the creation of a Pacific Basin Forum to deal with such issues as free trade and economic development. About two weeks before he introduced his bill, Senator Cranston had made the same proposal in an address at the annual meeting of the United States Committee of PBEC. "Washington," he declared, "should take the lead in establishing a Pacific Basin Forum to pursue cooperation on regional economic and security concerns. This initiative should include annual summit-level meetings styled after those by key NATO presidents and prime ministers. These meetings are part of the ongoing dialogue that has helped to keep the peace in Europe for over forty years. In similar fashion, the Pacific Basin Forum would convene high-level meetings to discuss such issues as the Korean DMZ, the Taiwan Straits, and the Chinese–Mongolian Border, among many others."[15]

In this address Senator Cranston chose to emphasize security issues. His bill gave more attention to economic and developmental issues. But it is quite obvious that he envisions a Pacific Basin Forum that would deal with economic, security, and many other issues and that its annual meetings would normally be held at the highest level and would give the leaders of the Pacific Basin countries a forum for the consideration of a wide gamut of issues and problems without restrictions on the topics that could be discussed.

In his approach to the matter of cooperation in Asia and the Pacific, Senator Cranston was far ahead of his own government. Until 1989 the U.S. government seemed to be lagging behind other countries in advancing and supporting proposals for an all-Asia–Pacific official institution. In public pronouncements, leading spokesmen of the Reagan administration often expressed approval of the general idea without doing much to advance it. Secretary of State George Shultz referred to it occasionally in public addresses. His successor, James Baker, has given the idea more active and concrete support. The *Wall Street Journal* of 27 June 1989 gave some details regarding "a secret initiative Mr. Baker mounted last year, when he was Treasury secretary during the Reagan administration. At that time, he was attempting to put together an economic coordinating body covering the U.S., Japan, and the four newly industrializing countries of Asia: South Korea, Taiwan, Hong Kong, and Singapore. But the effort foundered on the diplomatic difficulties of treating Hong Kong and Taiwan as full-fledged nations because China regards both as part of its territory."[16]

Mr. Baker's public endorsement of an all-Asia–Pacific regional organization, focused primarily on economic cooperation, was first brought to general attention in a widely publicized address to the Asia Society in New York on 26 June 1989. "Last year," he pointed out,

> intra-Asian trade approached $200 billion, reflecting the rapid pace of Pacific rim economic integration. Yet unlike Europe, there are inadequate regional mechanisms to deal with the effects of interdependence. Many distinguished statesmen and influential organizations have suggested ways to fill the gap. . . . All their suggestions share the objective of improving economic cooperation and offering a regional forum to discuss a range of common problems.
>
> Clearly, the need for a new mechanism for multilateral cooperation among the nations of the Pacific rim is an idea whose time has come. Our involvement in the creation of this new institution will signal our full and ongoing engagement in the region. . . .
>
> The United States will not offer a definitive blueprint. We will be looking instead for consensus, drawing on the best elements from various plans. . . . If a consensus can be reached, we would support the Prime Minister's [referring to the proposal of Prime Minister Robert Hawke of Australia] call for a ministerial meeting this fall as a first step toward developing such a new Pacific institution.[17]

In January 1989, in a meeting in Seoul with President Roh Tae Woo of South Korea, Mr. Hawke proposed the establishment of some structured form of regional economic cooperation on the governmental level. In April Hawke's special envoy, Richard Woolcott, visited nine countries—all the ASEAN countries, South Korea, Japan, and New Zealand—to solicit their cooperation in setting up an Asia–Pacific economic organization. In May Mr. Woolcott also visited the United States, Canada, and China to explore the possibility of securing their agreement to join the proposed new organization. Australia, and possibly South Korea, might be the sponsors (Woolcott used the term "catalysts"). They would be more generally acceptable in this role than the economic giants of the Asia–Pacific region, Japan and the United States.[18]

After this sounding out of opinion in major Asia–Pacific states, and after the leaders of the ASEAN countries had agreed to attend an "exploratory" meeting to discuss the Australian prime minister's proposal, the government of Australia invited twelve countries to send high-level representatives to a conference in Canberra in early November 1989 to consider Mr. Hawke's all-regional proposal and its possible implementation. The twelve countries were the six ASEAN nations, Japan, South Korea, Australia, New Zealand, Canada, and the United States. Mr. Hawke had originally suggested that the founding members of his proposed organization be limited to East and Southeast Asia and the Southwest Pacific, thus excluding Canada and the United States; but Mr. Woolcott on his travels soon discovered that most of the countries he visited, except Thailand and Malaysia, favored the inclusion of the United States and Canada, "largely to avoid the perception that this was the beginning of a closed bloc."[19]

All of the states invited to the Canberra conference accepted the invitation. It was, in the words of Daniel Sneider, a staff writer of the *Christian Science Monitor,* "a moment rich in historical portent." The conference, formally called the Asia–Pacific Economic Cooperation Conference, was "the first Cabinet-level meeting of virtually all the major free market economies of the Pacific Rim." Mr. Sneider gave a concise summary of differing evaluations and differing attitudes toward the new venture:

> For some, it marks the emergence of the Pacific century, the shift of the economic and political center of gravity in the world from Europe and the Atlantic to Asia and the Pacific.
>
> For others, the gathering is a sign of growing economic rivalry, of rising protectionism, and the division of the world into warring economic blocs in Europe, Asia, and the Americas.
>
> And there are those who dismiss the possibility of this new grouping as an impossible dream, trying to wed nations separated by the vast distances of the Pacific Ocean and by widely diverse cultures.[20]

The ASEAN representatives at the conference made it plain that they considered the meeting an "exploratory" one, not involving any further commitment on their part. Obviously Prime Minister Hawke and some of the other sponsors had larger goals in mind. The group was so diverse that the best that could be hoped for was slow progress in mutually agreed-upon directions. The conference participants discussed the possible shape of the proposed new all-regional organization, its membership, and the follow-up steps that should be taken. They agreed to meet annually, at least in the initial stages. At a preliminary meeting in September the ASEAN representatives had offered to host the second meeting, sometime in 1990, and South Korea's representatives made a similar offer for the third. The conference agenda also covered "several other major items, including global trade liberalization and regional cooperation on issues such as investment, technology transfer, human resource development, and environmental protection"[21]—all of which had often been considered at other Asia–Pacific forums of a less comprehensive nature.

It is still too early to tell whether the 1989 APEC conference will prove to be the "historical portent" that Mr. Sneider envisioned; but it may well be what he called the "beginning" of "what is sure to be a long and difficult path toward creating a new force in the world."[22] Even if the momentum continues, it will be some time before this promising initiative will lead to the establishment of an all-Asia–Pacific economic organization of an official nature—a goal that has eluded all previous efforts.

A Concluding Note

Trends toward regional economic cooperation could be a phase of the larger trends toward greater globalization and interdependence. "In a world now tightly knit and interdependent," observed Ruth Leger Sivard, "only the development of positive links between countries and concerted international action can ensure the common security. Today's world calls for a new global vision, one less diverted by military fantasies and more attuned to the realities of human needs."[23]

The new regionalism could contribute to this "new global vision" and could help to translate this vision into concrete reality. Dr. Young Seek Choue, chancellor of Kyung Hee University in Seoul, a renowned internationalist, sees the possibility of "Regional Common Societies (RCS)" becoming "integrated and developed into a Global Cooperation Society (GCS)," and this GCS in turn into a "Global Common Society."[24] If such an evolution does indeed take place, the many trends toward greater interaction and cooperation in the Asia–Pacific region, in spite of all handicaps and difficulties, will contribute to a happier and more peaceful world order.

3
Regionalism in East Asia

I n terms of political, economic, and military power East Asia is clearly the most important of the four subregions of Asia and the Pacific. It is the economic powerhouse of the entire Asia–Pacific and one of the three economic powerhouses of the world. It is the homeland of a quarter of the human race, mainly due to China's immense population. The dominant economic power is obviously Japan, but three of the rapidly growing newly industrialized economies (NIEs) of Asia—South Korea, Taiwan, and Hong Kong—are also located in this region. It is heavily militarized, especially if Soviet troops along the Sino–Soviet border and elsewhere in the Soviet Far East, U.S. and Soviet naval forces in the Western Pacific, and the U.S. troops in Japan and South Korea are added to the formidable forces of China (the world's second largest), North and South Korea, Taiwan, and the smaller but highly developed Self Defense Forces of Japan.

Limited Regionalism in the Past

In the past, for reasons of history, cultural diversity, foreign control, and geographic distance and isolation, very little real regionalism ever existed in the entire East Asian area. Much that did develop was imposed by foreign conquerors, including Western colonial powers in recent centuries, lasting up to the end of World War II, or by powerful regional dynasties, notably those of China and Japan, over centuries past.

In a recent work entitled *New Tides in the Pacific: Pacific Basin Cooperation and the Big Four (Japan, PRC, USA, USSR)*, Professors Roy Kim and Hilary Conroy refer to the heritage of three East Asian regional systems: the Confucian system, "perhaps the most successful regional system on the Pacific," which, in cultural terms at least, extended over most of East Asia, much of Southeast Asia, and in more limited ways even beyond; the "Open Door Policy," a policy of foreign economic and political pressure on China that, as Kim and Conroy admit, was "not so much a system as a balancing act," and that was a relatively recent feature of the much more extensive pattern of direct and indirect foreign control over most of the Asia–Pacific region, excluding Japan and Russian Asia, over a period of many decades; and Japan's more recent "Greater East Asia Co-Prosperity Sphere," which in the 1930s and early 1940s provided a thin facade for Japan's ruthless expansionism in China, and which would have been the framework for Japan's longtime control over East and Southeast Asia and the Western Pacific if the Japanese had been victorious in World War II.[1]

But while all three of these "East Asia regional systems" are important legacies of the past, they were obviously examples of imposed regionalism. Examples of this type of regionalism still exist, in more limited and modified forms, in other parts of the world.

These are not the kinds of regionalism that are now developing in most of the world, including the Asia–Pacific region. They are not good examples of genuine regional cooperation, nor are they the focus of studies by students of international regionalism. They provide some basis for investigation and some warnings for those who are concerned with voluntary and cooperative regionalism and with the interrelationships among nationalism, regionalism, and internationalism in the latter years of the twentieth century, as a prelude to whatever other political and economic patterns may emerge in the twenty-first.

In the period of the "old regionalism" one interregional organization was formed among countries of East and Southeast Asia and the Western Pacific, largely at the initiative of an East Asian country, South Korea. This was the Asia and Pacific Council (ASPAC), formed in June 1966 at a conference at the Walker Hill resort, outside of Seoul, by representatives of nine states—Australia, Japan, Malaysia, Nationalist China, New Zealand, the Philippines, South Korea, South Vietnam, and Thailand (Laos sent an observer). Its affairs were handled by a standing committee in Bangkok, and its policies were determined at an annual meeting at the ministerial level.[2] "It was agreed that the new organization would give primary attention to the promotion of economic cooperation, and would be nonmilitary, nonideological, and not anticommunist. This might, it was hoped, provide a sufficiently flexible framework for enlisting the eventual cooperation, and perhaps the membership, of other Asian states."[3]

It was obvious that ASPAC was formed for political and security as well as economic reasons. It also had less obvious but important implications for regionalism in Asia and the Pacific. For its main founder, South Korea, as Walt W. Rostow noted, ASPAC, it was hoped, would help "to define South Korea as a part of the Asian and Pacific community quite apart from its special security link to the United States."[4] The security concerns of ASPAC were clearly reflected in a statement in the joint communiqué at the founding meeting in 1966, in which the representatives of the nine founding member states expressed their "determination to preserve their integrity and sovereignty in the face of external threats."[5]

ASPAC never realized the hopes of its founders. Only South Korea, in fact, showed much enthusiasm for the organization. It was strongly denounced by the Soviet Union and its Asian allies. It had a short life. After the change in the U.S. position regarding the People's Republic of China in 1971 and 1972, the Japanese recognition of the PRC in 1972, and the declining fortunes of the South Vietnamese regime and the U.S. military operations in Vietnam, the presence of the Republic of China on Taiwan and of South Vietnam among its members became a source of weakness—and of embarrassment—for ASPAC, and some member states withdrew. It was officially ended in 1973.

Prior to World War II much of the region was under foreign influence or control, including the spheres of interest of Western powers in China, the Japanese rule in Korea and Formosa, and the Greater Co-Prosperity Sphere of Japan. Although virtually the entire region had long shared, in varying degrees, the common traditions and orientation of Confucianism and the Sinic culture, with Buddhism as another unifying force, much of the region was largely isolated from external contacts of any kind, except through the Western colonial powers. The two major states of the region, China and Japan, for various and differing reasons, had little contact with each other, and what contact there was was largely imposed by the Japanese, especially in the years preceding and during World War II. After the war Japan was a defeated and occupied nation—indeed, not really a nation at all until 1952—and China was devastated by the long war with Japan and rent by the civil strife between Nationalists and Communists. The Communists assumed control in October 1949 under the strong leadership of Mao Tse-tung (Mao Zedung) and proclaimed the People's Republic of China. This new regime was a disturbing factor in East Asia and beyond.

After Japan reemerged as a sovereign state, it devoted most of its efforts to internal reconstruction and export-oriented policies, most of its major trading partners being outside the region. The Nationalist regime on Taiwan managed to assume control over the island where its mainland supporters had taken refuge and to develop a booming economy; but its status as an independent nation was increasingly dubious after many of the countries that had recognized it, including Japan and the United States, withdrew recognition while maintaining contacts and recognized the Communist regime on the mainland as the legitimate government of China. South Korea, established as an independent nation in 1948, managed to survive partition and, with the assistance of United Nations forces, mostly American, a bloody war of resistance to North Korea's efforts to reunify the entire peninsula under its rule. In spite of heavy defense burdens and concerns and a series of authoritarian leaders, South Korea finally achieved an extraordinary rate of economic growth.

By the late 1970s and 1980s China had passed through the years of estrangement from the Soviet Union, limited regional and international contacts, and the excesses of the Cultural Revolution to a more stable political system and some hope of success in its "four modernizations" efforts, which required more export-oriented, less dogmatic policies, more contacts with other states of the region and elsewhere, and more participation in the international economy. Recent developments, however, have raised doubts about its political and economic stability and about its future course, both at home and abroad. Will China be the "rolling cannon" on the East Asian deck, or will its leaders learn to rule without continued reversion to brutal repression and how to function as a cooperative member of the regional and world community?

By the late 1970s and 1980s the stage finally seemed set for greater contacts and cooperation among the states of East Asia, between these states and those of other subregions of Asia and the Pacific, and with the international community. In an improved strategic, economic, and political environment the countries of East Asia began to develop a "web of cooperative realities," to borrow again the words of former U.S. Secretary of State Shultz, within the region and beyond. At the same time nationalism and demands for national self-reliance became stronger in virtually every nation in the region.

This heightened nationalism seemed to be a barrier to growing association with other nations; but it also provided new incentives for economic development, which was only possible by following export-oriented economic policies and developing other contacts in the region and elsewhere in the world. Hence, in spite of the nationalist revival, a new regionalism began to emerge where an old regionalism had hardly existed.

The general patterns of this new regionalism in East Asia are already beginning to be clear. It is developing rapidly, in spite of the countervailing trends in the direction of national self-reliance and of increasing global involvement. It is manifest especially in increasing and usually indirect contacts between governments that do not recognize each other—for example, China and Taiwan, South Korea and China, Japan and North Korea—in more extensive contacts, both direct and indirect, between influential groups in the societies of the East Asian states—members of opposition parties, businessmen, academics, journalists, et. al.—in wider participation from virtually all the countries of the region in professional conferences and associations of a regional nature, in increasing trade within the region, and, in general, in a growing sense of regional consciousness, mutual interests, and identity.

There are increasing interactions, primarily economic but also political and cultural, among the nations of East Asia. These interactions have led to more extensive and more cooperative relationships, especially since Japan has become more active in the region, as it has in Southeast Asia and other parts of Asia and the Pacific and to an increasing degree on a global scale, and since the People's Republic of China, in the decade 1978–88, began to play a larger and more cooperative role in East and Southeast Asia (a trend at least temporarily reversed by the traumatic events in the PRC in 1989). Increasingly these interactions are bridging the once seemingly unbridgable gap between East Asia's Communist and non-Communist states. This is illustrated by many of the new departures in East Asian regional cooperation—departures that would have seemed almost inconceivable not so long ago. Examples are the growing economic and political contacts between Japan and the PRC, the Soviet Union, and North Korea, and between South Korea and China, the Soviet Union, Vietnam, and even, to a lesser degree, with North Korea.

All of this adds up to an impressive "web of cooperative realities," far more extensive than ever before. But it is a web that is in the early stages of development, one that could be easily disrupted or even destroyed by adverse trends in the region.

Thus far, the growing contacts within the East Asia subregion have been mainly bilateral; but they provide the basis for a series of multilateral relationships as well. In fact, such contacts are essential building blocks for the new regionalism, which requires the breakdown or at least the bypassing of many deep-rooted divisions and attitudes and the development of variegated patterns of multilateral as well as bilateral relationships and organizations.

In each of the other three subregions of Asia and the Pacific the trends toward the new regionalism, in spite of many strong countertrends and counterforces, have led to the establishment of a comprehensive regional organization, which in each case has developed greater support and has served wider purposes than was originally envisioned by its critics. No such organization has come into being in East Asia, nor is there much likelihood that one will emerge in the foreseeable future. The reasons can be found in historical experience and longstanding suspicions and rivalries.

Japan is clearly the economic giant of the region, but China and the East Asian NICs are developing greater economic strength and would be wary of entering into too close association with Japan, for political and psychological as well as economic reasons. A Japan-dominated regional organization would probably be unacceptable, and a China-dominated one even more so. China and the NICs are not yet sufficiently strong to cooperate—or compete—on equal terms with Japan in any possible regional organization. Some sharing of power and responsibilities would have to be agreed upon before an overall regional organization could be established.

Instead of a full-fledged regional organization, comparable to ASEAN, what may be emerging in East Asia, as Professor Bernard Gordon perceives, is "an East Asian structure of multiple nations, with no one of these unilaterally capable or likely to achieve hegemony."[6] Professor Gordon believes that such an "East Asian structure" is now assured. He may be correct in this belief, but, in view of the rapidly changing scene in East Asia, his confidence may prove to be premature. In the meantime, to use Robert Scalapino's words, East Asian regionalism will continue to be a "soft regionalism . . . because it lacks a formal structure."[7]

But even a "soft regionalism" can be quite extensive and significant. This is preeminently the case in East Asia, where there are innumerable kinds of bilateral and multilateral associations, mostly without a high degree of institutionalization. Some are associations that link East Asia with other regions of Asia and the Pacific, especially Southeast Asia. Even more link East Asia with international regimes, in a wide variety of issue areas.

The Growing Web of Regional Interactions

In spite of the increasing interactions, now to some extent even bridging the Communist–non-Communist divide, East Asia seems to be no closer to real institutionalization on an all-regional scale than it was before the web of regional interactions became so extensive and before intraregional relations became more cooperative and less confrontational. But an increasing web of interactions, especially of a more cooperative nature, indicates an increasing degree of real regionalism, even in the absence of comprehensive institutionalization.

In the institutional sense the East Asian countries seem to have developed formal relations more successfully and more extensively with countries in other parts of the Asia–Pacific region, notably in Southeast Asia, with regional organizations outside of East Asia, notably ASEAN, and with a wide variety of international organizations, from the United Nations and its family of organs, agencies, commissions, etc. to more specialized international organizations. East Asian countries also have extraregional links with nongovernmental as well as governmental organizations, both on an all-regional scale, such as the Pacific Economic Cooperation Conference (PECC), and on a global scale, including a large number of international professional associations.

Japan, of course, is a full participant in several prestigious international associations to which it has been admitted by virtue of its position as a major global economic power. Outstanding examples on the official level are its participation in the Organization for Economic Cooperation and Development (OECD) and in the annual economic summits, and on the unofficial level the participation of many of its most distinguished citizens (including many who at one time held high official positions) in the Trilateral Commission, an unofficial organization of great influence that consists of distinguished citizens of all three of the centers of economic power in the world—Western Europe, North America, and Japan.[8]

Because of its status as the most highly developed nation in all of the Asia–Pacific region, its special ties with other highly developed countries through such organizations as OECD and the Trilateral Commission, and its growing international connections and aspirations, Japan is sometimes referred to as a "Western" state. Apparently many influential Japanese regard this characterization as a compliment, a recognition of their country as a global power. Some top Japanese leaders, notably former Prime Minister Yasuhiro Nakasone, and a number of highly publicized government-sponsored reports, notably the Maekawa Report of 1986, have described Japan as an "international state";[9] but other Japanese, especially those belonging to opposition parties or to highly nationalistic groups, and many people in other countries of East Asia are more critical of the concept of Japan as either a "Western" or an "international" state. In any event, this trend in official Japanese policy and outlook is another reminder that Japan is becoming more active in interregional and international affairs, while at the same time, like virtually all of the other East Asian states, it is becoming more nationalistic and more assertive. And it is by no means neglecting another of its main goals, namely to play a leading role in the promotion of regional ties and associations.

More and more, in this period of nationalistic resurgence and self-assertion, Japan, in common with its neighbors in East Asia, is fostering the notion that the countries of the region themselves, acting with as much constructive cooperation as possible, should determine the nature and pace of East Asian regionalism. And in this scenario Japan obviously believes that it can, and should, take a—perhaps *the*—leading role, a belief that most other nations of the region view with mixed acceptance and apprehension. Memories of Japan's past stand in the way of full acceptance of contemporary Japan as the leader of East Asian regionalism, while a recognition of Japan's great power and special status suggests the inevitability that Japan will play such a leading role and the dire consequences to them if the region's economic giant refuses to accept such a role or even opposes effective regional institutionalization.

China has been an uncertain factor in the East Asian regional picture. As long as the region was sharply divided between Communist and non-Communist states any all-regional cooperation and institutionalization was obviously impossible. When the ideological divide in the region became less serious and when the main ideological and political rivals on the world stage entered into the era often referred to as "Detente II," opportunities for really significant regionalism in East Asia seemed to open up, although many other conditions had to change before these opportunities could be realized.

After the death of Mao Zedong, the end of the Cultural Revolution, and the rise to power of leaders who deliberately embarked on new directions in both domestic and foreign policy, the PRC, for the first time on a major scale, showed an interest and desire to cooperate with non-Communist states in East Asia and beyond. The new directions led to a greater degree of openness and restructuring—Chinese versions of *glasnost* and *perestroika*—and to growing interactions with virtually all other Asian states, notably Japan, and even South Korea (without the establishment of formal diplomatic relations or a withdrawal of support from North Korea). This new orientation changed the whole environment in East Asia and opened up new prospects for effective regional cooperation.

These prospects were greatly dampened in 1989, when student-led demonstrations and demands for changes in political leadership, an end to growing abuses, including large-scale corruption, and the granting of further democratization were answered, after weeks of turmoil and uncertainty, by the massacres in Tiananmen Square and elsewhere and by the ruthless pursuit and severe punishment of leaders of the protest movement. Until and unless a new leadership takes over in China and reverses the trend backward to the old patterns of authoritarian control and repression, China will again be a great barrier to regional cooperation and peace in East Asia.

The sudden reversal in China of what appeared to be a new, more promising, and more cooperative course has cast a pall over the entire East Asian scene. In such a climate regional cooperation will be more difficult than ever.

It is impossible to conceive of real regional cooperation in East Asia without the positive participation of both Japan and China, the major indigenous powers. Much will depend on the nature of the relations between them, which in the short period since the end of World War II have undergone such remarkable changes. Regional peace and cooperation would be jeopardized if these states either allowed their rivalry for political, economic, and military power and influence in the region to dominate their relationship or entered into too close collaboration to exert a kind of joint condominium of power. Recent developments in both China and Japan—especially in China—have raised fresh doubts about the capacity or willingness of either power to assume roles of constructive leadership and cooperation in East Asia; but from a broader perspective it should be noted that Japan has shown a greater interest and has been playing a larger role in regional, interregional, and international associations, and that China, for a decade before the tragic events of 1989, had been showing similar encouraging signs of becoming a more cooperative member of the Asian and world community.

Even if the two major indigenous powers of East Asia could reach a consensus on joint initiatives, a comprehensive East Asian regional organization could not come into being or function effectively without the cooperation and support of the other political entities in the region. (The words "political entities" are used instead of "countries" because of the uncertain political status of Taiwan and the dependent status of Hong Kong until 1997, when it will become a part of China and may lose its status as an important international actor and one of Asia's NICs.) Three of the four political entities that are usually included in the Asian NICs, namely South

Korea, Taiwan, and Hong Kong, are in East Asia. Though dwarfed by the two giants in the region, they are becoming increasingly assertive, increasingly competitive in economic relations, and increasingly influential in regional and even in interregional and international affairs. They are therefore factors that must be reckoned with in any efforts toward regional institutionalization.

This is particularly true of South Korea, which has long had extensive ties with Japan, Taiwan, and Hong Kong and which in recent years has expanded ties with China and the Soviet Union, a major goal of its so-called *Nordpolitik,* or "northern policy."[10] South Korea also seems to be particularly interested in promoting cooperation within the region and indeed throughout the entire Asia–Pacific area. It would undoubtedly aspire to an important if not leading role in any comprehensive organization that might emerge in East Asia, or in all of Asia and the Pacific.

It is quite clear, however, as has been noted, that there is little prospect that such an organization will be established in East Asia in the foreseeable future. This should not obscure the fact that a great deal of regional cooperation in various forms already exists and that the network of regional ties is growing all the time. Progress in overall institutionalization will be slow, and the growth of less comprehensive and less formal organizations will continue to be vulnerable to the effects of events within the region and elsewhere. For example, regional cooperation was greatly stimulated by the new relationships among Communist and non-Communist states in East Asia, elsewhere in the Asia–Pacific region, and in the world and by the improvement in Sino–Soviet relations; and it was greatly retarded by the Cultural Revolution, the turmoil of 1989 in China, and by the continuing tensions between the Soviet Union and Japan. But beneath this pattern of *yin* and *yang,* of cooperation and conflict, of varying relations among nations and cultures—all phenomena that East Asian people seem to regard as a normal part of their life experience—one can discern that growing "web of cooperative realities" that is giving a new underpinning to regional cooperation in East Asia and that may be a more enduring factor in East Asian regionalism than the headlines suggest.

Regional Military Alliances: The External Factor

The new assertiveness that East Asian countries are demonstrating in national and regional affairs does not mean that the nations of East Asia refuse to accept the important roles that external powers, notably the United States and the Soviet Union (a "semi-external" power) have played, are playing, and will continue to play in East Asia, or the importance of the growing ties with the rest of the world. But it does mean that the countries of East Asia are determined to have a larger voice in shaping their own destinies and the character and future of their own region. This attitude can lead—indeed, is already leading—to friction with major external actors; but it can also lead to a healthier and more realistic relationship both among the nations of East Asia and with other countries with which they have longstanding ties that may become even more important and extensive in future years. In this difficult but also hopeful new order of affairs in East Asia, regionalism may play a useful intermediary role, thus, as has been frequently stated, helping to channel the often conflicting currents of enhanced nationalism and internationalism in cooperative and complementary directions.

The nature, dimensions, possibilities, and limitations of regional institutionalization in East Asia may be illustrated by a summary of some of the forms of institutionalization that exist or that have been proposed.

A fairly extensive pattern of military alliances or security arrangements has developed in East Asia; but in every case but one, one or the other of the superpowers has played the dominant role. This is the case in the alliances of the United States with Japan and South Korea, and with Taiwan (Nationalist China) for almost two decades, and of the Soviet Union with North Korea and Mongolia, and with China in the 1950s. The only exception is the loose alliance relationship between the People's Republic of China and the Democratic People's Republic of Korea (North Korea). These alliances have involved a variety of cooperative activities on the part of the East Asian members, which paved the way for various kinds of security cooperation with each other; but they could hardly be called examples of indigenous regionalism. As Valéry Giscard d'Estaing, Yashuhiro Nakasone, and Henry A. Kissinger pointed out in a report on East–West relations to the Trilateral Commission in 1989, "Asia is a region of bilateral alliances . . . and shifting alignments."[11]

From time to time the Soviet Union has charged that a series of trilateral, or even quadrilateral, military blocs directed at the USSR were in the making in East Asia. Among these perceived blocs were those involving the United States–Japan–China, the United States–Japan–South Korea, and the United States–Japan–China–South Korea. Needless to say, none of these ever became a working reality. For some time, when the Communist world seemed to be a monolith under the direction of the Soviet Union, the perception of the United States and the non-Communist states of East Asia that the Soviet Union, the People's Republic of China, Mongolia, and North Korea formed what amounted to a bloc, directed against the non-Communist nations of East Asia as well as against the United States, seemed to have some basis; but the outlines and actual operation of such a bloc, if it ever really existed, were never clear. Fears that this bloc was becoming operational dissipated with the Sino–Soviet split. Again, one could observe that while all of these alleged blocs had a clear regional focus, they could not be regarded as examples of real regionalism.

A more recent proposal, of a different sort, might also not pass the test of true regionalism, but it is an interesting one nevertheless. This is the proposal of Mikhail Gorbachev in his second major address outlining a new policy in Asia, made in Krasnoyarsk in September 1988, for a cooperative relationship among the Soviet Union, China, and Japan, on the basis of mutual benefit.[12] It is a part of Gorbachev's many-faceted "charm offensive" in Asia. It is the kind of proposal that would have been inconceivable from a Soviet leader before the era of *glasnost* and *perestroika*. It would be another bridge across the Communist–non-Communist divide in East Asia. Moreover, it raises the possibility of significant rapprochement between the Soviet Union with the other Communist giant, the basis of which seems to have been laid in the 1980s, and with Japan, with whom the Soviet Union has had strained and very limited relations ever since World War II.

Neither of the countries that Gorbachev would link with the Soviet Union has responded favorably to his demarche. Relations of both, especially Japan, with the Soviet Union would have to improve considerably and be tested for some time before either would even consider the kind of offer that Gorbachev has advanced. Clearly neither China nor Japan is yet ready for the proposed relationship, and in all probability, in spite of Gorbachev's offer, or feeler, neither is the Soviet Union.

Prospects for an East Asian "Trading Bloc"

The limitations of nationalism in a world of growing interdependence and the uncertainties regarding the forms and directions that interdependence will take in a world of revived and often virulent nationalism have led to the emergence of a new and stronger regionalism. One of the forms that this new regionalism is taking, as has been noted, is the movement toward the establishment of so-called trading blocs in two of the three major economic regions of the world—North America and Western Europe, the major laboratories of the old regionalism of the 1950s and 1960s.[13]

As both of these regions move toward the creation of a single common market, powerful external pressures are being exerted on the third major economic zone, East Asia, a region where internal pressures for greater economic cooperation are also strong. These pressures for the creation of some kind of trading bloc in East Asia, to counteract the increasing competition from the North American and West European trading blocs, which may resort to a growing number of restrictive measures against countries outside their enlarged free-trade zones, are already quite visible and are certain to grow exponentially in coming years.[14] They could be largely abortive, however, if the countries of East Asia continue to experience the phenomenal economic growth that made most of them, along with a few states of Southeast Asia, the most rapidly developing countries in the world, if the states of North America and the European Community demonstrate that they will still be open to outside competition on fair terms, and if the countries of East Asia are unable to cooperate effectively (as their past history would seem to indicate), even in the face of new imperatives for cooperation, both in the region and in the world.

The scenario that will probably emerge is that of increasing regional cooperation among most, if not all, of the nations of East Asia, well short of the formation of the kind of trading blocs that seem to be in the process of formation in the other two great economic regions. There can be no doubt that the kind of economic and other forms of cooperation that have existed in Western Europe and between the United States and Canada for a long time, and that has taken a quantum jump with the entry into effect of the U.S.–Canada free-trade treaty, as of 1 January 1989, and with the progress toward a single market in Western Europe in 1992, is far greater, far more deeply rooted, and has larger political overtones and implications than is the case of the growing economic and other forms of cooperation among the countries of East Asia.

The overall conclusion that emerges from all the current discussions about "trading blocs" is that Western Europe and North America are well along toward the formation of such blocs, whereas East Asia is not, and in all probability will not take a similar course. A supplementary conclusion obviously is that the East Asian countries, especially Japan, will follow the development of the two great "trading blocs" with close attention and considerable concern. They will probably be stimulated to take many steps that they would otherwise not take to counter the negative effects of the growing economic institutionalization of the other major economic regions. They will be compelled to develop new economic and political policies that will enable them to continue to compete on advantageous terms with any "blocs," and to promote international economic cooperation and minimize protectionism throughout the world. This will almost certainly lead to greater reregional economic cooperation, and to greater political cooperation as well.

Here we have another reminder that while regional institutionalization in East Asia lags behind that in the other three subregions of Asia and the Pacific, other forms of economic and political cooperation are developing in an impressive, if less spectacular, way. Thus regionalism is becoming an increasingly important feature of the East Asian scene, even if comprehensive regional institutionalization is not.[15]

A New Era in East Asian Regional Cooperation?

Major changes have occurred and are occurring in East Asia and in the world that seem to presage a new era, one in which the nations of East Asia, especially Japan, China, and South Korea (and also Taiwan, if it maintains its political identity and its economic strength) will be impelled toward closer association, and in which the superpowers, the major intrusive powers, will seek to improve their relations with all of the states of East Asia as well as with each other and thereby help to reduce tensions and further cooperation in this increasingly important world region.

This is, of course, a hopeful scenario, which may prove to be too optimistic, for the historical and psychological obstacles to closer regional cooperation still remain. Moreover, new obstacles have arisen because of difficulties within and among the states of the region and the continuing rivalries of the superpowers and their continuing pursuit of policies widely regarded by East Asian countries as both dishonest and detrimental to their interests.

Clearly the nations of East Asia are being subjected to pressures that provide strong incentives for greater regional cooperation while at the same time they make increased cooperation more difficult and dramatize its limitations as well as its necessity. These pressures come from the economic and military presence and policies of the superpowers in the region; from the increasingly assertive and abrasive nationalism in almost every East Asian state and in other subregions of Asia and the Pacific; from the internal instabilities and turmoil in most of the East Asian countries; and from the increasing impact and seriousness of many global problems that call for radical revision of national and regional as well as international behavior and policies.

It is in such an environment, and within such a framework, that the new regionalism in East Asia and elsewhere in Asia and the Pacific is developing. Again we are reminded of the potential importance of this new regionalism, and of the necessity of considering the difficulties as well as the opportunities that are open to it in a world where trends in nation-states, still the major actors in the international system, and in the international system more generally, are both encouraging and discouraging.

Donald Zagoria has pointed out that "because of several new factors, especially economic development, international relations in East Asia are undergoing a substantial change." Among these "new factors" he singles out three as being of special importance, and all three are of special relevance for regional cooperation:

> First, the region's extraordinary economic growth, which has now been sustained over several decades, is leading to the rise of many new sources of power, including Japan, China and such middle powers as the Republic of Korea. As a result, the old bipolar world is eroding and a new multipolar system is emerging. . . . Second, the vigorous expansion of trade, investment and other economic ties within the Pacific region is contributing to a new type of "positive sum" international relations in which all the players

benefit from a growing pie, develop a stake in maintaining an open trading system and, in the process, create a new set of peaceful and friendly relations among themselves. . . . A third prominent feature of East Asian international relations is that, for the first time in postwar history, a major reduction of tensions among all four major powers in the region is now taking place. There is no "odd man out." The United States and the Soviet Union . . . are at the foothills of a new detente, Sino–Soviet relations are improving rapidly and Soviet–Japanese relations will probably also improve in the near future.[16]

Zagoria tempers this hopeful analysis with the precautionary reminder that "there will be many barriers in the road toward a more peaceful and stable environment" in East Asia.[17] He might also have included the emergence and development of a new regionalism as another new and significant factor in contemporary East Asian international relations. All of the factors he mentions will have a profound bearing on the new regionalism and, it is hoped, will help to create and shape the kind of environment in which this new regionalism will become an increasingly important factor in the East Asian, Asian, and global systems.

4
Regionalism in Southeast Asia: Focus on ASEAN

F or a case study of regionalism, both "old" and "new," Southeast Asia offers perhaps the best laboratory of any region in the so-called Third World. Since World War II more regional experiments, many of them abortive, have been tried in that region and a more extensive pattern of regional contacts and organizations has been developed than in any other part of Asia and the Pacific.

A study of Southeast Asia will reveal the many obstacles to regionalism in a region that has so many divisions and so little previous experience in regional cooperation. It will also reveal surprising progress in overcoming these barriers and the possible gains of all participating members from regional cooperation, not only within the region but also in relations and contacts with other regions or subregions in Asia and the Pacific and with other countries and international organizations.[1]

But for all the impressive progress in cooperation, Southeast Asia remains a divided and conflict-prone region. It still falls far short of the kind of significant movement toward real integration that was the professed goal of many of the founding fathers and leading promoters of the "old" regionalism in Western Europe. It does, however, provide ample evidence, of both theoretical and practical value, of a central feature of the "new" regionalism, namely its new and enhanced role as a catalytic agent, a kind of middleman, between resurgent nationalism and growing internationalism and interdependence.

Southeast Asia under Foreign Control

The history of Southeast Asia over many centuries provides few examples of anything approaching regional cooperation, and innumerable examples of the adverse impact of isolation, noncooperation, and conflict, within the region and in relation to outside predators, many of which were much more powerful than any indigenous empires or ruling groups. As was the case with some other parts of the world, such as nearby South Asia and more distant Africa, whenever a kind of unity seemed to prevail—always breaking down sooner or later—this was an imposed unity, either by transient hegemonial powers within the region, or more effectively by outside powers, notably China and India long ago and European colonial powers in more recent centuries.[2]

Neither the Chinese nor the seafaring empires of South India were able to control the entire region. Moreover, their techniques of partial control by indirect means were more subtle and effective than their military might. In a sense, Southeast Asia became for a time an arena of competition between India and China. The lasting legacies of the two neighboring giants have been more cultural and philosophical than political or economic. The presence of large numbers of persons of Chinese and Indian origin—particularly Chinese—and the persistence of Chinese and Indian customs, traditions, and ways of life are constant reminders of the major external influences on Southeast Asia.

In the early stages of Western colonial expansion into Asia, England, France, Portugal, Spain, and Holland established footholds in South and Southeast Asia. In time the British exercised control over all or much of what is now Burma, Malaysia, and Singapore, and the Dutch over what is now Indonesia. In the late nineteenth century the French established control over Indochina, and shortly thereafter the United States, following the Spanish–American War, annexed the Philippines, which had been under Spanish rule for more than 350 years. Only Siam (now Thailand) escaped direct European rule. But none of the Western colonial powers ever established direct control over all, or nearly all, of Southeast Asia. This was probably due more to their own rivalries in the region than to any effective resistance by indigenous groups or rulers. In any event, the lasting impact on the region by Western "imperialists" was far less than that of China and India.

During World War II, for the first and only time in its long history, all of Southeast Asia was occupied and controlled by a single external power, Japan. Internal resistance movements, many aided or even organized by the Allied powers, and eventually Allied military operations in the region, especially in Burma, began to undermine Japan's stern rule; and of course the final defeat of Japan deprived it of all the territories in East and Southeast Asia and the Western Pacific that its forces had occupied.[3]

Regional Organizations in the Era of the Old Regionalism

Obviously regionalism could hardly develop in Southeast Asia until the region became independent of external control. Before 1945, only Siam was an independent state. Now the entire region is carved out among sovereign nations. Thus a major precondition for meaningful regionalism has been met. But other preconditions are still lacking, or are still in an embryonic state. Among these are other heritages of the past, including the relative lack of contacts within the region as well as with the outside world, except through foreign rulers; centuries-old strife among tribal, ethnic, religious, and other groups, and among rival rulers and kingdoms; differing cultures and traditions; generally authoritarian and controlled political systems; and practices and outlooks that were not conducive to cooperation on any level. Moreover, Southeast Asia is still a divided region, with the major political division being the great divide between the Communist states of Indochina and the non-Communist states of the rest of the region. Under these circumstances, the proliferation of regional organizations, in spite of all the formidable barriers to true regionalism, and, even more importantly, the development and broadening of the regional process and the linkage of regional and interregional and global organizations and processes have been most impressive.

In Southeast Asia, more than in the other three regions of Asia and the Pacific, special attention to the organizational dimensions of regionalism is particularly warranted. This applies mainly to the non-Communist countries of the region. But these countries also participate in and are affected by a large number of international regimes in particular issue areas, notably the areas of trade and development. If the longstanding objective of the ASEAN countries to make their region a "Zone of Peace, Freedom and Neutrality" (ZOPFAN) ever becomes a reality, the region would become a part of the so-called nonproliferation regime, following in the footsteps of the member nations of the South Pacific Forum.

The headquarters of two of the most comprehensive organizations in all of the Asia–Pacific area are based in Southeast Asia. These are the Economic and Social Commission for Asia and the Pacific—ESCAP, formerly the Economic Commission for Asia and the Far East (ECAFE)—with headquarters in Bangkok, and the Asian Development Bank (ADB), with its central offices in Manila. It should be pointed out that ESCAP is a regional commission of the United Nations, and not a product of Southeast Asian initiative, and that the ADB is less comprehensive in its functions than an overall all-Asia–Pacific organization should be and that some of its major contributors, particularly the United States, are external financial powers that have special interests in Asia–Pacific development.

Above all, Southeast Asia is the birthplace and home of ASEAN, the most important and vital regional organization in the entire Asia–Pacific area—and indeed in the entire Third World. It deserves special study by all students of regionalism, old and new.

Before turning to ASEAN, some reference should be made to four earlier organizations, whose experience—eventually ill-fated—had a pronounced bearing on ASEAN's formation and development. These are the Southeast Asia Treaty Organization (SEATO), the Association of Southeast Asia (ASA), "Maphilindo" (an acronym formed from the first letters of the names of its member countries), and the Asian and Pacific Council (ASPAC). The majority of the members of the first and fourth of these organizations (which were also discussed in chapter 2), however, were not Southeast Asian states, and the second and third of these organizations were composed of only three Southeast Asian countries.

SEATO

Formed at the instigation of the United States, with Secretary of State John Foster Dulles in the leading role, SEATO can be more accurately described as a part of the worldwide U.S.-led system of anti-Communist military alliances, or security arrangements, than as a true Southeast Asian regional arrangement. It emerged out of a conference in Manila in 1954, shortly after the Geneva conference on Indochina following the final victory of the Viet Minh over the French with the fall of Dienbienphu. At this conference the participating nations—Australia, Britain, France, New Zealand, Pakistan, the Philippines, Thailand, and the United States—signed the Southeast Asia Collective Defense Treaty (the Manila Treaty) and proclaimed a Pacific Charter.[4] Although only two nations of Southeast Asia, the Philippines and Thailand, and only one other Asian country, Pakistan, were signatories to the treaty, the "treaty area" was designated as "the general area of Southeast Asia" and a protocol specifically extended the provisions of the treaty to Indochina. The treaty contained provisions for collective action in the event of an armed attack on any of the Southeast Asian countries (much more general and less binding than the comparable provisions in the North Atlantic Treaty of 1949, for countering "subversive activities from without," and even for cooperation in strengthening "free institutions" and the promotion of "economic progress and social well-being."

In a separate protocol the United States made it clear that it interpreted the Manila treaty as a commitment to provide collective defense to Southeast Asia against *Communist* aggression only. In 1962, in another unilateral protocol to the Manila Treaty, the United States pledged that it would come to the assistance of Thailand in the event of Communist aggression, whether other SEATO members did or did not.

In spite of continuing support from the United States, SEATO became "dead in the water" not long after its formation. It never had much potential as a collective security instrument. Most of its members were reluctant to make the commitment that would be required to achieve this objective. It was widely criticized, not only by the Soviet Union and other Communist states, but also by influential groups within some of its member countries and by most of the non-Communist states of Southeast Asia that were not signatories to the treaty, notably Indonesia.

As the world's political climate changed with the ebbing of the cold war, SEATO gradually lost the support of some of its members. France and Pakistan ceased to take an active role in the alliance, and Britain showed an increasing reluctance to associate itself with any SEATO military preparations and exercises. In a kind of confirmation of Parkinson's Law, SEATO developed an increasingly elaborate organizational structure, mostly based in Bangkok, its headquarters, while it was losing the support of its members and was becoming increasingly irrelevant as a security organization. It never had much relevance in terms of regionalism in Southeast Asia, even though it presumably focused on this region. It is a leading reminder of the problems of developing a really effective collective security arrangement with disparate membership, lacking the essential bases and incentives for cooperation, and of trying to promote any significant regional cooperation from the outside. By the early 1960s it was clearly losing its effectiveness and support. But, as John Stirling noted, "it survived (with occasional military exercises) until 1977, when it was dissolved and its grandiose headquarters in Bangkok taken over by the Thai government."[5] Technically the Manila Treaty, but not SEATO, "is still in force. . . . The alliance remains on paper but in fact is defunct."[6]

ASPAC

Even more ill-fated, and even more irrelevant from the point of view of regionalism in Southeast Asia, was the Asian and Pacific Council (ASPAC), organized in 1966 at the initiative of President Park Chung-hee of South Korea. It did have some significance as perhaps the major example to date of a multi-regional organization designed to bring together most of the leading non-Communist nations of the Western Pacific to deal with external threats (many stemming from the developments in Indochina) and to provide a framework for more widespread cooperation. Its members were Australia, Japan, Malaysia, Nationalist China (Taiwan), New Zealand, the Philippines, South Korea, South Vietnam, and Thailand (with Laos having an observer status).[7] It should be noted that only four of its members were Southeast Asian states and that the largest nation of the region, Indonesia, refused to join. ASPAC was, in fact, never given more than halfhearted support by any participating member except South Korea. Nor were its main objectives and areas of concentration ever clear.

In a joint communiqué issued at the close of the organizational meeting in Seoul, the participating countries announced their "determination to preserve their integrity and sovereignty in the face of external threats"; but at the same time they agreed that the new organization should be "nonmilitary, nonideological, and not anti-Communist." Even the most closely knit regional organization would face difficulties in working toward these conflicting objectives, and ASPAC was anything but closely knit. It is not surprising that it survived for only seven years. What is surprising is that it was formed at all, and that countries of such disparate character would agree to adhere to it. As the Vietnam War gradually began to wind down, with a Communist victory in sight, and, more importantly, as the United States, Japan, and other non-Communist nations began to "normalize" their relations with the People's Republic of China, "the writing on the wall" was clear for all to read. ASPAC was dissolved early in 1973.[8]

ASA and "Maphilindo"

The Association of Southeast Asia (ASA) and "Maphilindo" were different types of organizations, more limited in membership and objectives, each involving only three Southeast Asian states. In 1959 the Prime Minister of Malaya, Tunku Abdul Rahman, formally proposed that an Association of Southeast Asia should be set up. In spite of the fact that most of the Southeast Asian states gave the proposal a cool reception and that China, the Soviet Union, and the Communist states of Indochina denounced it as an offshoot of SEATO, the Philippines and Thailand agreed to join Malaya in forming ASA.

The new organization was launched in 1961. But it had a short life. In 1963, in accordance with a British proposal, two territories on the island of Borneo—Sarawak and Sabah—were brought together with Malaya (which then included Singapore) to form the Federation of Malaysia. The Philippines refused to recognize the enlarged federation, because it had longstanding claims to Sabah. ASA in effect was a victim of this dispute, although a small secretariat continued to carry on a shadowy existence for some time.[9]

The formation of Malaysia was also the *coup de grace* for "Maphilindo," an association of Malaya, the Philippines, and Indonesia, as its name suggests. Its establishment was proclaimed in a declaration of the foreign ministers of the three states in August 1963. It received a mortal blow a month later, when Malaysia came into being. Neither the Philippines nor Indonesia recognized the new federation. Sukarno soon launched a guerrilla war against Malaysia, a bitter and sometimes bloody confrontation—*Konfrontasi*—that lasted until Sukarno's fall in 1967. "Maphilindo" was only one of the many casualties of this conflict, which created the most serious divisions in Southeast Asia until the prolonged war in Vietnam reached new heights shortly afterward.[10]

ASEAN: A "Success Story"

Against the background of longstanding internal divisions, foreign intervention and partial control, limited cooperation and frequent conflicts since independence, the failure of these experiments in organized regional cooperation was certainly no occasion for surprise. Indeed, any other outcome would have been regarded as at least a minor miracle, which might not be repeated. But the miracle was repeated, on a much grander and more inclusive and comprehensive scale, with the founding and evolution of the Association for Southeast Asian Nations (ASEAN).

Proposals for a wider regional organization in Southeast Asia were advanced by responsible leaders of the region even before the Philippines and Indonesia had fully resolved their disputes with Malaysia and had extended recognition to the enlarged Federation. After recognition was extended, the outlook was more promising, even considering the separation of the Communist states of Indochina from the non-Communist nations of the region and the brooding isolation of Burma under Ne Win.

The First Decade

ASEAN was formed at a meeting of representatives of Indonesia, Malaysia, the Philippines, Singapore, and Thailand in Bangkok in August 1967. Much of the credit for this major and unprecedented step forward in regional cooperation should be given to the foreign ministers of Thailand and Indonesia, Thanat Khoman and Adam Malik.

The formation of ASEAN was announced in the historic "Bangkok Declaration," which stated that the main purposes of the new organization were "to accelerate economic growth, social progress, and cultural development in the region," "to promote active collaboration and mutual assistance . . . in the economic, social, cultural, scientific, and administrative fields," and "to promote regional peace and stability."[11] In spite of the last of these stated objectives, the framers of ASEAN insisted that the new organization would not deal directly with security matters and would also avoid controversial political issues. This stated aversion to formal involvement with problems of security and defense and delicate political issues is characteristic of almost all the regional organizations in Asia and the Pacific.

Although ASEAN got off to a slow and cautious start, it soon developed a bewilderingly complex organizational pattern (see fig. 4–1). The machinery provided for in the Bangkok Declaration was quite modest, however— a Standing Committee, "Ad Hoc committees and Permanent Committees of specialists and officials on specific subjects," and a national secretariat in each member country.[12] ASEAN did not get its own secretariat until almost a decade after its founding; but many committees were soon appointed, as were ASEAN-affiliated committees and organizations in all of the member countries. "Asean inherited from ASA and ASPAC a congeries of committees on trade, transportation, 'rehabilitation of Indochina,' relations with the EEC, cultural cooperation, and so on. These committees churned out almost endless proposals; by 1974, the total had risen to 289, of which only 83 had

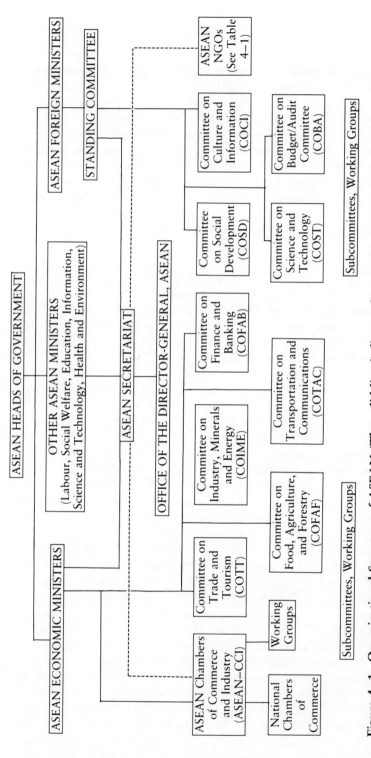

Figure 4–1. Organizational Structure of ASEAN (The solid line indicates the organizational hierarchy; the dotted line indicates an information channel.)

Source: Adapted from Jun Nishikawa, *ASEAN and the United Nations System* (New York: United Nations Institute for Training and Research, Regional Study No. 9, 1983), 13.

been implemented."[13] A large number of regional nongovernmental organizations were also associated with ASEAN (see table 4–1).

Each year several conferences on specific subjects were convened under ASEAN auspices. Annual meetings of the foreign ministers of ASEAN states proved to be important promotional and decision-making affairs, in addition to providing the foreign ministers with a unique opportunity to exchange views and often to reach agreements on many important matters which were not on the official agenda of the meetings.

Table 4–1
ASEAN: Nongovernmental Organizations (June 1981)

1. ASEAN Tours and Travel Association
2. ASEAN Motion Picture Producers' Association
3. ASEAN Inter Parliamentary Organization
4. ASEAN Council of Museums
5. ASEAN Women Circle of Jakarta
6. ASEAN Port Authorities Association
7. ASEAN Council of Petroleum Cooperation
8. ASEAN College of Surgeons
9. ASEAN Cardiologists Federation
10. ASEAN Consumers Protection Agency
11. ASEAN Federation of Jurists
12. ASEAN Bankers' Association*
13. ASEAN Trade Union Council
14. ASEAN Federation of Women
15. ASEAN Pediatric Federation
16. ASEAN Federation of Accountants
17. ASEAN Council of Japan Alumni
18. ASEAN Law Association
19. ASEAN Confederation of Employers*
20. ASEAN Banking Council
21. Confederation of ASEAN Journalists
22. Committee for ASEAN Youth Cooperation
23. Federation of ASEAN Shippers Council
24. Federation of ASEAN Shipowners Association*
25. Federation of ASEAN Newspaper Publishers
26. Federation of ASEAN Economic Association
27. Federation of ASEAN Public Relations Organizations*
28. ASEAN Cooperative Organization
29. ASEAN Association for Planning and Housing*
30. Medical Association of Southeast Asian Nations (MASEAN)*
31. ASEAN Chambers of Commerce and Industry (ASEAN–CCI)
32. Music Industry Association*
33. ASEAN Federation of Engineering Organizations
34. Confederation of ASEAN Societies of Anaesthesiologists
35. ASEAN Standard Trade Directory

Source: Jun Nishikawa, *ASEAN and the United Nations System* (New York: United Nations Institute for Training and Research, Regional Study No. 9, 1983), 48.

*Indicates affiliation as ASEAN NGO. Other applications are still pending.

ASEAN since 1976

ASEAN was given greater momentum in 1976, when the heads of government of the member states held their first summit meeting, on Bali. At this meeting, for the first time, agreement was reached to establish an ASEAN secretariat. Jakarta was designated as ASEAN's headquarters, and an Indonesian, General Hartono Rekso Dharsono, was named the first secretary general.

Two important agreements were signed at the Bali summit. One was a Treaty of Amity and Cooperation, providing a broad framework for cooperation among ASEAN states and potentially for the entire region. A more specific program of action was outlined in a second agreement, a Declaration of ASEAN Concord. This envisioned concrete programs of cooperation in the political, economic, social, cultural, informational, and security fields.[14]

After the Bali summit ASEAN became a more active, more organized, and more effective regional organization. There was considerable basis for the observation of an informed American diplomat in 1980 that ASEAN had achieved "a stature and weight which now make it a primary consideration in the foreign and even some of the domestic policy decisions of every ASEAN country."[15] But it was still hampered by internal difficulties and divisions in its member states.

The whole nature of ASEAN's operations and concerns was altered by the developments in Indochina. New and inescapable security problems arose as tensions between the Communist states of Indochina and ASEAN states escalated, thus moving ASEAN in directions that made it more difficult to concentrate on its original objectives of economic and social development and nonmilitary cooperation. These concerns were manifest at a hastily convened second summit in Kuala Lumpur in 1976, and also at the third summit in Manila in December 1987.

The fact that a decade elapsed between the second and third summits suggested that ASEAN was not being given continuous and sustained direction by the heads of government of the member states. But the ongoing work of the Secretariat and various committees and special technical groups reached new levels; and the annual meetings of the foreign ministers provided the kind of high-level supervision and review that was needed on a continuous basis. The many evaluations of its record that were made in 1986 and 1987, twenty years after its formation, were generally laudatory.

By any realistic standards of assessment ASEAN could be viewed as a "success story,"[16] indeed a surprising and unprecedented success. It had achieved its promise of developing into the most important regional organization of a comprehensive nature in all of Asia and the Pacific.

Naturally there was also considerable basis for less positive evaluations, and the organization received a great deal of open criticism in the ASEAN countries and elsewhere.[17] One of the most scathing publicly expressed criticisms by the head of an ASEAN state was made by Mrs. Corazon Aquino, president of the Philippines, at the nineteenth annual meeting of the foreign ministers of ASEAN states, in 1986. In her opening address Mrs. Aquino said: "After nineteen years of existence ASEAN should already be evaluating the impact of regional economic cooperation; instead, it is endlessly discussing how to get it off the ground." "ASEAN," she continued, "has problems which . . . threaten to render meaningless our continual association."[18]

Concerning the meeting that Mrs. Aquino addressed, a correspondent of *The Far Eastern Economic Review* reported that, "many delegates said ASEAN has now reached a point of no return; it must either move toward genuine independence or accept increasing drift." The foreign ministers, he found, were in "a self-questioning mood." He also called attention to the fact that the directors-general of the "national secretariats" of ASEAN countries had met only twice, in Malaysia and Singapore, "in an emergency mood," and he quoted one of them as saying: "We are basically very worried. This may be our last chance to re-invigorate the grouping." But the correspondent followed up this quotation with a less gloomy statement by the foreign minister of Indonesia, at a meeting of ASEAN foreign ministers in 1987, to the effect that "there is a sense that Asean has reached another plateau, calling for a 'thorough reassessment' of its program and potential."[19]

ASEAN and Security Issues

Three features of the ASEAN experience are of special interest to students of the new regionalism. These are the growing importance of security considerations, even though the framers of the organization insisted that they were not setting up a security-oriented organization; the special associations that have been established between ASEAN and the industrialized nations with which its members have the closest economic relations; and the role of ASEAN in interregional and international affairs.

As a leading Indonesian scholar has pointed out, "ASEAN spokesmen often take pains to explain that ASEAN is never intended to become a military alliance in the model of the now defunct SEATO. . . . Indeed, no evidence is to be found in any ASEAN documents of an intention ultimately to develop the association into the formation of a military alliance. Nevertheless, however paradoxical it may sound, security concern forms an important part of the considerations for the establishment of ASEAN in 1967."[20] The Bangkok Declaration contained a statement that the member states were "determined to ensure their stability and security from external interference in any form or manifestation in order to preserve their national identities in accordance with the ideals and aspirations of their peoples."[21] The ASEAN states are particularly concerned and sensitive about security from external interference, and they find evidences of this kind of threat everywhere.[22] The ASEAN formula, however, was to eschew security problems as much as possible, leaving these problems to national action and multilateral cooperation through other channels, and above all to resist any attempts to convert ASEAN into a military alliance or other form of security organization. The task for ASEAN in this respect was to enhance economic and other forms of nonmilitary cooperation among Southeast Asian states. This would be the kind of contribution that ASEAN could best make to stability, development, and security in the region, and to peace and security elsewhere in Asia and the Pacific and throughout the world.

Preoccupation with "security from external interference" was reflected in the Kuala Lumpur Declaration of the ASEAN foreign ministers in 1971. This included the affirmation that the member states are "determined to exert initially necessary efforts to secure the recognition of, and respect for, Southeast Asia as a Zone of Peace, Freedom and Neutrality, free from any form of manner of interference by outside powers."[23] This proposal was reaffirmed in the Treaty of Amity and Cooperation and the Declaration of ASEAN Accord, signed by the heads of government of the ASEAN states in 1976, and in many other statements by ASEAN spokesmen. But the ZOPFAN proposal was a non-starter from the beginning, except as a statement of an ultimate goal. It has received a cool reception by most other states involved in Southeast Asian affairs, and no more than lip-service endorsement from others. While keeping the ZOPFAN proposal on the "backburner," the ASEAN countries have been forced to turn to other measures to promote their security, mainly outside of ASEAN but to an increasing extent, from the mid-1970s, within the ASEAN framework as well.[24]

With the fall of Saigon and the withdrawal of American forces from Vietnam in 1975, the ASEAN states faced new and greater security threats from the hostile Communist states of Indochina. The ASEAN countries were ill-prepared to meet these enhanced threats. The oft-predicted "domino effect" did not extend militarily beyond the borders of Indochina; but the repercussions of the traumatic developments in Indochina extended throughout the other countries of Southeast Asia, and far beyond as well. The threats seemed to be even greater for ASEAN, at least after the Vietnamese invasion of Cambodia (Kampuchea) and the fall of Pol Pot's Khmer Rouge regime in December 1978.

ASEAN has not been turned into a security organization, and military topics are still kept off the formal agenda of the meetings of the foreign ministers of ASEAN states; but the top officials who have attended these meetings have taken advantage of the opportunities to exchange views, outside of formal sessions, on the problems arising from the developments in Indochina. Moreover, to the surprise of many observers, ASEAN has openly backed an opposition coalition, in which Khmer Rouge forces are the major component, has recognized that coalition as the legitimate government of Cambodia (as has the United Nations General Assembly, mainly because of ASEAN's initiative and support). It has sponsored annual resolutions of the General Assembly condemning the Vietnamese occupation of Kampuchea and demanding the withdrawal of Vietnamese armed forces from that country, to be followed by a coalition government and free elections. More recently, ASEAN states have played a major role in negotiations with all four Cambodian parties (the three opposition groups and the Heng Samrin–Hun Sen regime in Phnom Penh) and, with Indonesia in the lead, in negotiations with Vietnam for support in resolving the Kampuchean–Cambodian question and for steps toward "normalization" of relations between Vietnam and the ASEAN countries following Vietnam's withdrawal from Kampuchea (completed in 1989).[25] All of these concerns were a central topic for consideration at the third ASEAN summit in Manila in December 1987. Indeed, security matters have tended to dominate recent meetings of top ASEAN leaders.

If the tensions between ASEAN and the Communist states of Indochina begin to ebb, and especially if the Communist–non-Communist divide in Southeast Asia is bridged, the prospects for peace, stability, security, and development in all of Southeast Asia will be greatly enhanced. Under these happier circumstances, ASEAN can concentrate more extensively, with greater prospects of success, on its basic objectives. But its experience, like that of some other comprehensive regional organizations that have started out with a firm and publicly announced determination to eschew security and "controversial" political questions, demonstrates that almost any comprehensive regional organization of an official nature cannot avoid political and security issues, however controversial they may be. This is especially true in regions like Southeast Asia, where regional organizations have to function in an unstable and threatening political and security environment.

ASEAN and Its "Dialogue Partners"

ASEAN has provided a channel for more concerted consultation between its member states and the countries with which it has the most extensive economic and, to a more limited extent, security relationships. This has been very important in the evolving relations between regional organizations and countries outside the region with which the organizations and their member states have special and continuing ties. It gives new interregional and international dimensions to regionalism, and links it more closely to the international system.

In the 1970s some of the Pacific countries with special ties and interests in Southeast Asia expressed an interest in periodic consultation with ASEAN. The ASEAN response to these early overtures was guarded and temporizing.

Apparently the member countries feared that ASEAN was too weak to deal on equal terms with more powerful Pacific nations.[26] Old suspicions of outside powers, including the underlying fear of external intervention and domination, were formidable barriers to even informal consultative procedures. Yet these fears and obstacles were eventually largely overcome, thus demonstrating that ASEAN would be an outward-looking rather than an inward-turning regional organization—an essential feature of the new regionalism in an increasingly interdependent world.

At the second ASEAN summit meeting, held in Kuala Lumpur in 1977, the Prime Ministers of Japan, Australia, and New Zealand had informal meetings with the heads of government and other top representatives of the ASEAN countries. This practice soon became standardized procedure. It has been regularized, but not elaborately institutionalized, in the "post-ministerial meetings" that the foreign ministers of ASEAN's main "dialogue partners"—the United States, Japan, Canada, Australia, and New Zealand, plus a representative of the European Economic Community (EEC)—hold with their ASEAN counterparts immediately after the annual meetings of the ASEAN foreign ministers.

These have proved to be very important meetings, at which the foreign ministers of ASEAN and its "dialogue partners" not only have an opportunity to get acquainted under pleasant conditions, but also to discuss a wide range of matters of mutual concern, ranging from economic problems and relations to major international trends and developments.[27] While economic issues tend to predominate, these meetings have also been a main forum for the consideration of developments in Vietnam and Kampuchea (now renamed Cambodia), the resulting tensions in ASEAN–Indochinese relations, and the problems posed by the migrations of the "boat people" from Vietnam and the flood of Kampuchean refugees and resistance groups opposing the long Vietnamese occupation of Kampuchea and the Vietnam-supported Heng Samrin–Hun Sen regime.[28]

ASEAN and its "dialogue partners" are also cooperating in many other ways. Each "dialogue partner" has signed cooperation agreements and/or has established a joint business council with ASEAN. This kind of cooperation is also developing with other nations as well. As early as 1979, for example, a Korea-ASEAN business clubs association was established. It has held a number of joint meetings.

In these and other ways ASEAN is creating a network of linkages with its "dialogue partners," which include the major market-oriented economies in the world. With these partners alone it has contacts with three continents. In the Asia–Pacific region it is also developing contacts with other states, as the growing relations with South Korea, Australia, New Zealand, and Papua New Guinea illustrate. In recent annual meetings of the ASEAN foreign ministers a representative of the latter country has been permitted to attend as an observer.

ASEAN in Interregional and International Affairs

Although its members are still rather hesitant to become deeply involved in organizations and programs outside of Southeast Asia, they are associated with many regional, interregional, and international organizations and associations, such as ESCAP, ADB, the General Agreement on Tariffs and Trade (GATT), the United Nations Conference on Trade and Development (UNCTAD), and several other organs, specialized agencies, commissions, committees, and programs in the United Nations system. After considerable hesitation and prolonged negotiations the ASEAN countries agreed to send representatives to the Conference on Asia–Pacific Economic Cooperation (APEC), held in Canberra in early November 1989. This conference was convened to consider proposals for greater all-Asia–Pacific economic cooperation, and specifically the proposal of Prime Minister Robert Hawke of Australia for the establishment of some kind of comprehensive official all-Asia–Pacific mechanism.[29]

Most of the contacts of ASEAN states with other states in Asia and the Pacific and other parts of the world, to be sure, are still carried out on a bilateral and not a multilateral basis; but increasingly ASEAN is involved in such contacts. One of the most convincing evidences that ASEAN is developing as a regional organization and has earned a high degree of confidence, cooperation, and support from its member states is that, like the EEC, its members are taking a common position on many international issues, and increasingly they are sending a single representative to international organizations and conferences.[30]

ASEAN gained new stature and visibility on the world stage by its leadership in the campaign to get the Vietnamese forces out of Cambodia, to condemn the Vietnamese occupation of that country, and to work out some basis for a broader coalition government of a more representative, democratic, and human type. Other countries holding the same views, in many parts of the world, including the United States, England, and West European states, have generally deferred to ASEAN's leadership and have given strong support to the ASEAN-led demarches.

ASEAN has been a main venue for some of the most promising negotiations to end the Kampuchean/Cambodian impasse, and by so doing to lay the basis for a gradual bridging of the ASEAN–Indochina divide. U.S. and Japanese support for these initiatives can be developed in a constructive way through the many channels of contact between ASEAN and its two most important "dialogue partners." It is quite possible that the other two major powers most directly involved in Southeast Asia, the Soviet Union and the

People's Republic of China, will also improve their relations with ASEAN, especially if their relations with each other continue to improve and if the new, more relaxed, and in an increasing number of areas even more cooperative relations between the United States and the Soviet Union that have developed since Mikhail Gorbachev took over as leader of the Soviet Union continue to become more extensive and more meaningful.

All in all, then, ASEAN seems to have established itself as a comprehensive regional organization that is growing in strength and in support from its members, its "dialogue partners," and many other countries, and that is beginning to function as a collective entity on the international stage. It is becoming, in short, an important international as well as regional and interregional actor.[31]

One should not, however, exaggerate ASEAN's regional and international, or even its subregional, role and importance. It is still a rather weak organization, even in Southeast Asia. Only six of the ten states of this region, or subregion, are members. Cooperation even among these states is still limited. They are inclined to work through ASEAN only to a limited degree, and to be more concerned with national than regional "resilience," to use a term that the Indonesians favor.[32]

ASEAN's first priority, often proclaimed, is the development of greater economic and social cooperation and support in that part of Asia and the Pacific in which it is located. It is still a hesitant and often reluctant participant in larger endeavors in the Asia–Pacific region, although it endorses the goal of greater all-regional cooperation, especially in the economic sphere. It is even more reluctant to get involved in larger international affairs. It is still fearful of being dominated by more powerful states. It is at best an underdeveloped regional organization. But it is the most important truly regional—or subregional—organization in all of Asia and the Pacific. It is worthy of careful examination as a leading example of the limits and possibilities of institutionalized regionalism in an increasingly important part of the world where the few experiments in official regional organization in the past have generally failed to live up to expectations, or have failed completely after a short life.

Will ASEAN prove to be the exception to the experience of the past? Much of the future of comprehensive regionalism in Asia and the Pacific rests on the answer to this question. If the answer is positive, it will be because a new brand of regionalism has arisen in a seemingly uncongenial environment and has been able to overcome much of the legacy of the past.

5
Regionalism in South Asia: Focus on SAARC

S outh Asia is a particularly interesting laboratory for the study of regionalism, old or new. There are many commonalities which should have provided a solid basis for regional cooperation; but there are also special obstacles in the way of real cooperation. Throughout the long history of the subcontinent the obstacles have generally been predominant. The result has been a notable absence of real regionalism, both over the centuries and in the brief post-independence period.

As Peter Lyon observed some years ago, South Asia has been "a region without regionalism." Yet in recent years a promising but still underdeveloped regional organization, the South Asian Association for Regional Cooperation (SAARC) has emerged and has developed quite impressively. The reasons for the emergence of the second most important comprehensive regional organization in all of Asia and the Pacific in "a region without regionalism" merit careful examination.

Obstacles to South Asian Regionalism

South Asia was relatively unaffected by the "old regionalism" of the 1950s and 1960s, the kind of development that reached exciting proportions in Western Europe, when the formula of joining federal and functional features seemed to offer a way out of the impasse among the federalists, the functionalists, the neo-functionalists, the integrationists, the staunch defenders of sovereignty, and the advocates of a "United States of Europe." But the South Asian region may prove to be a center of the new regionalism, or at least one of the best areas for testing the thesis that in an era when nationalism is experiencing a revival, when regionalism is taking on new forms, and when internationalism is an ever-present and unavoidable reality, what might seem to be the weakest of these three trends, namely regionalism, may prove to be a central unifying link between the other two trends, thus to some extent, at least, making all three trends more compatible and complementary than historical experience and conventional political analysis might suggest.

To fulfill this function, regionalism in South Asia will have to be greatly expanded and strengthened. It is still characterized by a relative paucity of linkages, either formal or informal, official or unofficial. The emergence of SAARC has given it a comprehensive regional organization, and has provided a greater impetus to further regional institutionalization. There are also a number of technical and professional associations in existence, with varying degrees of cohesion and effectiveness.

South Asia, in its regional dimensions, should also be analyzed in terms of the concept of international regimes. This is a little-examined dimension of South Asian regionalism, but it is an important one. The countries of the region, especially India, are active participants in many of these regimes, and in some, notably nonaligned, riparian, oceanic, nonproliferation, and developmental regimes, they have long been playing a leading role.

In terms of geography and history South Asia is one of the most clearly delineated and most easily identified regions in the world. It is a region of continental proportions, even though it is but one of the several great peninsulas that jut forth from the Eurasian land mass. It encompasses what was formerly called the Indian subcontinent and is now usually described as South Asia. Geographically it is easily demarcated. It is the area extending from the eastern borders of Afghanistan and Iran to the western borders of Burma, and from the Himalayas in the north to Cape Comorin at the southern tip of India and the offshore islands of Sri Lanka and the Maldives. This region is now divided among seven independent nations of very disparate size and power but sharing common burdens of poverty and underdevelopment. These nations are India, Pakistan, Bangladesh, Sri Lanka, Nepal, Bhutan, and the Maldives.

Historically the regional identification is less clear, for the region was never completely controlled by any would-be ruler. In some periods of its long and complicated history, to be sure—for example, during the reign of the Mauryan Emperor Ashoka in the third century B.C., the Moghul Emperor Akbar in the fifteenth and early sixteenth centuries A.D., and especially during the century of direct British rule, roughly from the middle of the nineteenth to the middle of the present century—most of the region was under the control of a single kingdom or foreign ruler; but only the British extended their control over virtually the entire region, and their rule was marked more by superficial dominance than by deep penetration. In other words, even such obvious commonalities as geography and history could also be interpreted as being obstacles to real regionalism, which South Asia in fact has never experienced.

The same observation could be made about many other commonalities. They provided the basis for regional cooperation, but they also were obstacles in the path to true regional association. This is true of such basic factors as traditions, cultural traits, value systems, problems of poverty and development, which all the states of the region share, but with such disparities and asymmetries, both within and between the nations that have emerged that they are often more obstacles to than unifying factors for effective cooperation.

All of the South Asian states, except Nepal, have been independent for only a few decades in the post–World War II period. All of them have been preoccupied with internal problems of development, political stability, social cohesion, and national integration, and have hardly been in a position to develop strong regional ties. Internal upheavals and civil strife within some of the states, as in the case of Pakistan, which split apart in 1971, and Sri Lanka since 1983, have had adverse spillover effects on their neighbors, especially on India. Similar effects have been created by the flow of refugees across newly created borders, notably the vast migration of Muslims from India into Pakistan and of Hindus and Sikhs from Pakistan into India, accompanied by massive slaughter, immediately before and after the partition of August 1947, and the flood of refugees from East Pakistan/Bangladesh into India during the civil war in East Pakistan in 1971 and during and after the Indo–Pakistan war in December of that year.

Other major post-independence obstacles to regional cooperation arising from the adverse political and security environment have been the great diversity in political systems in the South Asian states, and especially the recurring tensions between some of these states. Tensions between India and Pakistan have been a permanent feature of their uneasy relationship, and on three occasions—in 1947–48, 1965, and 1971—have led to armed conflict. Until the 1980s these internal problems and intraregional tensions effectively blocked the development of any comprehensive regional organization, although they did not completely block many cooperative bilateral relations, a few multilateral agreements, and a large number of intraregional associations of a less than comprehensive nature, especially in professional and technical fields.

One major obstacle to real regional cooperation in South Asia is what may be called the India factor. In no other region in the Third World does one nation occupy such a dominating position as India does in South Asia.[1] This creates a dangerously skewed situation, further complicated by the strained relations that have existed between India and Pakistan and occasionally, to a lesser degree, between India and most of the other South Asian nations. Fear of India is overt and pervasive in all of India's regional neighbors. Indeed, neighboring states often charge that India seeks to expand its dominance into hegemony.

Indians, of course, deny having such ambitions. They point out, quite correctly in a formal sense, that they have generally had good official relations with all of their regional neighbors except Pakistan, and that even with Pakistan official relations are correct and extensive. These relations improved substantially after Rajiv Gandhi came to power in India in late 1984 and improved further after Benazir Bhutto became prime minister of Pakistan in November 1988; but, in spite of the professed objective of the prime minister of India, V. P. Singh (who heads a shaky coalition that brought Rajiv Gandhi's rule to an abrupt end in the ninth general elections in November 1989) to bring about a new and happier era in Indo-Pakistan relations, these relations deteriorated alarmingly in the early 1990s. There was even widespread fear that for the fourth time since their emergence into independence, the two nations might become involved in a war that almost nobody wanted.

The dominant position of India in South Asia, and the suspicions and fears shared by all its South Asian neighbors, are formidable barriers to effective and comprehensive regional cooperation in South Asia. This pronounced asymmetry explains in large measure why India prefers to deal with regional matters on a bilateral rather than a multilateral basis, whereas the other South Asian countries often try to enlist outside assistance, if only to provide a counterweight to India.

Obviously no comprehensive regional organization or organizations can prosper in South Asia without India's full support and participation; and despite their fears the other South Asian states recognize the indispensability of India's participation. They have been more enthusiastic about multilateral cooperation than has India, perhaps because they hope that in cooperation they will gain added strength and because they realize that they cannot possibly deal with some of the problems they face without regional—and international—cooperation and support. One of the major reasons why India has been hesitant to enter into any comprehensive South Asian organization is that it fears that its smaller, weaker neighbors might try to use such an organization as a means of "ganging up" on India.

In spite of these serious obstacles to regionalism, the nations of South Asia have developed a large number of official and unofficial contacts and agreements. Numerous proposals for limited forms of regional cooperation were advanced in the years following their independence, and a few led to specific agreements or some institutionalized patterns of cooperation. These were mostly in the areas of economic and social development.

Examples of bilateral arrangements were the treaties of Peace and Friendship that India signed with Bhutan in 1949, Nepal in 1950, and Bangladesh in 1972. These were primarily security agreements, and at the time of their conclusion the smaller states regarded these treaties as necessary for security purposes. They later came to believe that they had given India undue say in their internal affairs.

Another example is the series of agreements between India and Pakistan over the use of the waters of the rivers flowing through India into the Indus River system in Pakistan, and between India and Bangladesh over the division of the waters of the Ganges River. The Indus Waters Agreement was reached only after years of rancor and failure to reach agreement on a bilateral basis, with the final agreement eventually worked out only under the aegis of a third party, the World Bank.[2] India and Bangladesh disagree more than they agree over the use of the waters of the Ganges.[3] This issue is still sensitive and largely unresolved. It clearly calls for some kind of regional solution (in which Nepal should probably also be involved, in spite of India's reluctance to participate in a tripartite arrangement).

The Origins of SARC (SAARC)

Regional cooperation in South Asia on a truly comprehensive scale was conspicuously absent until the late 1970s and early 1980s, when events forced the preliminary steps in a unique experiment in all-regional organization. South Asia can no longer be accurately described as "a region without regionalism," at least in the institutional sense.

Not until President Ziaur Rahman of Bangladesh made his historic formal proposal in May 1980 and until the other South Asian states reacted favorably, if cautiously, and gradually agreed on a substantially revised form of Rahman's original proposal did concrete steps get under way for the establishment of the first comprehensive regional organization in the subcontinent. This was originally known as South Asian Regional Cooperation (SARC), and then as the South Asian Association for Regional Cooperation (SAARC).

According to Professor S. D. Muni of the School of International Studies of Jawaharlal Nehru University in New Delhi, "The question of regional cooperation appeared for the first time during the talks of [the] Bangladesh Foreign Minister and his Sri Lankan counterpart in Colombo in 1977." Apparently the two officials agreed on the desirability of a regional organization in South Asia. The growing effectiveness of the Association of Southeast Asian Nations may have planted the idea of a similar organization in their region, but the Sri Lankan Foreign Minister seemed to be thinking in even larger terms, suggesting "a regional Asian grouping that could include [an] Asian common market."[4]

At about the same time a group of scholars in the South Asian countries began to exchange ideas on possible lines of regional cooperation, with a focus on economic and social development. "In September 1978 their efforts were formalized when academic institutions in 6 South Asian countries agreed to set in motion a concerted and systematic program of studies under a Committee on Studies for Co-operation in Development in South Asia" (CSCD).[5] During the next five years, while SARC was gradually taking shape on the official level, these scholars held a number of meetings and made a number of proposals that helped to provide the kind of background analysis and information which proved to be useful to those who worked out the details of the new organization, under the direction of the foreign secretaries and foreign ministers of the South Asian states.

The Soviet intervention in Afghanistan in late December 1979 changed the entire context in which the proposal of the President of Bangladesh was being framed. It undoubtedly led him to place a greater emphasis on security cooperation than he might otherwise have done, and it created a more difficult atmosphere for regional cooperation while it made such cooperation all the more desirable. The great divide was between India, which was hesitant to criticize the Soviet action in Afghanistan, and Pakistan, which regarded this action as a major threat to its security and the security of all of South Asia. It also put President Ziaur Rahman in a difficult position, since he was compelled to take the new realities into consideration but was at the same time seeking a formula for regional cooperation that would be acceptable to all the South Asian countries.

After informal soundings in other South Asian capitals, Rahman sent a formal proposal in May 1980 in the form of a letter to the heads of the other South Asian states. In it he proposed a South Asian summit meeting to consider the desirability and feasibility of establishing a framework for regional cooperation and the steps necessary to create "a climate for regional harmony;" but he also linked this approach with the goal of maintaining "peace, stability, and security" in the region.

The response to this demarche was quite lukewarm. Virtually all of the other South Asian countries had reservations and doubts about this bold proposal. Most of them shared India's reservations regarding the reference to security considerations and the lack of clarity regarding the theme of economic and social development, which most of countries believed should be the central focus of any movement toward formal all-regional institutionalization.

All of the South Asian states, however, expressed a willingness to discuss Rahman's proposal. "What followed was a series of quiet diplomatic consultations . . . at the U.N. Headquarters among the South Asian countries." As a result Rahman's proposal "was reformulated in the form of a working paper circulated to all South Asian countries in November 1980."[6] While endorsing the idea of a regional organization, this paper dropped almost all references to security matters, and suggested that the areas of cooperation should be confined to those of a "non-political" and "non-controversial" character.

This working paper became the basis of the discussions that began in Colombo in April 1981, at the foreign secretaries level. During four meetings over the following year and a half these third-echelon officials hammered out specific proposals for a new organization. They agreed that this organization was to begin modestly with a step-by-step approach and with the "veto power" of each member state, however large or small, assured by the adoption of the principle of unanimity. They also established five Study Groups and a Committee of the Whole, and they decided on the areas of cooperation that should receive detailed attention. Their first meeting identified five such areas: agriculture, rural development, health and population, telecommunication, and meterology. In subsequent meetings they added four more areas: transport, postal service, science and technology, and sports, arts, and culture.

At their fourth meeting, held in Dhaka in March 1983, the foreign secretaries announced that a new organization, to be known as South Asian Regional Cooperation (SARC), would be launched by the foreign ministers of the South Asian states at a meeting in Delhi in August 1983. This meeting was held as scheduled. At its completion the foreign ministers issued a Declaration of Regional Cooperation and a joint communiqué. The Delhi Declaration stated that cooperation should be "based on respect for the principles of sovereign equality, territorial integrity, political independence, noninterference in internal affairs of other States and mutual benefit" (the famous "Five Principles of Peaceful Coexistence"), that regional cooperation should "not be a substitute for bilateral and multilateral cooperation," and that it should be "based on mutual trust, understanding and sympathetic appreciation of the national aspirations." The Declaration reaffirmed the principle of unanimity for all SARC decisions, and it stipulated that "bilateral and contentious issues shall be excluded from the deliberations" (a stipulation that has been adhered to in principle but not in practice).[7]

The Declaration on South Asian Regional Cooperation "marked the completion of the preparatory phase and the beginning of a new phase of active implementation of joint programs in a number of specific areas,"[8] of both a short-term and long-term character. Some of these were spelled out in the joint communiqué under the heading of an Integrated Programme of Action for South Asia Regional Cooperation. The foreign ministers also decided to give the new organization institutional shape—or at least the skeleton of institutionalization—by providing for the establishment of a Standing Committee of the Foreign Secretaries, a Technical Committee, and an Action Committee. It did not, however, provide for a headquarters for SARC or a permanent secretariat. The foreign ministers would have overall supervision as the Council of Ministers.

From SARC to SAARC

The decision of the foreign ministers at the Dhaka meeting brought SARC into being as a functioning regional organization. "The formal launching . . . opened up for the first time a new horizon of interstate cooperation among the regional countries and augured the emergence of South Asia as a regional entity within the international system."[9] A new and important comprehensive regional organization had been born in a region that has been noteworthy—or notorious—for the virtual absence of organized regional cooperation.

While SARC became an actively functioning organization soon after the foreign ministers' meeting in Dhaka, with a widening network of technical and action committees and programs and with annual meetings of the foreign ministers, it still needed the public endorsement of the heads of government of the member states. This was bestowed, with considerable fanfare, at the first South Asian summit, held in Dhaka in December 1985. This gave greater stature to the new organization, and also greater institutional form, mainly through agreement to establish a modest headquarters in Kathmandu, the capital of Nepal, with a Secretary General (Abul Aharan, a career diplomat of Bangladesh) and a small permanent secretariat. At the Dhaka summit a decision was made to change the name of the organization from South Asian Regional Cooperation (SARC) to South Asian Association for Regional Cooperation (SAARC).

The Dhaka summit also broadened SAARC's mandate. It called for an expansion of the activities of the technical and action committees, the strengthening of infrastructure support in the areas selected for cooperative development, the creation of linkages among existing national institutions in these designated areas (to which others were soon added), and the establishment of a number of regional institutions of a specialized nature, especially institutions for training and research. Thus, as Dr. S. D. Muni explains, "The establishment of SAARC in December 1985 can be considered as the culmination of this process as a whole."[10] After this meeting SAARC was a working reality.

The list of areas for possible cooperation among the seven nations of South Asia, under the aegis of SAARC, is a reminder of the wide range of mutual interests among these states and of the necessity for regional cooperation in dealing with many issues of mutual concern. Among those suggested, over and above those already on SAARC's agenda, are the following: the formulation of common policies in the field of trade, both within the region and between the region and other countries throughout the world, including trade relations with both Third World and developed countries; shipping and other maritime services; developing and harnessing natural resources, especially energy sources (including oil, hydroelectric power, and atomic energy) and sea bed resources; the joint sharing and control of river waters that run through two or more of the countries of the region; a regional food policy, perhaps patterned after ASEAN's successful Food Security Reserve; the development of cooperative policies in dealing with multinational corporations, with a view to the furtherance of national and regional development programs, foreign investment, and technology transfer without being forced to make too many concessions to the multinationals; the promotion of tourism throughout the region, through such means as joint advertising, "package deals" for more than one country, and the development of regional transport networks along the lines of the West European network; and regional security cooperation.

SAARC and Regional Security Issues

It is obvious that some—perhaps most—of these possible areas of cooperation raise "contentious issues," which the Delhi Declaration of 1983 declared should be excluded from the agenda of SARC; but the fact is that almost all issues on the agenda that are being dealt with almost continuously at various levels of the SAARC network are "contentious issues," on which there are considerable differences in approach and policies among the states of South Asia. A strict adherence to the direction to exclude "contentious issues" would doom SAARC to futility, and probably to extinction. Such issues have arisen from the earliest stages of SARC, and they have become a normal feature of SAARC's activities as the agenda has broadened.

For some time, as S. D. Muni notes, "many of the SAARC leaders have been expressing their preference for taking up political and bilateral/contentious issues for discussion in the SAARC forum. India has been the lone exception in this regard." The reasons for India's objections to this practice are frankly stated by Dr. Muni:

> India has been particularly keen on this provision [that bilateral and contentious issues should be excluded from SAARC deliberations, as mandated by Article X of the SAARC Charter] since the composition of the South Asian region is such that any bilateral issues would most likely involve India as one of the parties. As for the contentious issues, debate on these in the SAARC forum can only vitiate the regional atmosphere without resolving the given controversies. Here again, most of the regional contentious issues are essentially bilateral in character.[11]

"However," Dr. Muni admits, "not all SAARC members seem to be happy with this provision, and there have been occasions when pressure has been exercised for diluting this provision."[12] India has been increasingly the "odd man out" in SAARC; but in recent years it has made some concessions to the wishes of the other South Asian states and has agreed to the inclusion of some bilateral and contentious issues on the SAARC agenda. The contentious aspects are particularly obvious with respect to the control and division of river waters and the touchy area of security.

The need for some kind of agreement for the control of rivers that run through more than one South Asian nation has been dramatically, and sometimes tragically, demonstrated by the controversies between India and Pakistan over the control and use of the waters of the Indus basin and by the prolonged and still continuing controversies between India and Bangladesh over the control and use of the waters of the Ganges River.

The latter issue was dramatized again in 1988, when much of Bangladesh was inundated by disastrous floods. The government and people of that country placed a good deal of the blame on India for not controlling the flow into Bangladesh of the Ganges, whose swollen waters were said to have added to the floods, and for refusing to seek a cooperative solution to the Ganges water problem, either by negotiations with the other two countries in the Ganges basin, namely Nepal and Bangladesh, or by seeking outside assistance, as was done in the case of the Indus waters dispute.[13]

In South Asia security issues have always been particularly delicate and controversial. The reasons for this are quite clear. Security is always a controversial issue. It is particularly so in South Asia because the major perceived threats are seen as arising from internal tensions and conflicts, especially in India, Pakistan, and Sri Lanka, which have had serious spillover effects, jeopardizing the security of neighboring states as well, and from tensions and conflicts with each other, notably between India and Pakistan.

There has thus been a marked disparity in security orientations and threat perceptions among the members of SAARC, both with respect to internal and intraregional threats. This disparity also extends to external relations, beyond the borders of South Asia.[14] The South Asian countries do, however, share a large number of common interests, including the promotion of peace in their region and in the world, the desire to concentrate on economic development, and active participation in the affairs of the Third World and in international organizations and agencies. They also share a common determination to resist any forms of imperialism and external interference. All of the South Asian states are members of the nonaligned movement, with Pakistan, long an aligned state, being a relative latecomer in this movement. But even in their external relations, and particularly in their relations with major world powers, there are many differences in policies, orientation, and threat perceptions.

Even in their external relations the special impact of internal and intraregional tensions and conflicts is particularly obvious and particularly important. It is difficult for nations to unite and agree on ways and means of dealing with security threats when they perceive that their main security threats arise from within or from each other. This is an aspect of the security problem in South Asia that makes cooperation in this field particularly difficult, that adversely affects efforts to cooperate in other areas, and that casts a pall over the future prospects for SAARC, even if security issues are kept off the formal agenda. These special complications are well delineated by a leading Indian student of foreign affairs:

[E]xternal threats to South Asian countries are perceived to emerge primarily from other members of SARC, and external involvement is perceived primarily as a function of regional conflicts. . . . [M]embers of SARC tend to identify regional countries as the primary and/or major sources of threat to their security. The classic "security dilemma" that dominates Indo–Pakistani relations is the most glaring example of this fact. But Bangladesh and Sri Lanka (and for that matter Nepal) also tend to identify India, although this usually goes unstated, as the major external threat to themselves. This is largely a function of India's "bigness" . . . and its obvious preeminence in the region which the other countries, except for Pakistan, can do precious little to challenge. But the fear of India is also intimately connected with these various countries' search for their own identity. Since they are all offshoots of India in one form or another and find it extremely difficult to define their identities except in relation to India, their search for identity in non-Indian terms often leads them in anti-Indian directions and forms a significant psychological input in their process of threat perception and perception of India.[15]

India seems to be particularly insistent that SAARC must not be in any sense a security arrangement and that it must not be pro-Western in its security or political orientation. A typical Indian view is that SAARC is, and should be, quite different from ASEAN in this respect. This view was expressed by S. D. Muni when he wrote that "The SAARC, unlike its predecessor the ASEAN . . . , is far from being a Western sponsored example of regionalism or having pronounced security pretensions."[16]

India does not want to be associated with any organization that is primarily a security arrangement or that is "Western sponsored" (as SEATO and CENTO, with both of which Pakistan was affiliated, obviously were). Indeed, insists Dr. Muni, "the absence of external security sponsorship is almost a precondition for the viability and vitality of the SAARC." He admits, however, that "SAARC, no doubt, has considerable potential for evolving a common approach to security problems," and he recognizes that other members of SAARC seem to be increasingly interested in developing this potential. He also believes that "SAARC should acquire its indigenous strategic moorage," and he even states, seemingly with equanimity, that "there is a possibility of the SAARC providing impetus for [a] collective approach to internal security problems like antiterrorist measures, counterinsurgency training, suppression of political opponents, sharing of intelligence on internal problems, etc."[17]

As has been pointed out, in his letter to the other heads of South Asian states of May 1980, Bangladesh President Ziaur Rahman placed considerable emphasis on possible security dimensions of a proposed new all-regional organization; but this was virtually eliminated in the revised formulation of his proposal that was embodied in the working paper of November 1980.

Since SARC, as it was then called, proclaimed that it would avoid all "bi-lateral" and "controversial" issues, it was committed to avoid most security issues, which were almost always "controversial" and political as well as military (another controversial dimension) in nature.

The primary concern of SARC/SAARC, from the beginning, was with economic and social development; but from the beginning there was also an avowed objective of promoting "peace and security" in South Asia. This was clearly stated in the Dhaka Declaration, which launched SAARC as a formal organization: "The Heads of State or Government reaffirmed that their fundamental goal was to accelerate the process of economic and social development in their respective countries through the optimum utilization of their human and material resources. . . . They were conscious that peace and security was an essential prerequisite for the realization of this objective."[18] But the preamble of the SAARC Charter, of which the Dhaka Declaration was a part, contained the significant modification, or explanation, that the framers were "desirous of promoting peace, stability, amity and progress in the region through strict adherence to the principles of . . . non-use of force . . . and peaceful settlement of all disputes."[19]

In recent years India has somewhat relaxed its opposition to the inclusion of security-related issues on SAARC agenda, especially those of a regional nature. In late November 1985 Prime Minister Rajiv Gandhi said that SAARC could become one of the approaches to regional security in South Asia.[20] India's willingness, however reluctant, to allow issues of terrorism in South Asia to be discussed in formal high-level meetings of SAARC is evidence of this partial shift in India's previously adamant position. It may be an indication that India has recognized and come to terms with the implications of the comprehensive nature of SAARC. As Dr. Muni has observed, the "stated and apparent thrust of the process that led to the establishment of SAARC has been on developmental issues. But underneath that thrust, political and strategic issues have remained the major concern of the activities related to the regional forum."[21]

While the South Asian states have recognized that security issues are bound to intrude on their discussions in SAARC, they still try to keep these issues off the formal agenda as far as possible. Such issues are discussed and dealt with more extensively, and in a more uninhibited way, at the informal talks that occur between and among the leaders of the region whenever they assemble for high-level meetings of SAARC.

The lessons of ASEAN with respect to security issues are instructive for SAARC.[22] Both regional organizations began in a modest and cautious way, and tended to concentrate on economic cooperation. Both quickly established the principle of unanimity, and agreed to keep security and other controversial issues off the formal agenda. In both the role of the foreign ministers has been central, and summit meetings, while of great importance, came later. Both were deliberately slow in establishing permanent head-quarters and a permanent secretariat, and in each the level of institutionalization has been low.

For ASEAN the great divide came in 1975, with the end of the Vietnam War and the withdrawal of U.S. forces, soon followed by the Vietnamese occupation and virtual control of all of Vietnam. Security concerns became even more demanding when Vietnam entered into close relationships with the Soviet Union in 1978, sent troops into Kampuchea, and became involved in military hostilities with China.

For SAARC, security issues loomed larger in the late 1980s as a result of new tensions between India and Pakistan and between India and Sri Lanka. Spillover effects of ethnic and religious strife were decisive causes for these new levels of tension. Thus SAARC, like ASEAN, soon learned that it could not avoid "contentious issues," including those with major security aspects.

The ASEAN formula for seeking some concerted action in dealing with regional security threats was to keep such matters off the formal agenda (at least by direct reference) and to provide a forum for discussion of these problems by the foreign ministers or heads of state or government outside the formal sessions. These discussions became even more meaningful when they were held "in the corridors" not only during top-level ASEAN meetings but also during the "post-ministerial meetings" that have been held in recent years with ASEAN's so-called dialogue partners, that is, with the foreign ministers (and occasionally heads of state or government) of those countries with which the member states of ASEAN have the most extensive economic relations. This is an ingenious and apparently highly successful innovation that might well be considered at some stage by the member states of SAARC; but for the time being, at least, in the security area top SAARC spokesmen might be well advised to develop the practice of taking advantage of their attendance at SAARC meetings to discuss security problems with each other outside the formal SAARC sessions. The extension of these discussions beyond the SAARC membership, as is happening in the case of ASEAN, may be introduced at a later stage, when preparations and attitudes are more highly developed.

In SAARC, therefore, the main forum for the discussion of security and other "controversial" issues remains the informal talks that are held during SAARC sessions between and among top leaders of the South Asian states. These talks often seem to be more fruitful than the deliberations of SAARC itself. But the SAARC high-level meetings provide the only regular and most frequently held forum for such exchanges.

Apparently the informal talks during SAARC sessions are regarded as useful supplements to the formal meetings by all South Asian countries, with the possible exception of India. In fact, these talks have been formally approved by the South Asian foreign ministers. "The Ministerial meetings held in Maldives . . . in July 1984 had . . . decided that there could be 'regular informal meetings of representatives of South Asian countries in all the capitals' of South Asia. These meetings can help avoid misunderstandings arising from routine communication gap and may also be a viable forum for dealing with unforeseen contingencies. Other organizations like ASEAN and Nordic Council have found such arrangements very useful." Thus, "informally SAARC is already providing opportunities for bilateral talks between the member states on all important occasions of SAARC gatherings."[23]

Sri Lanka has taken the lead in proposing that an "informal forum" be created within SAARC for the discussion of bilateral problems. It first made this proposal at a meeting of the Council of Ministers of SAARC, held in New Delhi in June 1987. Most of the other members of SAARC supported this proposal, with varying degrees of enthusiasm; but India was opposed, and was able to shelve the idea. Sri Lanka raised the issue again at the Kathmandu SAARC summit in November 1987, and will probably continue to promote it in future high-level SAARC meetings.[24]

In all probability, however, bilateral talks will be held at major SAARC meetings on the informal basis that have characterized them up to the present. Some of them have been of particular importance and seem to have helped reduce tension and avoid conflict in the subcontinent. Some outstanding examples have been cited by Professor Muni:

[A]s a result of talks between Indian and Pakistani leaders during the first SAARC Summit, the bilateral normalization process was reactivated and attempts were made to break [the] stalemate on trade matters. On his way back from Dhaka, President Zia of Pakistan broke his journey in New Delhi to meet Prime Minister Rajiv Gandhi on 17 December 1985 and the two leaders agreed not to attack each others' nuclear installations. The Banglalore SAARC Summit in November 1986 helped [the] Indian and Pakistani Prime Ministers to hold talks on diffusing the tensions resulting from India's military exercise (Brass Tacks) on the Indo–Pak border. During the Bangalore Summit, informal Indo–Srilankan talks outside the SAARC forum resulted in the formulation of "19 December" proposals on devolution of power to the proposed Tamil areas. There are many other such examples. The frequency of the SAARC meeting has thus facilitated greater personal interaction among the leaders and officials; created opportunities to ease bilateral tensions and generated proper understanding of each others point of view even on issues outside the SAARC agenda. One is not sure if discussion of such issues within the SAARC forum would be specially more effective.[25]

A more recent example of the usefulness of these informal talks was provided at the fifth SAARC Summit in Islamabad in December 1988, when India's Prime Minister, Rajiv Gandhi, and Pakistan's new Prime Minister,

Benazir Bhutto, met for the first time in their official capacities, discussed a wide range of issues between their two countries, and reached a number of agreements for steps to improve their relations. So much attention was given to these informal discussions between the representatives of a "new generation" in their countries that the important proceedings at the SAARC Summit were overshadowed.[26]

In developing SAARC the South Asian countries undoubtedly benefited from a study of the experience of ASEAN in a neighboring region; but thus far they have taken a curiously detached and standoffish approach to the major regional organization in their part of the world. They seem to have little interest in forging links between the two organizations, although they do keep in touch with ASEAN in various ways.

Whenever the question of establishing links with ASEAN has arisen in SAARC, India has usually tended to discourage this kind of orientation. The reasons for this position are doubtless very complex, but they seem to arise from India's desire to prevent external involvement in South Asian affairs, even from a similar organization in a neighboring region, and to keep SAARC from developing too close ties with any organization that India feels is too Western in its basic orientation. This explanation is candidly stated by Dr. Muni: "[India] has . . . resisted pressures for reorienting the SAARC on the basis of the ASEAN, which is a pro-Western organisation. India does not look with favour at the move on the part of some of the members to forge links between the SAARC and the ASEAN. Instead it has tried to bring such other neighbours like Burma and Afghanistan into the SAARC which do not readily endorse western strategic positions on Asian and international issues."[27]

As Dr. Muni indicates, India's position on this issue is not shared by other members of SAARC. This seems to be another indication of the basic differences in the whole conception of the proper role of SAARC that divides India, the giant of South Asia, from its smaller and weaker neighbors. India apparently would like to limit the outside connections of SAARC, although it is not opposed to SAARC's development as an international actor, whereas other SAARC member states, perhaps seeking ways to balance the inescapable predominance of India in South Asia, seem to be more interested in developing external ties.

Sri Lanka is a leading example of this trend. Some years ago it was even reported to have applied, or to be seriously thinking of applying, for membership in ASEAN; but this feeler was discouraged by the ASEAN states, and apparently Sri Lanka has abandoned the idea. It is still trying, however, to enlist regional support, through SAARC and other channels, and extra-regional and international support in its recent differences with India arising from its ethnic tensions and violence and India's role with respect to its internal difficulties.

If regional institutionalization develops significantly in Asia and the Pacific, as it seems to be doing, it seems inevitable that major regional organizations in the entire area, of which ASEAN, SAARC, and the South Pacific Forum are presently the leading examples, will establish closer ties with each other and perhaps will develop patterns and practices of cooperation that will further their mutual interests in Asia and the Pacific and also in the international community.

SAARC is still a fledgling regional organization, and its future is uncertain. It is greatly handicapped by the legacy of the past, the many tensions that exist within and among the South Asian nations, and the profound asymmetry because of the overwhelming size and weight of India. It is rather underdeveloped as far as institutionalization is concerned. There is still considerable doubt regarding the degree of genuine acceptance and support that it is receiving from its member states, in spite of strong verbal expressions of endorsement and support.

SAARC, however, has already proved to be a useful and unique agency for regional cooperation. As Mizanur Rahman Khan pointed out in a paper prepared for an international conference on "South Asian Regional Cooperation: A Socio-Economic Approach to Peace and Stability in South Asia," held in Dhaka in January 1985, "the proliferation of regional bodies under SAARC and participation in those by the member countries are expected to gradually inculcate among the leadership concerned a sense of belonging to the region, thus widening the psychological horizon from the national to the regional level."[28] This is an important consideration, especially at a time when we are witnessing, in South Asia and elsewhere in Asia and the Pacific, a revival of nationalistic feelings and identity, in both constructive and alarming forms, and when all of the South Asian countries are increasingly forced to try to cope with serious problems that have regional and international dimensions and cannot be resolved on a national level.

Thus SAARC is already playing a useful role in demonstrating the value of the new regionalism in mitigating some of the adverse effects and dangers of the revived nationalism, in helping to develop a sense of regional identity and mutual interests, and in establishing linkages between the nation-states of South Asia and the larger international system of which these states are increasingly a part. This important point is also noted by Mizanur Rahman Khan: "The interaction of SARC as a regional grouping with other countries, regional groupings and international organizations will reinforce the new reference make-up, such as 'We from SARC' as is usually done by the EEC, Arab League, OAU, or ASEAN member countries. Thus the changed reference make-up would gradually strengthen the sense of regionalism among the countries of South Asia while also promoting their interests as nation-states."[29]

SAARC as an Intraregional and International Actor

The potential of SAARC for representing the mutual interests and views of its member states in their international relations and for helping to win greater recognition, respect, and influence for South Asia in the international community is very great. Indeed, this may turn out to be one of its most important roles. But the organization is not yet ready to carry out this larger mission as effectively as the "objective conditions," to borrow a favorite term in the Communist vocabulary, would seem to call for. More importantly, the member states are apparently not yet ready to entrust SAARC with the assignment of representing their common interests and positions in international circles. This is a role that the member states of EEC regularly entrust to the organization—i.e., they often empower a representative or representatives of the EEC to act on behalf of all the members in certain international conferences, other multilateral gatherings and groupings, and negotiations. It is a role that ASEAN member states are beginning to entrust to a single ASEAN representative or representatives, still on a limited basis.

This may in fact be one of the ultimate tests of the value and effectiveness of comprehensive regional organizations, that is, how frequently they are empowered to speak for and represent all of their members, as a collectivity, and how effective they can be in representing the region, in promoting the interests of member states and the region as a whole, and in gaining new status and influence for the region in its international interrelationships. EEC already seems to have achieved this goal. Moreover, the European Community as a whole, of which the EEC is the central institution, may function even more effectively as an international actor, and as a representative of its members, after it becomes a single market and more clearly one of the world's three main centers of economic power, as is planned for 1992.

ASEAN is moving slowly in the direction of becoming an important international actor and spokesman for its members in the international community; but it is far behind EC and EEC in this respect, and is generally a much less developed and powerful economic or political organization.

SAARC is obviously even farther behind. There is little prospect that it will be able to equal the record of the European Community or even of ASEAN in the foreseeable future, if ever. But the South Asian states seem to be moving, however slowly, toward greater regional cooperation and institutionalization, and to be recognizing more realistically than ever before that they will not be able to gain the recognition, respect, and influence in international affairs to which they aspire and to which they think they are entitled until and unless they demonstrate to the world that they can "get their act together," both internally and intraregionally. With the full support of its members SAARC would seem to have the potential to function as a clarion voice of South Asia on the world stage. But this is a possibility—or perhaps no more than a hope—for the future.

SAARC is, however, beginning to emerge as an international actor, although obviously most of the foreign relations of the South Asian states are still conducted on a bilateral basis, or through participation in international organizations and conferences in the normal way, rather than through SAARC. Gradually, however, SAARC, like ASEAN, is acting as a spokesperson for all the South Asian states, through a single representative or delegation.

The Charter of SAARC clearly envisions such international representation, and later resolutions at SAARC meetings have reaffirmed the desirability of this practice. Article I of the SAARC Charter provides for cooperation "in international forums on matters of common interests." At their meeting in Islamabad in April 1986 the South Asian foreign ministers decided that "representatives of SAARC countries should co-ordinate their positions at the headquarters of international and regional organisations as well as in relevant international conferences to further the common objectives of member countries."[30]

Thus far, this practice has often been followed in terms of consultation and coordination of positions in international forums, but it has not yet led to extensive use of a single representative or delegation of SAARC to speak for all of the South Asian states.

SAARC in Its First Decade: An Evaluation

The experience of SAARC in its first decade as a functioning regional organization provides grounds for hope and for discouragement regarding the prospects for continuing regional institutionalization and the growth of effective regional cooperation in South Asia and other parts of the world where there are so many obstacles in the way to such cooperation and so little past experience in constructive regional cooperation. At this stage, any optimistic forecasts must be advanced with continuing reminders of the unprecedented nature of the SAARC experiment. Writing in 1987, Dr. S. D. Muni, a staunch and informed supporter of SAARC, observed: "Looking at the totality of present trends in South Asia, nothing significant may be expected out of SAARC in the coming months and years. . . . [I]t would . . . be a miracle if SAARC can develop as an autonomous regional factor for peace through development in the face of adverse regional and extra regional pressures."[31] A distinguished American economist concluded a generally favorable assessment of SAARC with a similar precautionary note: "[T]he SAARC effort will have to go forward against a counterpoint of chronic intervals of bilateral tension as between South Asian countries and of domestic political difficulties in particular countries; and quite often the two will be related."[32]

Dr. Muni is quite correct, however, in pointing out that one cannot expect an organization "which has been launched on a considerable small scale and with modest expectations" to do more than partially counteract, during its brief period of existence, "forty years of dissonance," with roots in a much longer past. "The achievements," he insists, "may not appear to be spectacular but they are by no standard mean."[33]

Among the achievements of SAARC Dr. Muni itemizes the exercise of "a benign influence on bilateral differences and problems;" the effective development of the organizational structure; the expansion of the Integrated Programme of Action (IPA), including such previously avoided areas of co-operation as the suppression of terrorism, the problem of floods and other natural disasters, now on the IPA agenda "under the wider canvas of 'protection of environment,'" and trade. Dr. Muni also calls attention to the development of SAARC "as an approach to mutual confidence building."[34]

This "intangible performance" of SAARC, together with the opportunities the SAARC meetings provide for the discussion of bilateral issues on an informal basis among the leaders of the South Asian states, may prove to be the most important constructive consequence of the emergence of this unique regional organization.

From the viewpoint of comparative scholarly analysis of the new regionalism, SAARC raises a number of interesting questions. For example, to what extent is it an atypical emerging regional organization in a region where there has been little regionalism of a comprehensive nature in the past, and to what extent is its evolution rather similar to that of other regional organizations elsewhere in Asia and the Pacific and in other parts of the world? Dr. Muni believes that it is atypical, both because of the peculiar nature of the political and social environment in which it has emerged and because of the different approach it has tried to follow *vis-à-vis* external pressures, especially from Western powers. His reasoning is thought provoking and worthy of careful consideration:

> The evolution and prospects of SAARC present a number of difficult questions to the scholars, statesmen and observers who are trained habitually to compare any such organization with similar previous examples. SAARC is an example in itself. It makes a significant departure from the conventional pattern of regionalism moves enshrined in its European predecessors like EEC and COMECON as well as its Asian neighbours and contemporaries like ASEAN and GCC.
>
> Regionalism has not really been a regional phenomenon as such. It has been a product of world politics, initiated most by major powers in the regions adjacent to them or even far off, to seek a desirable regional order

for a global balance that could cater to their respective regional and group interests.[35]

This is an intriguing interpretation. It can be criticized as being unduly influenced by the tendency in newly independent countries to see foreign machinations and pressures everywhere, and by the common tendency to view any regional development as even more ideosyncratic than it really is. It can also be argued that this interpretation exaggerates the distinctive aspects of regionalism in South Asia, and that it shows an inadequate realization of the similarities to other experiments in region institutionalization.

Obviously regionalism in any part of the world has distinctive and unique features; but it also has important commonalities as well. Both of these aspects must be considered in any balanced assessment of regionalism and regional institutionalization in South Asia, as elsewhere.

6
Regionalism in the Southwest Pacific and Oceania: Focus on the South Pacific Forum

T he fourth major subregion of Asia and the Pacific—the Southwest Pacific and Oceania—is a vast region in itself, covering one-sixth of the earth's surface. Only the two developed countries of Australia and New Zealand are important actors both within the region and in the international community. Until recently, however, their ties with the rest of the Asia–Pacific area were far less extensive than their ties with the Western world. This situation is changing rapidly, as they develop more contacts with the other subregions of Asia and the Pacific and with the island nations of Oceania.

The Island Nations of Oceania

There are literally thousands of islands in Oceania, but only nine island groupings have attained the status of independent nations, all within the past thirty years. In the order of their independence these are Western Samoa (1962); Nauru (1968); Tonga (1970); Fiji (1970); Papua New Guinea (1975); the Solomon Islands (1978); Tuvalu, formerly the Ellice Islands (1978); Kiribati, formerly the Gilbert Islands (1979); and Vanuatu, formerly the New Hebrides (1980). Three of the four groupings carved out of the former Strategic Trust Territory of the Pacific Islands (USTTPI), which was administered by the United States—the Republic of the Marshall Islands, the Federated States of Micronesia, and the Republic of Palau—are approaching independence. Guam, the Cook Islands, and Niue have self-governing status, the former in association with the United States, the latter two in association with New Zealand.

In a statement summarizing "the political arrangements and statuses" of the polities in Oceania, included in a paper on "Economic Security Issues in the South Pacific," which he prepared for a symposium at the National Defense University in February 1986,[1] Dr. Robert Kiste, Director of the Pacific Studies Program at the University of Hawaii, observed: "[T]here will be twenty-one countries in the insular Pacific after the termination of the USTTPI: the eleven island nations of the SPF (Australia and New Zealand excluded), the six with American connections, the three French territories, and Tokelau."[2] But only nine of these twenty-one "countries" have presently the recognized attributes of completely sovereign states. Dr. Kiste's "eleven island nations of the SPF" (South Pacific Forum) include the Cook Islands and Niue, which, as has been noted, have self-governing but not independent status in association with New Zealand. None of "the six with American connections" has yet achieved fully independent status, although, as has been stated, the Republic of the Marshall Islands, the Federated States of Malaysia, and the Republic of Palau, "are approaching independence." Of the three French territories of New Caledonia, French Polynesia, and Wallis and Futuna, only the first seems to have any prospect of independence before the end of this century, and this is by no means certain; and Tokelau, with four square miles and a population of 1,600 in 1987, seems destined to remain under New Zealand's administration into the indefinite future.

In terms of size and population Papua New Guinea is the giant among the nine island nations of Oceania. It is twelve times as large and has two and a half times as many people as all the others combined. The only other nations of Oceania with more than 100,000 people are Fiji (700,000 in mid-1987), the Solomon Islands (300,000), Vanuatu (200,000), Western Samoa (200,000), and Tonga (107,000). The smallest in population, with around 8,000 each, are Tuvalu and Nauru. The latter is often described as the world's smallest republic.[3] All the island nations except Papua New Guinea are very small, ranging from the Solomon Islands, with 10,985 square miles, to the tiny states of Tuvalu, with 10 square miles, and Nauru, with only 8.2.

These island nations are scattered about the vast expanses of Oceania, in the Southwest, South, and West Central Pacific. Until recently they had little contact with each other, or with Australia or New Zealand (except for Papua New Guinea), or with the other major subregions of Asia and the Pacific, or with the world beyond, except through the Western countries—mainly the United States, France, and Britain—that formerly controlled most of them. With their emergence into independence, however, they have been developing new and closer patterns of relations with each other and with other regions and countries. Hence, for the first time, a significant degree of regional cooperation is developing. This will be the central theme of this chapter.

These nations are now exhibiting the three characteristics that have been so marked in the other regions of Asia and the Pacific—a new and more assertive nationalism, a new and broader regionalism, and a growing consciousness of interdependence and internationalism. They all belong to the Third World of developing countries, and most of them rank with the poorest of the poor. They are among the most isolated of the world's nations. But the world is discovering them, and they are discovering the world. Politically, economically, and strategically they have little influence in the councils of the nations as long as they act individually; but collectively they are beginning to be heard, especially through the South Pacific Forum and other regional groupings, or when they can enlist the support of nations and groupings with similar interests and concerns, such as Third World countries, the nonaligned movement, and antinuclear forces. In their disputes with more powerful nations over at least three issues of deep concern to them, namely trade, fisheries, and nuclear testing, they have been able to act collectively with considerable success. In their quest for development they have had widespread support from many nations and international organizations.

All of these matters, plus growing tourism and cultural, historical, anthropological, scenic, and other attractions, have brought the island nations of Oceania more in touch with each other and with the outside world. On the whole, this has contributed to their development; but it has had many negative effects as well. Among these are threats to their cultures and ways of life, their physical environment, and their political stability—as illustrated by recent events in Fiji, Vanuatu, and New Caledonia.

Polynesia, Melanesia, and Micronesia

Conventional historical, ethnographic, and geographic analysis has divided the area we have called Oceania into three main regions, or subregions, based on distinctive racial and geographic characteristics. These regions are known as Polynesia, Melanesia, and Micronesia. It is still a convenient division, as even a brief description of the nature of and trends in each of these regions will reveal.

Polynesia ("many islands") includes the easternmost islands of the region described here as Oceania, plus the Hawaiian Islands. Because Hawaii is a state in the American Union, and is located far away from much of Polynesia, it will not be considered as a part of Oceania; but it should be noted that it is a focal point of contact with the entire Pacific area and is increasingly becoming a center for training, research, and development programs for the entire area. While the dividing line between the three subregions is not wholly clear, Polynesia may be said to include four of the nine independent Pacific island nations—Western Samoa, Tonga, Tuvalu, and Kiribati—as well as the extensive area of French Polynesia, an overseas territory of France whose best known islands are Tahiti in the Society Islands, a great tourist attraction, and Mururoa, where France's Pacific Nuclear Test Center is located.

In the vicinity of Mururoa, France has continued to conduct nuclear tests, in spite of strong protests by virtually all of the Pacific island nations, supported by Australia, New Zealand, and many countries outside the region. Indeed, a united front against all nuclear testing (and nuclear waste dumping) in French Polynesia and by the United States in the territory now embraced in the Republic of the Marshall Islands in Micronesia (the U.S. tests have been suspended) has been a major factor for greater regionalism in all of Oceania.[4]

Melanesia ("islands where black or dark-skinned people live") extends from Papua New Guinea to Fiji and embraces three more of the nine Pacific island nations—the Solomon Islands, Fiji, and Nauru—as well as the important French overseas territory of New Caledonia. Because it includes Papua New Guinea, Melanesia is by far the most populous region of Oceania, with about 80 percent of all the people of the entire region. Fiji, the second most populous nation in Oceania, is perhaps the best known island group and the nearest thing to an unofficial capital of Oceania. It is a hub of air traffic through the South Pacific and a popular tourist center (made less attractive in recent years by internal disturbances and tensions). The headquarters of the South Pacific Forum, the leading regional organization in the Southwest Pacific and Oceania, and the main campus of the University of the South Pacific are located in Suva, the capital of Fiji.

After World War II, when it was a major combat theater, Oceania became one of the most peaceful as well as one of the least known of the world's regions; but in recent years, because of the distressful conditions and political instabilities in many of the islands, the increasing activities in the region of outside powers, and disputes with these powers over such important concerns as development assistance, fisheries rights and policies, and nuclear issues, the region has been anything but peaceful. And the greatest instability has been in Melanesia, especially in Fiji, New Caledonia, and Vanuatu.[5]

In Fiji the instability has been caused by longstanding frictions between the native Fijians and the people of Indian origin in the islands, who slightly outnumber the native population. An Indian-dominated government, installed after elections in April 1987, was overthrown the following month by the Fijian-dominated army, led by Lieutenant Colonel Sitiveni, and a new government, structured to preserve Fijian control, was formed.[6] This led to an announcement at the Commonwealth summit meeting in Vancouver that Fiji's membership had lapsed, and to strained relations with England, Australia, and other countries. It also led to a marked decline in tourism, Fiji's main source of income. More recently internal conditions and external relations have improved considerably.

In New Caledonia the controversy has been between the French rulers and pro-French native peoples, on the one hand, and the majority of the major native group, the Kanaks, who have demanded self-government, on the other. After considerable violence in 1988, an agreement was finally reached between the two parties, and approved by the French voters in

November. This calls for a ten-year transition period, with increasing self-government, to be followed by a vote in 1998 to determine whether the people of New Caledonia wish to remain a part of France or become independent.[7]

Vanuatu has been a center of disturbances which, like those in Fiji and New Caledonia, have had repercussions far beyond the region. The leftist and anti-West Prime Minister, Walter Lini, a priest, has given special privileges to Libya, the Soviet Union, and Cuba. He has used strong-arm methods to suppress opposition within his own government and from opposition groups, especially those led by his chief political rival, Barak Sope.[8]

In Melanesia one finds some of the most conspicuous examples of a new trend characterizing the new regionalism in other parts of the Southwest Pacific and Oceania and in other regions of Asia and the Pacific, namely the rise of younger, more aggressive, and more nationalistic political leaders. Walter Lini of Vanuatu is in his early forties, as are Solomon Mamaloni and Sir Peter Kenilorea, both former prime ministers in the Solomon Islands. Paias Wingti, a former prime minister of Papua New Guinea and often mentioned as a man who might one day emerge as an all-regional leader, is still in his thirties.[9]

Four main polities have emerged, or are emerging, in Micronesia ("small islands"). They are the Republic of the Marshall Islands, the Federated States of Micronesia (comprising most of the Caroline Islands group), the Republic of Palau, and the Commonwealth of the Northern Mariana Islands. All of these polities have emerged out of the Strategic Trust Territory of the Pacific Islands, administered by the United States since 1947. Under considerable foreign pressure, the United States agreed in the 1970s to terminate the trusteeship and to work out a different political status for the inhabitants of the scattered islands that would be in accord with the wishes of the majority of the people of the subregion, that would assure these people continued economic and financial support, and that would take into consideration the strategic needs of the United States in that part of the West Central Pacific.

In 1976 the islands of the Northern Marianas (including Saipan and Tinian) became a Commonwealth under U.S. sovereignty, after a covenant was approved overwhelmingly by the people of these islands. Prolonged negotiations with the other three polities led to acceptance of a proposed Compact of Free Association with the United States.[10] The Compact became effective for the Republic of the Marshall Islands and the Federated States of Micronesia in November 1986. After being rejected no less than five times by the voters of the Palau Islands, the Covenant was finally approved, after much arm twisting by the United States and pro–U.S. groups in the islands; but it has not yet entered into effect because the U.S. government and the leaders of Palau, backed by the majority of the people, are still at odds over the right of the United States to maintain bases on the islands (with atomic weapons) and to use the islands, if the United States so chooses, as a forward base if and when the U.S. is forced to abandon the huge naval base at Subic Bay and the air base at Clark Field in the Philippines.[11]

These three polities, therefore, are in various stages of transition, leading to a much greater degree of autonomy and quite possibly to independence. If they achieve the status of independent nations, they will doubtless play a larger role in the new regionalism in the Southwest Pacific and Oceania; but their nominal independence will be greatly circumscribed by their "free association" with and their continuing dependence on the United States for their survival.

Australia, New Zealand, and the Crisis in ANZUS

Because of their developed status and far greater political experience and international associations, Australia and New Zealand are the most important nations in the Southwest Pacific and Oceania. They are turning more and more to the island nations of Oceania, as well as to Asia and the Pacific region generally.

Australia has long had a special relationship with the island of New Guinea. It occupied the huge island, then under the control of Germany, during World War I, and it retained jurisdiction over the eastern half of the island, first under a League of Nations mandate and then under a United Nations trusteeship, until September 1975, when Papua New Guinea was granted its independence. Since then Australia has continued to have many special ties with that new nation, by far the largest and probably, or at least potentially, the most influential of the new nations of Oceania. The changing relationship between the two countries, however, is an increasingly delicate one.[12]

New Zealand has had no similar relationship with any of the new nations of Oceania, but two of the members of the South Pacific Forum and other regional organizations in the Southwest Pacific and Oceania, the Cook Islands and Niue, have self-governing status in association with New Zealand.

Most of the Pacific Island states depend far more on developed countries of the Western world, and on Japan, than they do on either Australia or New Zealand; but Australia is the main source of imports for several of these nations, including Fiji, Papua New Guinea, and Vanuatu, and the second major source for Western Samoa, and New Zealand is the main source of imports for Western Samoa and the second most important for Fiji. Moreover, Australia is the second most important market for Fiji and the third for Papua New Guinea, while Western Samoa exports more to New Zealand than to any other country except the United States.[13]

In 1951 Australia and New Zealand took the initiative in the formation of an alliance with the United States, known as ANZUS. This was the only military alliance in the Southwest Pacific and Oceania. From the point of view of Australia and New Zealand the alliance with the United States was a powerful guarantee of their security. From the point of view of the United States ANZUS was a part of the Western alliance system.

For many years ANZUS was one of the most stable and reliable of all the world's multilateral security arrangements. Because of it, security cooperation among the three allies was extensive. It included "military exercises, unit exchanges, joint training, standardization and interoperability of equipment and weapons systems, intelligence and personnel exchanges, and regular high-level political exchanges."[14]

In the 1980s ANZUS became an alliance in crisis. Critics in Australia and New Zealand argued that the alliance had become unnecessary and indeed dangerous, in that it might involve their countries in Soviet–American regional conflicts, or even in a global war. This view was endorsed by the Labour parties in both countries; and in the 1980s these parties came to power in both.

In spite of its longstanding criticisms of ANZUS the Australian Labour government remained a cooperative member of the alliance; but in 1984 the newly elected Labour government in New Zealand, headed by David Lange, moved to implement the party's campaign pledge to ban visits by nuclear-powered and nuclear-capable naval vessels, even those of its allies. This provoked a major crisis in the alliance.[15] New Zealand would not permit U.S. warships to make port calls unless the U.S. gave assurances that these vessels were neither nuclear-powered nor nuclear-armed. New Zealand's demands for such assurances ran counter to the "neither confirm nor deny" policy of the United States. The United States feared that any deviation from this policy would set a dangerous precedent. It also argued that denials of port calls and other restrictions on U.S. nuclear-powered vessels—some 40 percent of U.S. naval combat ships fall into this category—were incompatible with the obligations of an ally.

In August 1986, after prolonged efforts to resolve the impasse proved to be unsuccessful, the U.S. government notified New Zealand that it was suspending its security commitments to that country under the ANZUS pact.[16] Technically, the pact remained in effect, but in reality it became inoperative. New Zealand took the position that it wished to remain in ANZUS; but in early May 1988 Prime Minister Lange, in an address at Yale University during an unofficial visit to the United States, when he was snubbed by high-level American officials, declared that New Zealand might soon officially withdraw from ANZUS. "Between the United States and New Zealand," he said, "the security alliance is a dead letter. The basis of the alliance was a commitment to consult. Consultation has stopped."[17]

Support for the New Zealand position was widespread throughout the

Pacific island nations and in influential circles in Australia; but the leaders of most of these countries urged the United States and New Zealand to resolve their differences promptly. The Australian Labour government made special efforts to persuade the sparring ANZUS partners—or former partners—to remain in ANZUS and to reach some mutually acceptable compromise on their nuclear disagreement. It also entered into bilateral agreements with the United States to continue to honor the mutual obligations under the ANZUS treaty, and it agreed to allow the United States to continue, under somewhat more restricted conditions, to maintain a number of communications and other facilities in Australia for at least another ten years.

The ANZUS crisis had repercussions throughout the Southwest Pacific–Oceania region. The South Pacific Forum was a channel for expressions of support for New Zealand, and for efforts to mediate the U.S.–New Zealand dispute. The crisis helped to strengthen the bonds uniting the disparate nations in the vast oceanic region. It also created new complications for the United States in a region where it had long been the dominant external power. In this case, as in many others, a localized crisis had national, regional, interregional, and international implications.

The South Pacific Commission and the South Pacific Conference

In such a disparate, isolated, and vast area as the Southwest Pacific and Oceania, with little past experience in regional cooperation, it is amazing that so much regional institutionalization has taken place. On the official level three all-regional, or nearly all-regional, organizations deserve special attention. They are the South Pacific Commission, the South Pacific Conference, and the South Pacific Forum.[18]

The South Pacific Commission is an interesting example of a regional organization that was originally formed by external powers with possessions in the region, in cooperation with Australia and New Zealand, and that eventually developed an indigenous all-regional character and identity. It was established by Australia, Britain, France, the Netherlands (which withdrew in 1962 when it ceased to administer the former Dutch New Guinea, now known as Irian Jaya, a part of Indonesia), and New Zealand under an agreement signed in Canberra, the capital of Australia, in February 1947.

In 1985, three years after it became the first Pacific island group to achieve independence, Western Samoa became a member. This step encountered some opposition in the new nation and elsewhere in Oceania, especially among nationalists who wanted to expel rather than join with the colonial or former colonial powers. But Western Samoa's membership was followed by that of every subsequent Pacific island nation.

The main purpose of the South Pacific Commission is "to advise and assist the participating governments and territorial administrations in promoting the economic, medical, and social development of the peoples of Oceania." Its work program, as described in a book on Oceania published in 1984, is a very comprehensive one in these broad areas. It includes "agricultural development, conservation, cultural exchanges, . . . the development of marine resources and research, environmental health, fisheries, nutrition, plant diseases and protection, regional communications, sanitation, [and] youth and community work. In recent years rural development and regional integration have received increasing attention."[19]

Headquarters of the South Pacific Commission are in Noumea, New Caledonia. There is a small secretariat, headed by a secretary general as chief executive officer. It is worthy of special note that since 1969 all of the secretaries general have been Pacific islanders. The annual budget is provided by contributions by the members. About 93 percent of the 1984 budget of $3.4 million was borne by the five remaining original members: Australia, 34%; the United States, 17%; New Zealand, 16%; France, 14%; and Britain, 12%.

In the 1987 edition of a standard guidebook—*Fodor's Australia, New Zealand and the South Pacific*—the South Pacific Commission was described as "an important body," "a kind of small United Nations of the South Pacific," "a heartening example of cooperation between the nations who administer territories in the South Pacific, the island territories themselves, and the increasing number of independent Pacific nations."[20] For some time it was the only comprehensive official all-regional organization in the Southwest Pacific–Oceania region. It has received much less attention in recent years, largely because it has been superceded in importance—or in generally recognized importance—both by the South Pacific Conference and the South Pacific Forum. But it is still an important regional organization, and it merits much more attention than it is now receiving.

Originally created as an auxiliary body of the South Pacific Commission, to provide advice to the Commission and to hold conferences of its members, the South Pacific Conference soon developed an importance and a momentum of its own, while retaining special ties with the Commission. By the early 1980s the Conference had become the most comprehensive regional organization in the entire region. It had twenty-six members—all the founders of the South Pacific Commission except the Netherlands, including Australia and New Zealand, all nine of the independent island states of Oceania, the Cook Islands, Niue, the Federated States of Micronesia, the Republic of the Marshall Islands, the Commonwealth of the Northern Mariana Islands, the Republic of Palau, Guam, American Samoa, French Polynesia, New Caledonia, the Pitcairn Islands (Britain's only remaining holding in the region), Tokelau (a four square mile island possession of New Zealand), and the Wallis and Futuna Islands (an overseas territory of France).

The first annual meeting organized by the South Pacific Conference was held in 1950. Thereafter, for more than a decade and a half, its conferences were held every three years; and then, in 1967, they became annual affairs. They were held immediately after the annual meetings of the South Pacific Commission, and made recommendations to the Commission. In 1974 a Memorandum of Understanding between the Commission and the Conference provided that the two bodies—the "parent" and the "child"—should henceforth meet annually as a single body, to be known as the South Pacific Conference.

Bunge and Cook (1984) described the Conference as the "principal decision-making body of the South Pacific Commission." Eventually, according to this volume, "the Conference became the superior body. . . . The child had become the parent; the parent had become the child."[21] And it was making a major contribution to Southwest Pacific–Oceania regionalism. "The conference was to become extremely important in ways that had not been foreseen. For the first time, representatives of countries from all over the Pacific met on a face-to-face basis. They found the experience very much to their liking, and there began to emerge a real regional identity— that of a 'Pacific islander'—as opposed to more local identities, such as Samoan, Maori, or Tongan."[22] This new identity is now sometimes referred to as "the Pacific Way."[23]

The South Pacific Forum

Both the Commission and the Conference were created as nonpolitical organizations. This was an advantage in that they were no threat to the sovereignty or autonomy of their members. Obviously political issues and considerations could not be wholly avoided, but they were not put on the formal agenda, which, as has been indicated, dealt primarily with a wide range of economic and social matters. This was a substantial contribution to regional as well as to national development. But as time went on leaders of the states and other political entities of the region increasingly felt the need for some official regional organization to present a united front in dealings with stronger outside powers and with international organizations and agencies. Hence growing frustration with the political restraints on the Commission and the Conference led Australia, New Zealand, the nine independent island nations, and the self-governing Cook Islands and Niue to form a new and stronger regional organization, the South Pacific Forum. This was inaugurated in August 1971 at a conference in Wellington, New Zealand, of the heads of government of all thirteen of its charter members.

The South Pacific Forum is the most important regional organization in the entire Southwest Pacific–Oceania region, and one of the three most important in all of Asia and the Pacific.[24] Two-thirds of the Forum's annual budget is provided by Australia and New Zealand (each contributing one-third), and the remaining members provide one-third, in equal shares. The headquarters of the Forum are in Suva, the capital of Fiji.

A particularly important affiliated agency is the South Pacific Bureau for Economic Cooperation (SPEC), established in 1972 as the Forum's major executive branch and coordinator of various programs in the fields of economic and social cooperation—essentially the same fields with which the South Pacific Commission and South Pacific Conference were also concerned, but with more political "clout" than these other regional organizations had. Eventually SPEC became more of a secretariat than the executive of the Forum; and it continues to have broader functions as well. It has played a primary role in developing cooperative relations with other regional organizations in the Southwest Pacific and Oceania, notably the Commission and the Conference, and outside the region, including ASEAN, ESCAP, and EEC.

The South Pacific Forum has set up a large number of other agencies, many under the aegis of SPEC. These include the Pacific Forum Line (1978), a joint venture regional shipping organization, the South Pacific Forum Fisheries Agency (1979), South Pacific Airlines (1979), the South Pacific Trade Commission (1979), and the Tourism Council of the South Pacific (1983).

In 1987 the Federated States of Micronesia and the Republic of the Marshall Islands became full members of the Forum, thus increasing the membership to fifteen and giving it a more truly all-regional character.

Political disputes between or among its members are usually kept off the agenda of the annual meetings of top leaders of the member states of the Forum, although they are inevitably a subject of discussion "in the corridors" and in behind-the-scenes meetings of leaders of countries most directly concerned. However, the Forum, especially at its annual meetings, has become a central agency for taking positions and exerting pressure on political and security issues on which there is fairly widespread agreement. This is particularly true of nuclear issues.

Antinuclear sentiment is strong throughout the Southwest Pacific–Oceania region. It was the central issue in the dispute between New Zealand and the United States that led to the disruption of the ANZUS alliance. It is manifest in the repeated protests against the testing of nuclear weapons in Pacific waters, by the United States in the vicinity of the Bikini and Eniwetok atolls in what is now the Republic of the Marshall Islands in the 1950s and by the French in the vicinity of the Mururea atoll in French Polynesia.

Other nuclear developments of particular concern are the dumping of nuclear waste and the presence of nuclear-powered and nuclear-armed warships in the Pacific, a major strategic as well as commercial highway. Underlying all of these protests are fears of involvement in nuclear conflicts and in the rivalries of nuclear powers—and basically, opposition to all things nuclear.[25]

The South Pacific Forum has become the major channel for the expression of regional views and demands on nuclear issues. At every annual meeting of the leaders of the member states, these issues have been discussed and antinuclear resolutions have been passed. The most specific and highly publicized product of these continuing discussions is the South Pacific Nuclear Free Zone Treaty (SPNFZT), also known as the Treaty of Rarotonga, which was signed by representatives of ten of the thirteen member states at the annual meeting of the Forum in Rarotonga, in the Cook Islands, in August 1986. It prohibits testing, stationing, storage, acquisition, and deployment of nuclear weapons and the disposal of nuclear waste in the South Pacific (expanded to include all of the Southwest Pacific and Oceania). It does not restrict port visits by nuclear-powered or armed ships or the passage through the region of such vessels and planes. The matter of port calls is left for individual nations to decide.[26] The treaty was not as strong or as comprehensive in its provision for a nuclear free zone as some of the delegates at Rarotonga had wished. It was, in fact, a compromise negotiated by Australia's representatives to accommodate American concerns and interests.

On most major nuclear issues Australia has acted in a mediatory role without abandoning its generally antinuclear stand. It has tried to heal the rift in ANZUS and the dispute between its two ANZUS allies. It has put pressure on all the nuclear powers to make concessions to the antinuclear feelings that exist in varying degrees almost everywhere, and in particular on the United States and France, the two nuclear powers that are most active in the Pacific, to make concessions to the strong antinuclear feelings in the Southwest Pacific and Oceania.

The SPNFZT was a somewhat watered-down product of these feelings. All five nuclear powers were invited to sign protocols to the Rarotonga treaty, committing them not to "use, test, or deploy" nuclear weapons in the region. After the Rarotonga meeting a delegation from the South Pacific Forum visited the five nuclear powers and urged them to sign the protocols to the SPNFZT. The delegation was given a polite reception in all five countries; but thus far only the Soviet Union and China have signed the protocols, thereby scoring a considerable propaganda victory in the Southwest Pacific–Oceania region.

France still seems to be determined to continue to test nuclear weapons in French Polynesia, and the United States and Britain appear to be of two minds about adherence to the protocols of the SPNFZT. U.S. adherence would help to improve its overall relations with most of the Pacific nations, and might, to some extent at least, along with other changes in policy, help to soften its image in the Pacific as a bully and a dangerous nuclear giant.

Although it has a more comprehensive mandate than the South Pacific Commission and the South Pacific Conference, the South Pacific Forum has been increasingly concerned with economic issues. In this respect it duplicates the activities of the Commission and the Conference. In fact, there is some feeling in the region that the latter two organizations should be abolished. The Forum serves a wider function in the economic field, but it is perhaps less well equipped for more technical economic activities than are the other two organizations. At the same time it could be argued that because of its wider mandate the Forum is better able to promote the common economic interests of the countries of the region. It has become a central agency for the promotion of both regional and international trade, for the economic development of the individual member countries and other political entities in the region, and for economic cooperation among them. It is also playing an increasingly useful and effective role in its negotiations with other countries and international organizations in economic and other fields.

The individual polities of Oceania are too weak and underdeveloped to be able to deal effectively with more powerful nations, and yet they are becoming more and more involved in the international economy and in the international system generally. "Moving from aid-dependent coconut economies toward self-sufficiency is challenging. Vast distances to export markets, high freight charges, poor communications, and limited resources and skills create formidable hurdles for Pacific nations."[27] In many cases their needs and interests can best be promoted through regional cooperation and representation; and here the South Pacific Forum is often their most effective mouthpiece.

An example of the constructive activity of the Forum in the economic field is its role in the prolonged and often acrimonious disputes between the United States and several of the Pacific island nations over fishing rights, especially over tuna fishing in the region. The peoples of Oceania are heavily dependent for their livelihood upon fishing—the main resource of the seas. "The Pacific island nations have very few resources. They look to the sea as we would look as if it was our land. That's where they have, if you will, their crops. This is the way that they can harvest, this is the way that they can live."[28]

The island people are particularly sensitive about any real or perceived violations or excessive exploitation of the waters about them by foreign fishing fleets. For many years American tuna boats were regarded as the worst offenders, as "modern buccaneers." After the Law of the Sea Treaty was signed by most of the nations of the world, including the Pacific island nations but not the United States, tensions between the Pacific nations and the United States became serious. The Treaty endorsed the concept of a two-hundred mile Exclusive Economic Zone (EEZ) around each of the world's nations, within which the oceanic resources were the exclusive property of these nations, and nationals of no other country could exploit these resources without permission. Applying this standard, most of the Southwest Pacific–Oceania region was embraced within the EEZs of the tiny and scattered island nations.

The American Tunaboat Association, backed by a powerful lobby in Washington, D. C., insisted that tuna are a migratory fish and could not be claimed by any particular nations.[29] Hence American tuna boats continued to fish in waters embraced within EEZs and refused to purchase licenses to do so. This led to many unpleasant incidents, including the impounding of American tuna boats on charges of illegal poaching. The United States government tended to support the position of the American Tunaboat Association, but it also made repeated efforts to resolve the differences by bilateral negotiations. Instead of getting bogged down in acrimonious negotiation on fisheries issues with each of the Pacific island nations, the United States preferred to seek some comprehensive agreement with these nations as a bloc.

In this difficult situation the South Pacific Forum's Fishing Agency was authorized to enter into negotiations with the United States. Talks began in 1984 in Fiji, and continued through several rounds for four years, culminating in a comprehensive fishing agreement in 1988. Compromises were made on both sides. The Pacific countries recognized the right of American tuna boats to continue to fish in their waters, some of the best for tuna fishing in the world, and agreed that some of that fishing could be in waters embraced within EEZs, with permission of the country or countries concerned and payment of specified fees. The United States, in turn, agreed that American tuna boats would recognize these conditions and would pay for the privilege of fishing within EEZs.[30]

The resolution of this long-drawn-out dispute between the United States and the Pacific island countries through the mediation of the South Pacific Forum's Fishing Agency was a great boost to the reputation of the Forum and removed one of the greatest irritants in relations between the island nations and the United States. It was a triumph of good sense on both sides, and a major demonstration of the usefulness of the regional approach in dealing with issues that are both interregional and international in character.

A year later the twentieth annual meeting of the South Pacific Forum, held in July 1989 in Tarawa, the capital of Kiribati (a famous and bloody battleground in World War II), devoted more time to another important fisheries issue than to any other item on the agenda. This time the target was not the United States but Taiwan and Japan. The issue concerned the threat of the depletion of fish resources in the Pacific—and elsewhere—by the growing practice of drift-net fishing, which, used over many square miles of water, garnered in not only huge quantities of tuna but many other types of fish and other marine life.

The Pacific nations became alarmed to the point of action when in the 1988–89 fishing season some 190 foreign fishing boats (two-thirds from Taiwan) came to the South Pacific to catch tuna through the use of drift-nets, called by opponents the "walls of death." At the Tarawa meeting of the South Pacific Forum a "Tarawa Declaration" was adopted, calling for the establishment in the region of a drift-net free zone, to be followed by concerted efforts to secure a worldwide ban on drift-net fishing. The delegates praised South Korea for its pledge to forbid its fishing boats to use drift-net techniques.[31] A few weeks later legal and diplomatic experts from the member states of the Forum met in New Zealand to draft a South Pacific "Drift-Net Free Zone" convention. From the South Pacific, therefore, has come a major initiative to ban a practice that threatens the depletion of a basic source of food in all the oceans of the world.

The delegates at Tarawa also considered another matter relating to their ocean-surrounded habitat that might in the foreseeable future threaten their very existence. This is another issue that now occupies an important place on the agenda of global issues, namely the "greenhouse effect." The peoples of the Pacific are particularly concerned about the consequences of rising sea levels that the "greenhouse effect" might produce. If this occurs, it could force the evacuation of a number of the Pacific island groups, many of which are a series of large and small atolls with little elevation above sea level.[32] At Tarawa the delegates to the South Pacific Forum meeting discussed the implication of the "greenhouse effect" upon their oceanic region, and they accepted an Australian offer of $4.7 million to initiate a climate and ocean monitoring program.

Delegates at Tarawa also endorsed a proposal to establish some formal links with ASEAN, especially between the two secretariats. This could be an important step in the development of closer regional cooperation between the countries of Southeast Asia and the Southwest Pacific and Oceania.

Another important evidence of the broadening scope of the South Pacific Forum was the convening of the first post-ministerial meeting immediately following the annual meeting of the Forum at Tarawa, with its "dialogue partners," in this case with high-level representatives from the major non-member aid-donor nations, Britain, Canada, France, Japan, and the United States.[33] Obviously this is the beginning of a practice that has been followed for several years by the ASEAN countries and their "dialogue partners" (their major trading partners). As has been pointed out in the discussion of ASEAN, this practice could develop into one of the most important and novel dimensions of the new regionalism in Asia and the Pacific. It will be greatly furthered by its adoption by the South Pacific Forum and its "dialogue partners."

In addition to these important new initiatives, the delegates to the twentieth annual meeting of the Forum approved a number of resolutions that were similar to those passed at every Forum meeting since its inception. For example, two resolutions restated the Forum's opposition to continued nuclear testing by the French in Pacific waters (French Polynesia) and its criticism of France for its slow movement toward the decolonialization of New Caledonia.

Regional Institutionalization: A Summing Up

There have been repeated suggestions that the three major official all-regional organizations in the Southwest Pacific and Oceania—the South Pacific Commission, the South Pacific Conference, and the South Pacific Forum—should be joined into a single regional organization. In this unification movement the South Pacific Forum would probably play the leading role. A major step in this direction was taken in 1988, when the Forum endorsed the proposed South Pacific Organizations Coordinating Committee (SPOCC), to be chaired by the Forum secretariat. If the other two major regional organizations agree to this proposal, which is by no means a certainty, it is possible that, as Michael Haas has predicted, "SPOCC may . . . be a turning point for regional cooperation in the South Pacific."[34]

In a region with as little previous experience in regionalism as the Southwest Pacific and Oceania, it is remarkable that three important nearly all-regional and quite comprehensive official regional organizations have emerged and have demonstrated their value in promoting the common interests of the scattered peoples of the region.

There are also several other regional organizations, official and unofficial, that are worthy of special attention. Examples are the Nuclear Free Pacific Conference, which has held general meetings about once every three years since 1975, and the Pacific Council of Churches, which includes major Protestant denominations and the Catholic Church as well.[35] Special mention should also be made of the University of the South Pacific, founded in 1967. Its main campus is located in Suva, the capital of Fiji, and it has extension centers in most Pacific island countries.

For reasons that have previously been indicated, Hawaii has not been included in this study; but it is located in the northeast part of Polynesia, and it has longstanding historical, ethnic, and cultural ties with Oceania. Moreover, its institutions, notably the University of Hawaii, the East–West Center, the Bishop Museum, and the Pacific Forum, are carrying on continuous research relating to Oceania, and are major centers for the education and training of Pacific islanders. In multiple ways, therefore, Hawaii has contributed much to the development of the peoples and polities of Oceania, and to the new regionalism in that part of the world.

Intraregional and Interregional Ties

Many examples have already been cited of growing ties within and among Australia, New Zealand, and the three main subregions of Oceania, ethnically and geographically defined. Since World War II intraregional cooperation has been common in Micronesia, but this has been largely through the United States as the administrator of the Strategic Trust Territory of the Pacific Islands, which embraced virtually all of the island groups in this subregion. With the emergence of four polities out of the former Trust Territory a new political order now exists. These new polities maintain special ties with the United States and are developing special ties with each other. Among their many common interests are improving the life conditions of their peoples, preserving and enriching their cultural heritage, maintaining their autonomous or semi-autonomous status, dealing with the United States and other external powers, and learning how to exist and function in the international system that intrudes upon them at every turn.

In Melanesia, where most of the people of Oceania live, a strange mixture and variety of intraregional ties have been forged among the five independent nations of this subregion; and new patterns seem to be emerging. A fascinating example of this latter trend is the development of such close ties among Papua New Guinea, the Solomon Islands, and Vanuatu—strange bedfellows indeed—that some informed observers speak of an emerging "Melanesian Union" among these three countries. This is a new development that deserves very special attention. It seems to have germinated in a most casual way through exchanges among the prime ministers of the three countries. According to Michael Haas, in 1986 these leaders "met together en route to the South Pacific Forum at Rarotonga" and "decided to announce the formation of the Melanesia Spearhead Group (MSG)." On 14 March 1988 "they issued a document entitled 'Agreed Principles of Cooperation,' in a ceremony in Port Vila (the capital of Vanuatu), thereby establishing MSG as an independent South Pacific regional organization."[36] It is still in a very early stage of institutional development. Its main activity thus far seems to be the convening of an annual summit conference. Through MSG these three important and diverse Melanesian islands will probably have a greater voice in all-regional and perhaps even in international affairs. An interesting question, still to be answered, is whether the existence of the MSG will promote or hinder the trends toward all-regional organization and cooperation.

Fewer intraregional ties are evident in Polynesia. A large part of this subregion is occupied by French Polynesia, controlled by France, whose chief contribution to regionalism in Oceania is a negative one, namely as an object of criticism because of the continuance of French colonial rule and the continued testing of nuclear weapons. Externally this subregion is best known for its tourist attractions, notably Tonga and Tahiti, for the division of Samoa into two parts—Western Samoa, an independent nation, and American Samoa—and perhaps also for remote Pitcairn Island, Britain's only remaining colony in Oceania, because of Captain Bligh and the *Bounty*.

Ties among the peoples and polities of the Southwest Pacific and Oceania, as distinguished from contacts within the three subregions of Oceania, have been illustrated by the frequent references to the relations of Australia and New Zealand with the island nations of Oceania, and by the discussion of the cooperation of all the polities of the region in regional organizations, notably the South Pacific Forum.

Multilateral ties among the peoples and governments of the region are much more extensive than a study of the operation of regional organizations might suggest. Indeed, the concept of international regimes may be more relevant to an analysis of this region than of any other region or subregion in Asia and the Pacific. In many issue areas of particular concern to the region and its peoples, international regimes of a fairly well recognized type exist, providing some degree of cohesion, order, and public attention to issue areas that would otherwise be overlooked. Notable examples of international regimes that are of particular importance in the Southwest Pacific and Oceania are the regimes in the issue areas of fishing and nuclear nonproliferation. Association with the first of these two regimes has at long last led to the conclusion of broad agreements between the nations of the region and outside governments and associations, notably with respect to tuna fishing; and the efforts of the governments and peoples of the region to end nuclear testing and nuclear waste disposal in their part of the world, and to keep warships carrying nuclear weapons out of their seas, have been greatly assisted by the existence of an international nonproliferation regime. To be sure, this wider association has also been a barrier to agreements in the region with major powers involved in nuclear activities in the Pacific, namely France and the United States, which have been reluctant to agree to the demands for nonproliferation in the region because this could set a precedent that could create more serious complications in other world regions of greater security concern and strategic importance.

Associations with the other three major subregions of Asia and the Pacific are growing rapidly, although they are still relatively underdeveloped. The closest ties are with Southeast Asia. Examples are the somewhat rocky relations of Australia with Indonesia, the association of Australia and New Zealand with Malaysia and Singapore—and Britain—in the Five Power Defense Pact, the presence of representatives of Papua New Guinea as observers at annual meetings of the foreign ministers of the ASEAN countries, and the increasing ties between the South Pacific Forum and ASEAN and between both Australia and New Zealand and Japan and, to a lesser extent, South Korea.

Similar ties may in time develop between the South Pacific Forum and SAARC, but thus far there have been fewer contacts with the peoples and countries of South Asia than with those of the other two subregions. One strong personal link, however, does exist, due to the presence in the countries of the Southwest Pacific and Oceania of large numbers of persons of Indian origin. Mention has already been made of the differences between such persons on Fiji and ethnic Fijians, now slightly outnumbered by Indian residents of the island group. These differences underlie the internal instabilities in Fiji in recent years.

Until recently contacts with the countries of East Asia, except for Japan, have been relatively limited; but now they are developing quite rapidly. Illustrations are the growing interest in Oceania of the People's Republic of China, which now has more resident diplomatic missions in the island nations of Oceania than has the United States, and the new interest of Korean businessmen in trade and investments in the countries of Oceania.

Japan's contacts with the region have been longer and quite different, and for the most part they have left a heritage of distrust and unhappy memories. During World War I the Japanese occupied many of the islands of Micronesia, and these islands were administered by Japan as a mandate under the supervision of the League of Nations between the two world wars. During World War II the Japanese occupied much of Oceania, which became one of the major combat theaters in the war in the Pacific.

This was a legacy of close association, of a distorted kind, but not one that was conducive to close cooperation. Nevertheless, since the end of World War II, and particularly after the emergence of independent nations in Oceania, contacts with Japan have been quite extensive, and of a different nature. Australia and New Zealand have participated in joint military and naval exercises with Japan—and the United States—including RIMPAC exercises in the Pacific, some of the largest naval exercises ever conducted. The two Antipodean nations, and to a lesser extent the island nations of Oceania, have been increasingly oriented toward Asia, and ties with Japan have been central to the new relationship. Trade between Japan and the region has been expanding, as have Japanese investments.

The countries of the region are also participants in various ways in the Asia–Pacific region as a whole through membership in the Economic and Social Commission for Asia and the Pacific (ESCAP) and the Asian Development Bank (ADB). Australia and New Zealand are active participants in the major private or semi-private all-regional organizations, the Pacific Trade and Development Conference (PAFTAD), the Pacific Basin Economic Council (PBEC), and the Pacific Economic Cooperation Council (PECC). Australia is taking a leading role in efforts to establish a more comprehensive all-regional official economic organization. Prime Minister Robert Hawke's proposal for such an organization, as has been pointed out in chapter 2, was endorsed by many of the nations of East and Southeast Asia. It led to the major all-regional conference in Canberra in November 1989.

International Ties

Australia and New Zealand have long been active participants in various international organizations and conferences, and in international life generally. They have been associated with the Western world in many ways. Both are members of the Commonwealth of Nations, the United Nations, and the Organization for Economic Cooperation and Development (OECD), whose other members are the developed nations of North America and Western Europe—and Japan.

The small Pacific island nations have, of course, been far less involved in international activities, organizations, and conferences; but they have been more involved than is generally recognized, and that involvement is growing.[37] It is notable, for instance, that all of the thirteen independent nations of the region, except Tuvalu and Vanuatu, are members of the Commonwealth of Nations,[38] and hence still have many special ties to Britain, and that all but Kiribati, Nauru, Tonga, and Tuvalu are members of the United Nations. Surprisingly, not one of these thirteen states is a member of the nonaligned movement, which embraces the majority of Third World countries (and all of the nine Pacific island nations belong in this category).

The fact is, as a correspondent of the *Christian Science Monitor* pointed out in an interesting report in July 1989 from Tarawa, the capital of Kiribati, "The South Pacific is going international." He noted that "the few days since the South Pacific Forum," which had just held its annual meeting in Tarawa, "provide the latest confirmation of the trend. For the first time, countries from outside the region were invited to a post-forum dialogue. Government delegates flocked from the United States, Japan, France, Canada, and the United Kingdom to discuss aid, trade, and regional issues. These and other nations are beefing up their diplomatic ties in the region and backing them with substantial hikes in assistance."[39] In short, as this article clearly documents, the countries of the "South Pacific" (i.e., of the Southwest Pacific and Oceania) are expanding their international ties and attracting increasing "global interest."

This trend illustrates the outward-turning nature of the new regionalism in the South Pacific. It demonstrates again that, if wisely developed, the new regionalism is quite compatible with the growing internationalism that is a marked feature of the contemporary world.

The Overall Picture

Of the four major subregions of Asia and the Pacific, the Southwest Pacific and Oceania subregion is the largest in area, the smallest in population and in territory, and the least examined as a region (or, for that matter, from almost any other perspective). While it has had, for many decades, more contacts with the other subregions than is generally recognized, it has nevertheless always been quite isolated, geographically, culturally, and politically, from the others. But it is the subregion that constitutes the Pacific component of the Asia–Pacific region. More importantly, since the emergence of nine new Pacific island nations, where none existed prior to the 1960s (one can, to be sure, argue about the status of Tonga over a much longer period of time), this subregion has developed an identity and assumed an importance in Asian and world affairs that it lacked in previous years.

Great changes, in short, have been occurring both within this subregion and in its relations with the other subregions of Asia and the Pacific and with major nations and organizations in the international system. Some of the major external powers that formerly exercised jurisdiction in Oceania, notably the United States, France, and Britain still have territorial holdings in the subregion (very small in the case of the U.S. and Britain) and continue to be important actors there; but they are no longer "the master of all they survey" in this vast area, for their relationships with their former and current possessions in Oceania and their role in the entire subregion are changing markedly and rapidly.

The same observation can be made about the changing relationships of the eleven independent nations of the Southwest Pacific and Oceania with each other (both intra- and interregionally), with the other subregions of Asia and the Pacific, and with external nations and organizations. These relationships have been greatly furthered by the emergence of an impressive pattern of regional institutionalization in the subregion. Of the new regional organizations the most important are the South Pacific Commission, the oldest, the South Pacific Conference, the most comprehensive in membership, with special ties to the Commission, and the South Pacific Forum. The latter has been described in greater detail than the other two because it is clearly the most important regional organization in the Southwest Pacific and Oceania and is one of the three major comprehensive regional organizations in all of Asia and the Pacific. The Forum has been the main multilateral channel for promoting the policies and interests of the entire subregion of major issues of common concern.

Beyond its subregion the countries of the Southwest Pacific and Oceania have been increasingly active in all-Asia–Pacific regional organizations, and in international organizations as well. On the all-regional level Australia and to a lesser extent New Zealand, have long been active promoters of and participants in virtually all of the major organizations of this type, but the participation and role of the Pacific island nations, for obvious reasons, has been more limited and selective.

The overall picture that emerges is that of an impressive degree of regionalism and regional institutionalization in a previously inchoate area that has recently become a more identifiable and important subregion. This development is noteworthy in itself, and it has larger implications. For students of the new regionalism, this subregion provides another developing laboratory for research, and possibly, as Michael Haas suggests, for a study of new patterns of regional and international integration. For all those concerned with the problem of understanding the changing times in which they live, developments in this little-known part of the world can no longer be ignored.

7
Interregional and International Cooperation: A Growing Trend

I n this interdependent world, cooperation as well as conflict can seldom
be contained within nations, or even within regions. They tend to have
spill over effects that extend across regions and often into the international community. This is definitely true of Asia and the Pacific, a region—
or superregion—that has witnessed the emergence of manifold forms of
regionalism to an unprecedented degree, and that has become much more
important on the world stage. The new regionalism developing in this superregion is one of the most significant, if relatively neglected, aspects of the
changing international scene.

"Everywhere in Asia," as an article in the *U.S. News and World Report*
in February 1989 pointed out, "relationships spawned by the cold war are
eroding as new U.S.–Soviet ties render them meaningless. In their place is
emerging a new order built on economic pragmatism but bringing with it
the danger of new instability."[1] This new order is being shaped not just by
the "new U.S.–Soviet ties" or the shift to "economic pragmatism," but also
by many other factors in the region and the world that have made a new
order possible—indeed inevitable. The nature of this new order is still not
wholly clear, and its creation may, as the article suggests, bring "new instability;" but whatever its nature, it will be characterized by new levels of
regional, interregional, and global interactions.

The pattern of regionalism or subregionalism in all of the four regions
or subregions of Asia and the Pacific has already been delineated. A similar
analysis should now be made of the pattern of interregional interactions in
this emerging superregion, and of the growing links with the outside world.

Interregional Cooperation

Cooperation among the peoples and countries of Asia and the Pacific has
usually been prompted by two main common objectives: security and development. Other common objectives of the countries of the region, which
are related to both security and development, include the development of a
greater capacity to protect their own interests in a world of power and
competitiveness, to learn how to cooperate more effectively with each other
in a part of the world where such cooperation has been quite limited in the

past, and to develop a sense of national and personal identity and dignity and a capacity to nurture and defend these national and human goals. Pursuit of all these goals requires cooperation within countries and between as well as in the subregions in which these countries are located.

Security Patterns

Security patterns of interregional interactions seem to be quite limited, as contrasted with other patterns that are developing within the four main subregions, and especially with forms of security cooperation that have strong international dimensions. Outstanding examples of the latter forms are the bilateral security alliances that the United States has with Japan, South Korea, the Philippines, and Thailand and the Soviet Union with North Korea, Mongolia, and Vietnam.

The increasing concern over security matters in the ASEAN countries, especially since the end of the Vietnam War in 1975 and the Vietnamese invasion of Kampuchea (Cambodia) in late 1978, has spilled over into the regional organization they have formed, even though when ASEAN was formed in 1967 its founding member states specifically excluded security issues from its agenda.[2] Hence in Southeast Asia, at least, we find a comprehensive regional organization that is concerned in various ways with security problems, perhaps more importantly by providing a forum for consultations on such problems by the high-level participants in the annual meetings, outside the formal ASEAN sessions. To a lesser but increasing extent the same practice is being followed at high-level meetings of the other two comprehensive regional organizations in Asia and the Pacific, SAARC and the South Pacific Forum.

ASEAN's interregional and international dimensions are shown by the presence of representatives of Papua New Guinea as observers at the annual meetings and especially by the now formalized practice of holding "post-ministerial" meetings, usually at the foreign ministers' level, with counterparts from the "dialogue partners" of the ASEAN countries—Japan, the United States, Canada, Australia, New Zealand, and the European Community. Participants in these meetings often discuss mutual security concerns.

Economic Patterns

Interregional cooperation is most obvious on the economic front. Much of this is bilateral in nature. This has become an ongoing and rapidly expanding aspect of the overall interactions of the countries of Asia and the Pacific. It seems to be a natural development, but it should be remembered that until quite recently economic relations within the region were quite limited, in spite of the fact that, with some major exceptions, the region's economies are more complementary than competitive. The economies of the region were oriented elsewhere, for their chief export markets and chief sources of imports, investment, and economic and technological assistance lay outside the region. This is still generally the case, but it is becoming less so. In fact, one of the most impressive evidences of the changing scene in Asia and the Pacific, and of the emergence of the Asia–Pacific region as a more integrated area and a more influential actor in the international system, is the remarkable shift from heavy external economic ties and dependence to an increasing amount of interregional economic relations and regional as well as national resilience, to use a term that the Indonesians first popularized.

This significant change in trade, investment, and assistance patterns has been under way for at least a decade, and it seems to be gathering momentum. As early as 1981 "more than half the trade of East Asia and other Pacific economies . . . was with other countries of the region."[3] And this interregional trade is assuming impressive dimensions. "Asian neighbors already export more manufactured goods to Japan than the U.S. does. Japan's total trade with Asian countries, even excluding China, now exceeds that with America."[4] And since its marked shift in economic policies and the pursuit of the "four modernizations," in the late 1970s, China has become a definite factor in inter-Asia–Pacific trade, with great potentialities for more rapid participation. The reversion of its leaders in June 1989 and thereafter to the authoritarian and repressive measures of the past, however, has slowed this trend, at least temporarily.

Japan: The Dominant Economic Actor

Since Japan has the world's largest trade surplus, it is not surprising that it has a surplus in its trade with most of its neighbors. In 1986 the surplus amounted to $6.135 billion with Hong Kong, $5.223 billion with South Korea, $4.029 billion with China, $3.710 billion with Taiwan, and $2.981 billion with Singapore. It had an adverse trade balance of $4.704 billion with Indonesia, $2.263 billion with Malaysia, and $1.243 billion with Brunei. In the same year the United States had an adverse trade balance of $13.579 billion with Taiwan, $7.142 billion with South Korea, $6.444 billion with Hong Kong, $2.135 billion with China, $2.729 billion with Indonesia, and smaller adverse balances with Thailand and Malaysia.[5] Prime Minister Lee Kuan Yew of Singapore has predicted that Japan will replace the United States as the dominant economic power in Asia in the next decade,[6] a prospect that Japan's neighbors view with very mixed feelings. On the positive side it may be pointed out that Japan has been a major factor in the amazing economic growth of the Asia–Pacific region, especially in most of the countries of East and Southeast Asia. The dimensions of this growth are not fully realized. "Within ten years, the combined GNP of ten

East Asian countries will be three-fourths of the GNP of all North America."
It will, however, not be surprising to learn that of the total regional growth
"Japan's share will account for nearly eighty percent."[7] This vast asymmetry
between Japan and the other Asia–Pacific nations, which are already suspicious of their powerful neighbor, is a major obstacle to increasing regional
and interregional cooperation, as well, no doubt, as an important engine for
economic development.

In foreign investment as well as in trade Japan is the dominant economic
actor in all of Asia and the Pacific. According to Japanese and Taiwanese
sources, in 1986 Japan's direct foreign investment was greater than that of
any other country in most of the countries of East and Southeast Asia, including South Korea, Indonesia, and Thailand. Its investments in China and
Taiwan were then less than those of the United States, in Malaysia less than
the combined investments of members of the European Community, and in
Singapore less than those of the European Community and the United States.[8]
Its investments in these two subregions have been increasing more rapidly
than those of any other country. According to an article in *U.S. News and
World Report* in February 1989, "It [Japan] is now the single largest foreign
investor in nearly every Asian economy, including China's."[9]

Japan is now the chief supplier of Overseas Development Assistance
(ODA) to most of the developing countries of East and Southeast Asia. Its
total amount of ODA to these countries is larger than those provided by the
United States, Canada, and the countries of the European Community combined.[10] Since its ODA contributions have increased substantially in recent
years, to the extent that its overall ODA throughout the world exceeds that
of the United States (a remarkable turnaround), its relative contributions to
its neighbors will undoubtedly continue to increase.

The Role of Other Asia–Pacific Countries

But while Japan will inevitably play a leading role in interregional economic
cooperation in Asia and the Pacific, other countries or economies of the
region will also be increasingly involved. This will be particularly true of
China, South Korea, Taiwan, and Hong Kong in East Asia; of the ASEAN
states and at some stage, perhaps earlier than most would now predict,
Vietnam, in Southeast Asia; of India and Pakistan in South Asia; and of
Australia and New Zealand in the Southwest Pacific and Oceania.

The Role of China. The role of China, like that of Japan, will obviously be
a central one. In terms of economic power, however, China is on the whole
a very underdeveloped country, while Japan is one of the world's most economically powerful nations. In 1978 China embarked on new policies that

greatly accelerated its rate of economic growth and promised to lead to considerable political development as well. Politically, economically, and psychologically, however, it has not recovered from the self-inflicted wounds of 1989, and its image as a self-confident nation moving with unexpected rapidity toward greater freedom, openness, and achievement has been sadly tarnished. Thus again—or perhaps one should say still—China remains a great question mark. Its future will determine the destiny of its huge population and will affect the destiny of the peoples of all of Asia and the Pacific, perhaps of all humanity.

The Role of South Korea. South Korea's regional and interregional links in Asia and the Pacific are expanding rapidly, even with nations with which it has no formal diplomatic relations. In the other three subregions of Asia and the Pacific it has growing ties with Australia, most of the ASEAN countries, and (to a limited extent) Vietnam, India, Pakistan, and some of the Pacific island nations. Its capacity to exert influence on regional, interregional, and global levels will depend greatly on its ability to deal with its internal political, economic, and social problems, to establish a better basis of coexistence with North Korea, and to expand its "northern policy" without jeopardizing its extensive but rather delicate relations with its two major trading partners, and security guarantors, Japan and the United States.

The Role of Taiwan. Although the Republic of China on Taiwan is officially recognized by only a few countries, and by only one—South Korea—in Asia and the Pacific (excluding the Middle East), it is still influential because of its remarkable economic growth, and it is becoming more generally accepted as an active participant in Asia–Pacific affairs. Its growing ties with the People's Republic of China, in spite of basic disagreement over the meaning of their joint agreement that Taiwan is a part of China, helps to legitimize its position as a participant in regional and interregional affairs and offers some hope that the continued dispute over its status with relation to the PRC will not erupt into armed conflict.

The Role of Hong Kong. If Taiwan's political status is still disputed, apparently Hong Kong's is not. Now a British crown colony, it will revert to the control of China in 1997. It is one of the four newly industrializing economies (NIEs), usually referred to as the newly industrializing countries (NICs), in East and Southeast Asia, and, like the other three, it has had a phenomenal rate of economic growth. Moreover, it is a major international financial center, and the main entrepôt for the PRC with the rest of the world, a role it will probably continue to play as a "special region" in China. If the PRC keeps its recent agreements with Britain, Hong Kong will be permitted to function as essentially a capitalist economy for at least a half century after it is rejoined to China.

Doubts about the reliability of the Chinese commitment, especially after the events of 1989, have grown as the date of transfer nears. Hong Kong's role and importance in the new Asia–Pacific regionalism depend largely on the future of its position in China.

The Role of Southeast Asia and ASEAN. The major barrier to regional cooperation in Southeast Asia, and to interregional cooperation as well, is the great rift between the ASEAN countries and the Communist states of Indochina. Fortunately, this division is becoming less threatening, although there are still some real problems in working out some kind of tolerable compromise among the contending parties affecting the future of Cambodia and the relations between the Communist and non-Communist states of Southeast Asia. This potentially explosive situation will continue to be a disruptive factor in Southeast Asia and in the entire Asia–Pacific region.

The surprisingly effective functioning of ASEAN, the most successful of the three comprehensive regional organizations that have arisen in Asia and the Pacific, has given a great stimulus to regional cooperation in Southeast Asia and throughout the Asia–Pacific region. It has developed some important extraregional linkages, especially in its "dialogue partners" around the Pacific Rim and in Western Europe, and also, to a more limited extent, with a number of countries in other subregions of Asia and the Pacific, such as Papua New Guinea, South Korea, and India, and with the South Asian Association for Regional Cooperation (SAARC) and the South Pacific Forum.

The Role of South Asia. The difficulties that the South Asian countries have experienced in their relations with each other have seriously handicapped their efforts at regional, interregional, and international cooperation. A particular barrier has been India's strained relations with the People's Republic of China since the late 1950s. In the 1980s the two Asian giants, with a third of the world's population, made some efforts to end their longstanding animosity, but limited contacts and continuing differences on border issues are still formidable obstacles to real rapprochement. China's close relations with Pakistan are another obstacle, from India's point of view.

There are extensive economic links between South Asia and the other Asia–Pacific subregions. These should increase, especially because of the interests that nearly all of the nations of Asia and the Pacific share and because of the emergence of SAARC as an increasingly important regional organization. SAARC has not yet developed the momentum and influence of ASEAN, but ASEAN is much older and more established, and it too experienced growing pains in its early years.

The Role of Australia. Australia and New Zealand are turning their attention increasingly to Asia and the Pacific and are becoming significant actors in the entire region. Australia has special security and economic relations with Malaysia and Singapore. Its efforts to play a greater role in Asia had been hampered by its strained relations with Indonesia, its nearest Southeast Asian neighbor, the most populous and potentially the most important nation of Southeast Asia; but in recent years these have improved considerably. Australia, in cooperation with Japan and more recently with South Korea, has taken a leading role in efforts to develop greater regional institutionalization in Asia and the Pacific, usually including the United States and Canada.

At the initiative of Prime Minister Robert Hawke of Australia, a major international conference was held in Canberra in November 1989, which was attended by delegations from twelve leading Asia–Pacific nations. The conference agreed to explore the desirability and feasibility of establishing an all-Asia–Pacific economic organization, usually referred to as Asia Pacific Economic Cooperation (APEC). If successful, this initiative could usher in a new era of comprehensive official all-Asia–Pacific cooperation and institutionalization.

Interregional Cooperation and the New Regionalism

This brief survey of the growing role in interregional cooperation of countries other than Japan suggests that a number of other countries of Asia and the Pacific are already active participants in the emerging new regionalism. They will probably be even more active in future years. This supports an observation in the *U.S. News and World Report* in February 1989: "Novel conditions are forming in Asia, causing a realignment in which the decisions of smaller nations, to an extent unimaginable as recently as a decade ago, will determine status. If the next century is to be the century of the Pacific, as many strategists now predict, and not merely of Japan, the other main players are only now emerging."[11]

Interregional institutionalization is not even as well developed as the still limited regional institutionalization, especially on the official level; but there are many examples of this growing trend, particularly private associations in economic, professional, scientific, technical, and other fields. These organizations range from virtually all-regional organizations, comprehensive or specialized in nature, often with international participation as well, to organizations that draw their membership primarily from only two of the subregions in Asia and the Pacific, often in highly specialized fields. Case studies of these organizations would be worthwhile and interesting in themselves. They would also help to fill out the broad picture of growing interregional as well as regional institutionalization presented in this volume.

In the analysis of interregional and international cooperation in Asia and the Pacific, the concept of linkages through international regimes complements the concept of the new regionalism. It provides a framework for understanding two important aspects of Asia–Pacific regionalism: (1) its international linkages, dimensions, and generally outward-turning character, and (2) the extensive pattern of regional and interregional interactions and associations, broader in scope than bilateral relations and less institutionalized than formal regional organizations.

In the economic field Asia–Pacific countries participate in a large number of international regimes, including those in trade, finance, investment, and development. Some important all-regional organizations are concerned mainly with these issue areas. Examples are ESCAP, the Colombo Plan, and the Asian Development Bank (ADB). Primarily regional organizations, all have significant international participation. Among the international agencies with extensive interests and operations in Asia and the Pacific are the General Agreement on Tariffs and Trade (GATT), the World Bank, the International Development Association, the United Nations Development Program, the United Nations Environmental Program, and many other organs, agencies, commissions, and committees of the multifaceted United Nations system. GATT is variously regarded as an international regime, or as symbolic of such a regime, or as simply the major international organization in the broader trade-barrier-removal regime. The same observation could be made about the Law of the Sea Conference, in which most Asia–Pacific states are actively involved. The Conference is not yet well organized, even though it has wide membership and support. It might be preferable to consider it as the most comprehensive organization, however ill-developed, among the oceanic regimes, which also embrace a wide variety of fishing, oceanic mining, sealane commerce, oceanic preservation, nuclear nonproliferation, and other kinds of regimes.

There is much speculation about the possibility of a trading bloc in East Asia, and perhaps in Southeast Asia as well. From an economic point of view a trading bloc in East, or East and Southeast Asia, anchored to the yen, may seem quite logical, perhaps even inevitable; but it is a long way from taking shape. Even if it does, it will probably not be correct to describe it as an international regime. A trading bloc, or a group of trading blocs, cannot be characterized as an international regime until and unless it can achieve a far greater degree of cohesion and cooperation than is likely to emerge in the Asia–Pacific area. But any developing bloc or blocs might become a part of the global trading bloc regime or regimes.

The security alliances in Asia and the Pacific, all of which are dominated by one of the superpowers (or powers that at least until recently were generally recognized as superpowers), also fall far short of being international regimes. They could be so characterized only if viewed as components of the nearly global security alliance systems associated with either the United States or the Soviet Union (which are now in varying stages of reduction and disarray). It is doubtful that this extensive pattern of alliances really constitutes an international regime, especially in Asia and the Pacific. In this region, and to a considerable extent elsewhere in the world, the dominant trend in the security field, as Robert Scalapino and others have observed, is in the direction of alignments rather than alliances. Throughout the world the whole question of security is being reexamined from much more comprehensive perspectives.

Whether these growing linkages within and between the subregions of Asia and the Pacific add up to a comprehensive pattern of organized and informal regionalism is a matter of semantics and debate. Most observers would doubtless take a cautious and generally negative view on this issue; but most would probably agree that a new regionalism is developing in the entire region, and that its outline and trends are already quite clear.

Some analysts go considerably farther in their interpretation. In a volume published in 1986, for example, Evelyn Colbert wrote: "While obstacles to some inclusive East Asian and Pacific organization remain extraordinarily high, more loosely structured, informal, special purpose, or even implicit linkages have nevertheless resulted in a Pacific system that, though not institutionalized and difficult to define, can nevertheless be perceived to exist."[12] Many observers are impressed with the growing linkages in the Asia–Pacific region, although they do not clearly perceive a "Pacific system" to be emerging. But most would certainly agree with an observation of Robert Scalapino in 1985 that "a process of Asianization is taking place in East Asia[13] as a whole, a process whereby the interactions between and among the Asian states themselves are intensifying, with the centrality of external powers (including the USSR and the United States) reduced, albeit by no means insignificant."[14]

International Cooperation and the New Regionalism

Asia–Pacific Regionalism and Global Trends: The Linkages

This "process of Asianization" could provide a strong underpinning and incentive for the new regionalism developing in Asia and the Pacific. It should be examined in relation to the trends toward a more assertive nationalism, on the one hand, and toward greater internationalism and international contacts, on the other. Are these as conflicting and contradictory as they seem, or are they encouraging stages in the development of this vast and increasingly influential international region? Will they enhance the importance of regionalism, perhaps elevating it to an equal status with nationalism and internationalism? Will they enable the new regionalism to play a useful intermediary role between these other two major trends? Will they contribute to an outward-looking regionalism, linked positively to the growing internationalization of all parts of the world, or will they lead to an inward-turning regionalism, reflecting the growing nationalism in most of the Asia–Pacific states?

These are important questions regarding basic trends in the international system. They are particularly relevant in the Asia–Pacific region. The evolution of the new regionalism in Asia and the Pacific, therefore, has great significance not only for this particular region but also for the entire world. In this respect, as in many others, the Asia–Pacific region has become a major laboratory where the shape of the emerging world order and the future course of international relations can be charted. In turn the course of world developments will do much to shape the course of the new regionalism in Asia and the Pacific, and in every other world region.

In his thoughtful analysis, "The Uncertain Future: Asian–Pacific Relations in Trouble," Professor Robert Scalapino identified "seven interrelated global developments" that in his opinion "underlie regional trends everywhere." These are summarized as follows:

1. Ours is an age of increasing interdependence—economic, political, and strategic. Yet because of the problems induced by this interdependence, nationalism is also rising.

2. We are confronted by a rising economic imbalance not only between North and South, but within both categories of states.

3. There has been a significant decline in secular ideology. One result has been a vacuum with respect to political values, a vacuum filled in certain instances by the largely unexpected resurgence of religion in politics.

4. Political institutionalization remains weak in many societies.

5. Political structures above the nation-state level are weak.

6. Violence will be endemic in coming years. Terrorism, undeclared wars (many combining civil and international elements), and small-state wars will be important phenomena in the decades immediately ahead.

7. Ours is an age in which the broad movement is from alliance to alignment. . . . For the United States as for the USSR, the management of alignments will be a crucial test of diplomacy and a crucial determinant of power.[15]

All of these developments "underlie regional trends"—and many other trends—in Asia and the Pacific, and are pertinent to any analysis of the situation in this region, including the developing new regionalism.

The distinguished authors of a report to the Trilateral Commission in 1988, "East Asia in Transition," stressed "the need to adapt global arrangements to accommodate the rise of this diverse region."[16] There is also an obvious need for the leaders of the Asia–Pacific nations to adapt regional arrangements to accommodate the great developments and trends in world affairs.

Thus far, at least, the new regionalism in Asia and the Pacific does not seem to be inward oriented. It has many links with the international community, links that give it greater strength and promise. This will probably become increasingly important with the further evolution of international interdependence and the increasing interactions of regional groups as well as nations.

The emergence of "trading blocs" in two of the three major economic regions of the world and the possible emergence of a similar bloc or blocs in the third major region, centered on East Asia, offer great possibilities for increased prosperity and cooperation not only among the peoples and nations of these blocs but also between the blocs and all other nations and peoples. Yet these blocs may still adopt "beggar-thy-neighbor" policies of economic discrimination vis-à-vis other blocs and other countries and regions. Hence the character and policies of the new regionalism, of which "trading blocs" may prove to be a major manifestation, will do much to shape the new economic order, and consequently the new political, social, and security order that, for better or for worse, will affect the destinies of nations and peoples in coming years.

Unless the new regionalism in Asia and the Pacific takes more of an inward-turning trend than it has thus far, perhaps as a result of reversion to more repressive, authoritarian practices in some of the key states of the region, the prospects that it will retain and enlarge its outward-turning character seem to be quite good.

Varieties of International Participation and Cooperation

Many of the regional organizations that exist in Asia and the Pacific have external as well as regional members, and these are particularly influential participants. This is true of all the organizations that have been mentioned as being the closest to all-regional organizations of an official type—ESCAP, the Colombo Plan, and the ADB. It is also true of the major unofficial all-regional bodies—PAFTAD, PBEC, and PECC. The same observation can be made of a large number of international professional and technical associations that have affiliated chapters in Asia–Pacific nations.

Through their regional organization, the six member nations of ASEAN have developed a novel and increasingly meaningful cooperative relationship with their "dialogue partners," which include not only major Asia–Pacific states—Japan, Australia, and New Zealand—but also the United States, Canada, and the European Community. This gives a strictly regional organization a significant transregional and international dimension.

For a region that in the past has been notable for its limited amount of regional and interregional cooperation, the extent of the participation of the countries of Asia and the Pacific in international organizations is truly remarkable. This is clearly brought out in Table 7–1.[17]

This table shows that membership in intergovernmental organizations (IGOs) between 1960 and 1982 varied from 17 each for Burma and North Korea and 18 for Mongolia to 57 for India, 58 for Japan, and 60 for Australia (Taiwan with 7 and Hong Kong with 9 were the lowest, but Taiwan is not universally recognized as a sovereign nation and Hong Kong is a British crown colony and will become a part of China in 1997). Participation in international nongovernmental organizations (INGOs) is even more im-

Table 7–1
Participation of Countries of Asia and the Pacific in International Organizations (1960–82)

	Intergovernmental (IGOs)	*Nongovernmental (INGOs)*	*Total*
East Asia			
China	24	275	299
Hong Kong	9	513	522
Japan	58	1210	1268
North Korea	17	114	131
South Korea	40	579	611
Mongolia	18	80	98
Taiwan	7	372	379
Southeast Asia			
Burma	17	137	154
Indonesia	49	547	596
Malaysia	46	498	544
Philippines	41	614	655
Singapore	36	450	486
Thailand	41	503	544
Vietnam	30	151	181
South Asia			
Bangladesh	32	286	318
India	57	1001	1058
Nepal	20	149	169
Pakistan	38	316	354
Sri Lanka	40	442	482
Southwest Pacific			
Australia	60	1162	1222
New Zealand	39	801	840

Source: *Yearbook of International Organizations 1988/89* (Brussels: Union of International Associations, 1988), vol. 2, table 3.

pressive, ranging from 80 for Mongolia, 114 for North Korea, and 137 for Burma to 1058 for India, 1222 for Australia and 1268 for Japan.[17]

These figures pinpoint the most and least internationally active nations of Asia and the Pacific. They also indicate that even the least internationally active nations of the region participate far more in international life than is generally realized. This is further stimulated by the growing number of regional and interregional organizations in Asia and the Pacific and will be given an added boost if the proposed official all-regional organization comes into being.

The extensive participation of Asia–Pacific nations and regional groupings and associations in international conferences of both an official and an unofficial nature also gives an international dimension to Asian regionalism. Hundreds of these conferences are held every year. Increasing numbers are being held in Asia–Pacific countries, and increasing numbers of people from the region are participating in conferences held elsewhere in the world. The successful staging in countries of the region of major world events—of which the twenty-fourth Olympiad in Seoul in 1988 is the most recent outstanding example—has helped to bring the Asia–Pacific region into the center of world attention. (Obviously the amazing economic dynamism throughout the region has done even more in this respect.)

Reference to the economic dimensions of external contacts is a reminder that these contacts can also create serious problems in the relations of states and regional organizations in Asia and the Pacific with outside countries and organizations. All of the Asia–Pacific countries, in various ways and for various reasons, are also experiencing difficulties in their dealings with outside nations and organizations. They depend heavily on the rest of the world for markets, for needed imports, and for economic and other forms of assistance. In innumerable ways they are affected by, as well as affect, the major trends in international life. Regionalism and regional organizations in Asia and the Pacific are deeply involved in this vast pattern of interactions.

The growing links between Asia and the Pacific and the outside world are also highlighted by the rapid increase in travel by officials, professional people, tourists, and others from other countries to the region, and by Asians to countries outside their region. According to an official of the U.S. Federal Aviation Administration (FAA), "some 18 million people traveled by air between the United States and Asia" in 1988, a figure "3.5 times higher than U.S.–Asia air traffic in 1975." The FAA forecasts "29.2 million passengers a year by 2000 and 82 million passengers a year by 2020."[18]

There are also large numbers of university students from most of the countries of Asia and the Pacific studying in Western countries. In the mid-1980s, in addition to at least 30,000 students from Japan, more than 130,000 students from East Asian and ASEAN countries were studying in Western universities and colleges, mainly in the United States (more than 97,000, one third from the People's Republic of China and Taiwan), in the European Community (over 22,000, mainly in the United Kingdom, mostly from Hong Kong, Malaysia, and Singapore, and in the Federal Republic of Germany, with a concentration of students from South Korea and Indonesia), and in Canada (nearly 13,000, more than half from Hong Kong).[19]

In 1989, according to the 1989 edition of the well-known publication of the Institute of International Education, *Open Doors,* of the 365,000 international students enrolled in U.S. colleges and universities 52 percent were Asians. Of the top ten countries in the world in terms of student enrollment in the United States, eight were Asian. There were 29,040 students from China, 28,760 from Taiwan, 24,000 from Japan, 23,350 from India, 20,610 from South Korea, 16,170 from Malaysia, 10,560 from Hong Kong, 8,950 from Iran, and 8,720 from Indonesia (Pakistan was in 11th place with 7,060, and Thailand in 13th place with 6,560).[20]

The Future Course of Asia–Pacific Cooperation

Almost all of the many proposals for a comprehensive official organization in Asia and the Pacific advanced during the past decade or more envision significant international linkages and usually international as well as broad regional participation.[21] These proposals have attracted considerable interest. They have led to some regional institutionalization, mainly of a private nature, in the field of economic cooperation. No official organization of comprehensive scope has yet emerged; but the Asia–Pacific Economic Cooperation (APEC) conference in Canberra in November 1989 may be the first step in that direction.

If a comprehensive regional organization is formed, at long last, in the Asia–Pacific region, if it is sufficiently comprehensive and open, and if it is given real and continuing support by all the member states, it will give a great boost to the new regionalism in Asia and the Pacific. It will mark the advent of a major new regional organization and a major new actor in the international system. But the odds against its formation on a truly all-regional scale are very great, and the odds against its effective functioning are even greater. The exploratory conference of November 1989 in Canberra, as has been noted, may have laid the basis for its formation. If so, this will be a landmark in the history of regional cooperation in the Asia–Pacific area; but it will be only the beginning of a new, and admittedly more promising, stage in the long history of the many efforts, thus far abortive, to introduce official all-regional institutionalization to the Asia–Pacific community.

In 1986 Dr. Saburo Okita, a former foreign minister of Japan and a leading advocate of greater cooperation and institutionalization in Asia and the Pacific, made a number of constructive suggestions for the future course of Asia–Pacific cooperation and development. Three will be mentioned by way of illustration:

1. The Pacific countries should strive for cooperation in nonmilitary, non-political fields, like economy, culture, and science and technology, thus leaving the way open for participation by countries with different political structures.

2. Every effort should be made to avoid institutionalizing discriminatory regional preference.

3. Cooperation should, in principle, be outward-looking—beyond the region itself. It is hoped that countries outside the region—the European countries, for example—will be able to participate positively in the Pacific region's development.[22]

Dr. Okita also called attention, in a novel way, to the constructive contribution that the growing regionalism in Asia and the Pacific could make to a "global dialogue" on North–South relations: "The Pacific region . . . offers an excellent opportunity to discuss North–South issues on a regional basis. . . . Promoting a North–South dialogue on a Pacific regional basis may open up new opportunities for the global dialogue."[23]

These thoughtful comments and recommendations by one of the wisest elder statesmen of Asia suggest some constructive directions and contributions for Asia–Pacific regionalism. In this vast and increasingly important superregion, regional cooperation is developing rapidly. It remains to be seen whether it can find a constructive role amid the crosscurrents of nationalism, Asianization, and internationalism.

8
Interregional Organizations: Six Major Examples, with Focus on PECC

I n the 1960s and 1970s many concrete suggestions and proposals for economic cooperation in Asia and the Pacific began to take shape and to attract region-wide attention, if not region-wide support. Four of these initiatives of an essentially private or unofficial nature were of particular significance, and had visible impact. In three of the four cases, these initiatives led to concrete implementation and institutionalization, well beyond the levels envisioned, or even desired by some participants, in their early stages.

Unofficial Regional Organizations

PAFTAD and OPTAD

The first of these initiatives was most clearly formulated by Professor Kiyoshi Kojima of Hitotsubashi University in Tokyo in the 1960s. His proposal, for a Pacific Free Trade Area attracted widespread attention, especially after he and a colleague at Hitotsubashi, Hiroshi Kurimoto, presented it at a conference in November 1965 of the Japan Economic Research Centre.[1] "The outcome of this initiative was the implementation of a series of Pacific Trade and Development (PAFTAD) Conferences, comprised primarily of regional economists."[2]

Between January 1968 and December 1989 eighteen Pacific Trade and Development Conferences were held. The place, general theme, and date of each of these conferences are given in the following list:[3]

January 1968
Pacific Trade and Development
Japan Economic Research Centre, Tokyo

January 1969
Pacific Trade and Development II
East–West Center, Honolulu

August 1970

Direct Foreign Investment in Asia and the Pacific
Sydney

October 1971
Obstacles to Trade in the Pacific Area
Carleton University, Ottawa

January 1973
Structural Adjustments in Asian–Pacific Trade
Japan Economic Research Center and Japan Institute of International Affairs, Tokyo

July 1974
Technology Transfer in Pacific Economic Development
National Science and Technology Council, Mexico City

August 1975
Cooperation and Development in the Asia/Pacific Region: Relations Between Large and Small Countries
Auckland

July 1976
Trade and Development in Asia and the Pacific
Pattaya

August 1977
Mineral Resources in the Pacific Area
San Francisco

March 1979
ASEAN in a Changing Pacific and World Economy
Australian National University, Canberra

September 1980
Trade and Growth of the Advanced Developing Countries in the Pacific Basin
Korea Development Institute, Seoul

September 1981
Renewable Resources in the Pacific
Vancouver

January 1983
Energy and Structural Change in the Asia–Pacific Region
Manila

June 1984
Pacific Growth and Financial Interdependence
Singapore

August 1985
Industrial Policies for Pacific Economic Growth
Tokyo

January 1988
The Challenge of Technological Change to Pacific Trade and Development
Centre for Strategic and International Studies, Jakarta

December 1989
Pacific Trade and Development: Lessons from the 1980s and Opportunities for the 1990s
Kuala Lumpur

The chairmen of the International Steering Committee of PAFTAD have been Professor Kiyoshi Kojima (1968–83) and Dr. Saburo Okita (1983–85), both of Japan, and Professor Hugh Patrick (1985–) of the United States. Dr. Peter Drysdale is the present director and Mr. John McBride is the present executive officer (both are associated with the Research School of Pacific Studies, Australia National University).

In 1984 Dr. Drysdale prepared a "brief history" of the PAFTAD Conference.[4] This useful publication contains the following comments on its purpose and contributions:

The conferences are private in the sense that economists from different Pacific countries are invited as individuals. Non-academic participants do not take part as representatives of their governments or of international organizations, but are invited in their private professional capacities. Participants are mainly from academic circles, although many have had considerable policy experience in government and elsewhere. . . . The conferences are designed primarily for the intelligent consideration of economic policy issues of importance to Pacific countries. The research papers, which serve as the basis for conference discussions, are intended to meet this aim. The focus on policy differentiates this work somewhat from purely academic economic research, though a major objective of the program is to generate substantial research and analysis of the Pacific economy. This intellectual contribution aims to assist and complement the contributions of practitioners, in government and in the business world, in dealing with the challenges of Pacific development. An underlying assumption of the PACTAD [*sic*] Conferences is that the distinctive contributions from these three sectors are critical to effective cooperation among the nations of the Pacific; and the history of Pacific cooperation and development over the past several years can be seen as validating this assumption to a remarkable extent. . . . A major contribution of the Pacific trade and development research activity over the years has been to build up in significant measure the network of persons and institutions involved in cooperative research and this continues to be an important task for the future.[5]

As Dr. Drysdale points out, "The geographic definition of the Pacific region has evolved over time." At the fifth PAFTAD Conference, in Tokyo, a representative from Mexico was the first participant from a Latin American Pacific nation. Thereafter, there was "a strong Latin American Pacific representation." At the sixth Conference, in Mexico City, "the first representatives from a socialist Pacific nation, the USSR," were present. "China finally accepted an invitation to send a participant to the Tenth Conference (in Canberra)," and Chinese economists submitted research papers for the Twelfth and Thirteenth Conferences (in Vancouver and Manila), "although there was no Chinese or USSR participation in these meetings. There has been some expression of interest from Vietnamese researchers in becoming involved in the research activity on the Pacific economy."[6]

The PAFTAD Conferences were soon given an institutional base in the Pacific Trade and Development Conference (also identified as PAFTAD). The international secretariat is located in the Research School of Pacific Studies, Australian National University, in Canberra.

PAFTAD was apparently conceived by Kojima and others who helped to frame it as a Japanese response to the European Economic Community; but it soon developed into a more truly regional proposal. An alternative proposal that emerged in the latter half of the 1970s seemed to be more along the lines of the Organization for Economic Cooperation and Development (an organization of the leading developed nations, mostly European but also including the United States, Canada, and Japan, the three leading Asia–Pacific economic powers). This alternative proposal was for an Organization for Pacific Trade and Development (OPTAD). It was recommended to their respective governments in 1976 by Dr. Saburo Okita, a leading proponent of Pacific economic cooperation, and Sir John Crawford, then chancellor of Australian National University. The proposal was given more concrete and detailed form in 1979 in a widely discussed report by Professors Peter Drysdale of Australian National University and Hugh Patrick of Yale University, both of whom were active participants in PAFTAD.[7] The report was prepared for the Committee on Foreign Relations of the United States Senate, which was beginning to take a special interest in the concept of Pacific Community and more particularly in that of Pacific economic cooperation.

For a time the OPTAD proposal seemed to attract more attention than PAFTAD, which was already assuming a loosely institutional form; but while OPTAD has not been forgotten, it has not yet led to effective implementation. One of the reasons probably is that, like OECD, it would have been essentially an association of more developed countries of Asia and the Pacific and as such would neither satisfy the need for an all-regional organization nor allay the fears of the less developed nations of the region—the vast majority—that they would either be excluded, or if admitted would be dominated by the richer member states. This latter fear has been, and continues to be, one of the major handicaps for any type of proposed comprehensive regional organization; but OPTAD was especially open to such criticisms.

PBEC

In the late 1960s a number of business leaders in several Pacific Basin countries formed the Pacific Basin Economic Council (PBEC). "Conceived at a meeting of the Japan–Australia Joint Economic Committee, PBEC was organized in 1967 as a private organization with five national committees: Australia, Canada, Japan, New Zealand, and the United States [again note the leadership of the only highly developed countries of the Pacific Basin]. It was enlarged in 1974 with a Pacific Basin Regional Committee, so that by the end of the 1970s it came to embrace more than three hundred influential businessmen throughout the Pacific Basin."[8] It has grown significantly since that time, in membership, activities, organization, and effectiveness (see figure 8–1). This is reflected in a brief description in late July 1989 by R. Sean Randolph, the international director general of PBEC:

> PBEC is an international business association composed of approximately six hundred corporations located in nine countries around the Pacific Basin. It was founded in 1967 as the pioneering multinational business forum in the region. In addition to operating as a network through which many business relationships have been established, PBEC seeks to encourage and develop the most favorable possible climate for business in the region. We do this by working with governments and international bodies such as the GATT to support open market policies and the lowering of barriers to trade and investment. The underlying philosophy of PBEC embraces active support for multinational economic cooperation in the Pacific region and the building of bridges between different economic communities.
>
> PBEC currently has full Member Committees in Australia, Canada, Chile, Japan, Korea, Mexico, New Zealand, Taiwan, and the United States. Each is fully independent. The International Secretariat is located in San Francisco.[9]

The twenty-first International General Meeting of PBEC, held in Sydney, Australia, May 22–25, 1988, was attended by senior representatives of PBEC's member committees; business leaders from Hong Kong, Indonesia, Mexico, the Pacific island nations, the Philippines, and Singapore; and a large number of journalists, observers, and representatives of regional and international

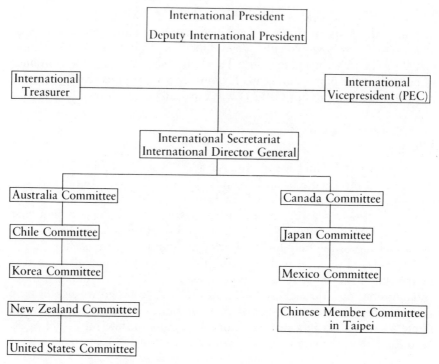

Figure 8–1. Pacific Basin Economic Council

Source: Chart prepared by R. Sean Randolph, International Director General, Pacific Basin Economic Council. Reprinted with permission.

organizations. The general theme of the conference was: "Beyond 2000—Toward 2000: Succeeding in a Changing World."[10]

The wide-ranging scope of the discussions and concerns is reflected in the topics for the plenary and concurrent sessions. For the plenary sessions the topics were: "The Pacific Basin in the Year 2000 and Beyond," "The Changing Structure of International Business," "Antarctica—The Awakening Giant," "The Demographics of Change in the Pacific," "The Age of the Pacific Economy," "Exploring Frontiers Beyond Trade," "Future Trade Prospects Following the 1987 U.S. Trade Bill," "Europe's Perception of Change in the Pacific," and "Deregulation, The Key to Economic Growth." Topics for the concurrent sessions were: "Corporatization of Government Enterprises," "Pacific Finance Post October, 1987," "LDCs and NICs, The Evolutionary Process," "Protecting the Environment," "Trade and Investment in Agricultural Products," and "The Future of the Pacific Island Nations."[11]

The Sydney meeting reaffirmed the commitment to "fight all protection-ism in all Pacific Basin markets," a commitment adopted at the twentieth International General Meeting in San Francisco the previous year. It ex-pressed strong support for the Uruguay Round of GATT, but it also called for a reform and revitalization of GATT and "endorsed the emergence of new mechanisms which promote free trade principles in conformity with the GATT." Specifically, it welcomed "bilateral mechanisms such as the Aus-tralia–New Zealand Closer Economic Relationship, the U.S.–Canada Free Trade Agreement, and the U.S.–Mexico Framework Agreement on Trade and Investment."[12]

PBEC has established a number of important special committees, in-cluding those on agriculture, tourism, environmental science and technology, and Pacific economic cooperation. In 1987 and 1988 the organizational structure of PBEC was strengthened by a reorganization of the International Secretariat.

At the 1988 meeting in Sydney the relationship of PBEC to the Pacific Economic Cooperation Conference (PECC) was discussed at some length. PBEC, along with PAFTAD, is a full member of PECC. The delegates at Sydney "discussed the need for active representation of PBEC within the PECC. It was widely agreed that PBEC's role should be to help focus PECC on pragmatic economic issues and to insure that the business aspects receive adequate emphasis within the organization."[13]

The Soviet Union has expressed an interest in establishing some regular relationship with both PBEC and PECC, perhaps even becoming a full mem-ber of each organization. At its request, it was permitted to send observers to the PECC annual meeting in Vancouver in 1986, and to the PBEC general meeting in Kuala Lumpur in December 1989. Admitting the Soviet Union to full membership in organizations dedicated to free market principles would create some complications and require some changes in basic Soviet policies and attitudes. Some countries with member committees in PBEC and PECC, notably the United States, seem to believe that the Soviet Union has not shown enough willingness to make the changes necessary to qualify for mem-bership. The position of the U.S. Member Committee of PBEC on this matter was frankly explained in a statement of "Policy Issue Positions Directed to the U.S. Government," dated May 31, 1989:

> The U.S. Committee welcomes the new economic policy directions indicated by General Secretary Gorbachev and believes that, if realized, these will work to the benefit of the Soviet people as well as to the international community. If these policies are to succeed, however, this must result from a willingness in the Soviet Union to directly grapple with the challenges of reform, not through concessions or other preferential treatment.[14]

PBEC was formed primarily to promote the mutual interests of businessmen and business organizations in the Pacific Basin. It has also been one of the many forums for the introduction and/or consideration of larger proposals for Pacific economic cooperation. For example,

> when PBEC met in Sydney on May 5–8, 1980, it had before it a draft proposal for a Pacific Economic Community (PEC) which the Japan National Committee had drawn up, presented for discussion to the Steering Committee the previous October and revised to accommodate the views of other member committees to which it had been circulated. . . . But it [PBEC] was not prepared to commit itself to any particular organizational formula for the PEC, either PAFTAD, OPTAD, or any other, and in fact did not reach a consensus on whether the coordinating mechanism should be at the governmental level at all.[15]

PBEC, like PAFTAD and PECC, has taken a cautiously supportive attitude toward the idea of a new all-Pacific official organization. As R. Sean Randolph stated in July 1989, "On the matter of a new governmental forum for the region, this is obviously a matter which the governments will decide themselves. PBEC has, however, supported this concept subject to a few qualifications. We are working to ensure that any new government process or institution has the input of the private sector, particularly the business community."[16]

PECC

Of all the unofficial regional and subregional organizations that have emerged in Asia and the Pacific in recent years, the most comprehensive and arguably the most important has been the Pacific Economic Cooperation Conference (PECC). Although, as its title suggests, the focus is on economic cooperation, it has proved to be a forum, and a network, for the consideration of many other matters of common interest and concern. Indeed, "since its beginnings in 1980, the PECC has grown to become the most important forum where all Pacific nations can gather to discuss common problems and policies."[17] A brief summary of its evolution in the 1980s will throw much light on both the possibilities of and the obstacles in the road to really meaningful all-regional cooperation in the vast Asia–Pacific area.

PECC came into being largely as a result of the initiatives of some far-seeing officials and scholars in Japan and Australia. Masayoshi Ohira deserves special recognition and credit. When he "began his final (and successful) struggle to become prime minister of Japan, he picked up the Pacific Basin Cooperation concept as one of the bold new ideas his administration would champion."[18] In March 1979, shortly after he became prime minister, he "appointed as one of his personal policy-advisory task forces the Pacific

Basin Cooperation Study Group," headed by a leading Japanese economist and politician, Dr. Saburo Okita, who had also been active in PAFTAD and PBEC and later (after Okita become foreign minister) by Professor Tsuneo of Nagoya University. This study group examined the whole concept of Pacific cooperation, and the advantages and disadvantages, the possibilities and prospects of moving ahead with more comprehensive Asia–Pacific cooperation. It submitted a preliminary report in November 1979 and a final report in the following May.

While the study group recommended a rather cautious approach and did not suggest any specific organizational form, it did point to the need to consider more comprehensive regional institutionalization, and it recommended that an international symposium be convened to consider the whole spectrum of issues and possibilities.

This idea appealed to Ohira, and he took concrete steps to secure its implementation. In January 1980, during a visit to Australia, where extensive interest in Pacific cooperation had also been evidenced, he discussed the proposal of an international seminar with the Australian prime minister, Sir Malcolm Fraser, and suggested that Australia would be an appropriate venue for the proposed seminar. The two prime ministers then asked Dr. Okita and Sir John Crawford, then chancellor of Australian National University, to arrange the conference.

The seminar was held in Canberra in September 1980. It was attended by tripartite delegations—one government official, participating in a "personal capacity," one business leader, and one prominent scholar—from each of eleven countries, the five Pacific members of OECD (Japan, the United States, Canada, Australia, and New Zealand), the five ASEAN nations (Indonesia, Malaysia, the Philippines, Singapore, and Thailand), and the Republic of Korea. In addition, a joint delegation from the Pacific island states (one each from Papua New Guinea, Fiji, and Tonga) participated. Representatives of several regional organizations, including PAFTAD, PBEC, and ADB (the Asian Development Bank), and a few officials and private citizens attended as observers.

The Canberra seminar was a highlight of a growing number of Asia–Pacific exchanges and meetings. It launched what soon came to be known as the Pacific Economic Cooperation Conference (PECC). "The seminar focused on the rationale, the format, and the agenda of a new consultative system. . . . It recommended that 'a standing committee of about twenty-five persons be established to coordinate an expansion of information exchange within the region and to set up Task Forces to undertake major studies on a number of issues for regional cooperation.' "[19]

The basic decision to form a new and more comprehensive regional organization in Asia and the Pacific was made collectively at the Canberra seminar—henceforth identified as PECC–I. There was still some uncertainty, however, whether its initiative and recommendations would be sufficient to overcome doubts about the advisability of such an organization, about its format and composition, and about the adequacy of the support base envisioned at Canberra.

The decision to make PECC an unofficial rather than an official organization, and the basis of the selection of representatives—tripartite delegations—seemed to meet with surprising approval. It was a novel method of selection and raised the question whether the delegates would have sufficient influence to launch successfully the most comprehensive regional organization in the Asia–Pacific area. The fact that the distinctive feature of tripartite representation has continued is testimony to the feasibility of the practice; but the further fact that governments are not directly represented, although for the most part they have been supportive, has raised questions regarding the centrality of PECC in the evolving movement toward Asia–Pacific cooperation. At Canberra the absence of official government delegations from both the countries represented by "unofficial" delegates, and also those not represented at all in the seminar, was keenly felt throughout the deliberations. "The recommendations of the Canberra conference were not implemented immediately because of an implied need for official governmental endorsement and commitment."[20]

At the second PECC Conference, held in Bangkok, 3–5 June 1982, the issue of government–PECC relations was faced more fully and more concretely. The conclusions of the conference on this important issue were well summed up in a report of the Pan-Pacific Community Association:

> There was a general consensus among the conference participants that although direct governmental interaction in the area of Pacific regional cooperation is premature, private initiatives, to be meaningful, must draw upon the views of governments. Rather than attempt to solicit the official consent and support of the governments, private task forces should develop trusting relationships with government officials and researchers on an informal basis. The appropriate government agencies should provide feedbacks to the task force efforts to ensure that the work is policy-relevant. . . .
>
> At present, governments are not obligated to deal with the regional cooperation issue. In the end, their active attention can only be maintained if it becomes apparent that regional tripartite consultations in the Pacific area serve national interests. To encourage their response, flesh will have to be put on the bones of the idea. The issues will have to be carefully selected in terms of what governments are oriented towards, particularly with respect to those areas of economic cooperation that may not be satisfactorily dealt with through existing bilateral contacts or global arrangements such as OECD, the Summits, and the GATT.[21]

Another problem that was frankly faced at the Bangkok Conference was that of the reservations of the ASEAN countries regarding PECC. Reflecting the suspicions of all of the developing countries of Asia and the Pacific, they feared that the new organization for Asia–Pacific cooperation would be dominated by the few developed states of the region, particularly by Japan and the United States, and would turn into a "rich man's club" that would not give adequate attention and assistance to less-developed members. ASEAN states also feared that their participation in PECC might weaken ASEAN, which was increasingly becoming the focus of their regional cooperative programs.

The Bangkok participants had the benefit of a series of eleven studies on ASEAN's economic relations with the Pacific region that had been commissioned by the Economic and Social Commission for Asia and the Pacific (ESCAP), a regional commission of the United Nations, with headquarters in Bangkok, and which had been considered by an ESCAP Experts Group prior to PECC–II. One of the most widely discussed papers, by Hadi Soesastro of Indonesia, entitled "Institutional Aspects of ASEAN–Pacific Economic Cooperation," well expressed some of the reasons for ASEAN's less than enthusiastic attitude toward the whole PECC process, while at the same time being willing to participate gingerly in it:

> It cannot be expected that ASEAN would come up with clear-cut responses at this stage, let along take some initiatives; indeed, it is unfair to expect and pressure ASEAN to do so. The idea is a big, new, uncertain and vague one; no prominent elements in the ASEAN bureaucracies would engage in such an undertaking; ASEAN could move only if it can be certain about the purpose and implications of the undertaking which appear to involve so many Pacific countries and complex economic and political issues.[22]

In his paper Soesastro referred to "five imperatives" upon which ASEAN's participation in Pacific regional cooperation programs and organizations would depend. These were first stated by another Southeast Asian scholar, Noordin Sopiee, in a background paper prepared for a conference on "The Pacific Basin Concept" that was held in Williamsburg, Virginia, shortly before the Bangkok Conference of PECC. These "five imperatives" were:

1. ASEAN must not be weakened nor its existence and prosperity jeopardized.
2. ASEAN must perceive clear benefits from regional cooperation which in totality far exceed the possible costs.
3. The concept must not compromise the non-aligned status of the ASEAN states nor enmesh them in political entanglements which they seek to avoid.
4. The concept must not be perceived as a Western, neo-colonial proposal devised for Western neo-colonial purposes.

5. It is important for the ASEAN states to feel that they are not being rushed into anything.[23]

These "five imperatives" have special significance for students of the "new regionalism." They call attention to some of the new regional momentum developing in Asia and the Pacific; but they also highlight the special difficulties and obstacles that stand in the way of regionalism on an all-Asia–Pacific basis. The movement from regionalism in the four major subregions in Asia and the Pacific, which, while impressive, is still in its early stages, to comprehensive all-Asia–Pacific regionalism has yet to gather momentum, or even demonstrate its feasibility at all.

The Third International General Meeting of PECC, held in Bali, 21–23 November 1983, took a major step in the direction of institutionalizing Pacific cooperation by implementing the two major organizational recommendations of the Canberra Conference of 1980, namely the establishment of a standing committee and four task forces, dealing with investment and technology transfer, trade in manufactured goods, trade in agricultural products, and trade in mineral commodities. In Bali the main outlines of the organizational framework that has existed since that time were agreed upon (see figure 8–2). They include the following major elements: (1) a general conference, such as had been convened in Canberra and Bangkok, to meet every year or two; (2) a standing committee composed of representatives of all countries and institutions having participant status; (3) task forces to develop cooperative programs in specific areas; (4) a coordinating group to supervise and coordinate the work of the various task forces; (5) a secretariat, based in the host country of the next PECC general conference; and (6) National Pacific Economic Cooperation Committees organized on a tripartite basis in each of the countries with participating members, "to serve as a focal point within each country regarding the PECC activities."[24]

Subsequent general meetings of PECC (PECC–IV in Seoul, 29 April–1 May 1985; PECC–V in Vancouver, 16–19 November 1986; PECC–VI in Osaka, 17–20 May 1988; and PECC–VII in Wellington in late 1989) have concentrated largely on the work of the task forces and on general discussion and exchanges about the problems and possibilities of expanding economic and to some extent other forms of cooperation among the nations of Asia and the Pacific. The Seoul Conference gave special attention to a report of the task force on Trade and Negotiations Policy. "The Conference supported the proposal submitted by the task force to work toward consensus positions on trade policy issues likely to be of priority importance to Pacific countries at the next round of GATT negotiations." This is an example of an important trend in the region, namely to work for the coordination of efforts to promote mutual interests through regional cooperation, a hitherto weak link in the national-regional-global chain, but at the same time to emphasize the

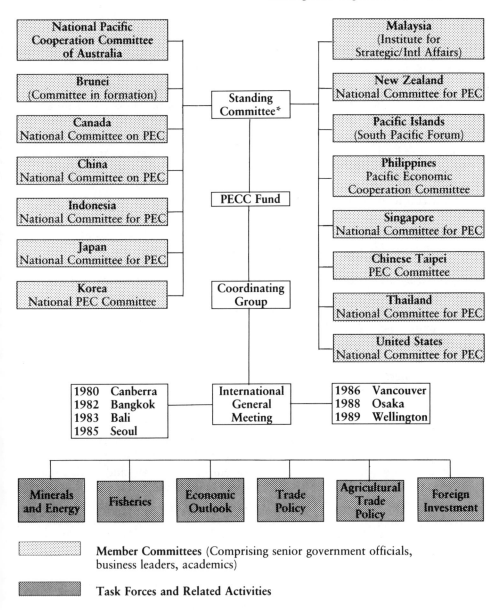

National Pacific Cooperation Committee of Australia			Malaysia (Institute for Strategic/Intl Affairs)
Brunei (Committee in formation)	Standing Committee*		New Zealand National Committee for PEC
Canada National Committee on PEC			Pacific Islands (South Pacific Forum)
China National Committee on PEC			Philippines Pacific Economic Cooperation Committee
Indonesia National Committee for PEC	PECC Fund		Singapore National Committee for PEC
Japan National Committee for PEC			Chinese Taipei PEC Committee
Korea National PEC Committee	Coordinating Group		Thailand National Committee for PEC
			United States National Committee for PEC

1980 Canberra	International	1986 Vancouver
1982 Bangkok	General	1988 Osaka
1983 Bali	Meeting	1989 Wellington
1985 Seoul		

Minerals and Energy   Fisheries   Economic Outlook   Trade Policy   Agricultural Trade Policy   Foreign Investment

Member Committees (Comprising senior government officials, business leaders, academics)

Task Forces and Related Activities

*Institutional members: Pacific Basin Economic Council (PBEC); Pacific Trade and Development Conference (PAFTAD)

Figure 8–2. Pacific Economic Cooperation Conference

Source: Brochure of the United States National Committee for Pacific Economic Cooperation (n.d.). Reprinted with permission.

need to deal with such problems as trade policies concurrently and cooperatively on national, regional, and international levels. In this case "The work of the Task Force was carried forward at the First Pacific Trade Policy Forum, held in San Francisco, March 20–22, 1986."[25]

A very important feature of the Vancouver Conference (PECC–V) in November 1986 was the presence of representatives of China and Taiwan (designated as "Chinese Taipei") as regular members, and of the Soviet Union as an observer. The Soviet Union had solicited an invitation to send observers and had indicated an interest in becoming a full and regular participant in PECC. There is still considerable resistance to full Soviet membership in PECC, mainly because of lingering suspicions, even in the Gorbachev era, of Soviet intentions and doubts whether the Soviet Union is really ready and willing to cooperate with the "capitalist" Asia–Pacific nations and business groups in market-oriented policies and broader areas of cooperation.

If the experiment of bringing China into PECC works out to the satisfaction of all PECC members—and to the PRC—and especially if this is followed by admission of the Soviet Union, a major breakthrough will have occurred in progress toward increasing all-Asia–Pacific cooperation, and in resolving one of the greatest obstacles in the past to such cooperation, namely the Communist—non-Communist divide. This would give new meaning and dimensions to the "new regionalism" in Asia and the Pacific, and might serve as a pattern that could be followed in other world regions.

The emerging mix of global and regional preoccupations in PECC was further illustrated by the adoption at the Vancouver Conference of a statement submitted by Dr. Thanat Khoman, then deputy prime minister of Thailand, perhaps the most enthusiastic supporter of any Southeast Asian leader of the immediate and larger aims of Pacific economic cooperation and of the PECC as a major agency for promoting these aims. Endorsed by PECC's Standing Committee and then by the delegates to PECC–V, and labeled the Vancouver Statement on Pacific Economic Cooperation, the document surveyed the background, premises, and organization of the PECC as the story of the evolution of the "PECC process," a term that soon came into widespread use to symbolize the larger aims and dimensions of the PECC. These were indicated most clearly in the following list of activities (really more objectives and proposed future directions than activities) which were incorporated in the final section of the Vancouver Statement:

1. Examination of key problems and issues influencing regional economic growth.
2. Provision of opportunities for identifying regional interests and consensus.
3. Stimulation of efforts to solve common problems through regional cooperation, reduce economic tensions and encourage new actions and creative development among Pacific nations.

4. Development, dissemination, and sharing of materials and analyses to encourage greater Pacific economic cooperation, and demonstrate how regional economic potential can be realized.

5. Encouragement of a Pacific voice in other multilateral organizations.

6. Promotion of greater awareness and understanding of the increasing interdependence of the Pacific economies.[26]

The increasing scope and significance of the PECC was demonstrated in the sixth general meeting (PECC–VI), held in Osaka, 17–20 May 1988. It was by far the largest PECC meeting up to that time. "A total of 862 business leaders, government officials, and economic specialists from the fifteen Member Committees, and the two institutional members (PAFTAD and PBEC) of the PECC attended the conference. Guests from sixteen nations and six international organizations observed the proceedings along with media representatives." New initiatives proposed by the standing committee and the task forces, or adopted at the initiative of delegates to the Osaka Conference, included the announcement of the creation of a Central Fund for PECC, an important trade policy statement by the standing committee, an agreement by this committee to "examine new possibilities for multilateral science and technology cooperation in the Pacific region," a statement by the same committee "inviting representatives of the South Pacific Forum to confer with the PECC and to help formulate suggestions for ways in which the Pacific island nations might become more involved in the PECC process," the establishment of a new task force on Agricultural Policy, Trade and Development and of a study group on Forest Reserves, a proposal by the Japanese National Committee for an examination of the "accelerated demands for transportation and communications services in the region," and the issuance of the first Economic Outlook report for the Pacific nations.[27]

Official Regional Organizations

Economic and Social Commission for Asia and the Pacific (ESCAP)

The most comprehensive official all-regional organization in Asia and the Pacific is the Economic and Social Commission for Asia and the Pacific (ESCAP). It is not just an all-regional organization, for it is one of the regional commissions of the United Nations and it has five influential nonregional members, France, the Netherlands, the Soviet Union (which is both a regional and a nonregional state), the United Kingdom, and the United States. Two Asian nations that are not in any of the four subregions of Asia and the Pacific, as delineated for purposes of this study—Afghanistan and Iran—are also members.

ESCAP includes almost all of the countries of Asia and the Pacific. Only Brunei, Kiribati, and North Korea are not full members. The first two are associated members, along with five political entities that are not fully independent—the Cook Islands, Guam, Hong Kong, Niue, and the Trust Territory of the Pacific Islands (which is in the process of being divided into four nearly autonomous units). Taiwan is also not a member, because of its anomalous international status, but this important NIC, or NIE, does participate indirectly in ESCAP's operations and derives considerable benefit from them.

Established in 1947 by the Economic and Social Council of the United Nations (ECOSOC) as the Economic Commission for Asia and the Far East (ECAFE), this regional commission was renamed the Economic and Social Commission for Asia and the Pacific (ESCAP) in 1974, to reflect more accurately its expanding geographic scope and its broader mission. It has become an active and comprehensive organization. It now has thirty-seven member states, and seven associated members. Its headquarters from the beginning have been in Bangkok. Its main governing commission—subject to the overall supervision of ECOSOC—usually consists of the ambassadors in Bangkok of the member states; but occasionally it meets at the ministerial level. Much of its work is done by nine "legislative committees," whose names suggest their scope and major functions: agriculture; development planning; industry; technology; human settlements and the environment; natural resources, population, and social development; statistics; trade and shipping; and transport and communications.[28] Moreover, ESCAP emphasizes increasingly the theme of "human resources development."[29]

Since ESCAP has been in existence for more than fifteen years, and its predecessor organization, ECAFE, functioned for twenty-seven years before 1974, it can hardly be called primarily an example of the "new regionalism"; but because of its broader scope and its growing associations with other regional and subregional organizations as well as with its member states in and outside of the Asia–Pacific region, and its increasingly international character, it has taken on some of the major characteristics of the new regionalism as well. It is also convincing proof of the thesis that regional organizations are stronger rather than weaker when they have significant interregional and international linkages and that because of these wider associations they have an enhanced status and effectiveness. All-regional organizations, in particular, help to bridge the gap between national and international interests and institutions.

The Asian Development Bank (ADB)

Another all-regional organization with growing scope and influence is the Asian Development Bank (ADB). It was established in 1965–66 under the auspices of ECAFE. It began operations in December 1966. Its headquarters, with a large staff of some sixteen hundred people, are in Manila. Its largest shareholders and contributors are Japan and the United States. During most of its existence each of these countries made equal contributions to the Asian Development Fund, administered by the ADB; but recently contributions by the United States have decreased, while those by Japan have increased. Every president of the Bank has been a Japanese financier.

The selection of the president and the determination of overall policies are entrusted to a Board of Governors, on which every member country is represented. The president serves as chairman of the Board of Directors, a body of twelve persons (eight regional and four nonregional) that supervises the day-to-day operations of the Bank.

Presently forty-seven countries (thirty-two from the region and fifteen from outside) are members of the ADB. Regional members include all of the countries of East, Southeast, and South Asia except Mongolia and North Korea, plus Australia, New Zealand, and most of the island nations of the Pacific. The Republic of China on Taiwan was a charter member. When the People's Republic of China was admitted, at the ADB's twentieth annual meeting of the Board of Governors in Osaka in 1987, the ROC was permitted to remain a member, but its designation was changed to "Taipei, China." In protest against this change the ROC boycotted the next annual meeting, but it sent representatives to the twenty-second annual meeting, held in Beijing,[30] 4–6 May 1989, while students and other dissidents were staging demonstrations, especially in Tiananmen Square in Beijing, near the site of the ADB meeting. This was the first time since the Communist victory in China in 1949 that a high-level official delegation from Taiwan went to the Chinese mainland. ADB is the only regional (or international) organization of which both Chinas are members with an equal status.[31]

The fifteen nonregional members are developed nations of Western Europe, plus the United States and Canada. In recent years, in keeping with Gorbachev's expressed interest in cooperating in the development of the Asia–Pacific region, the Soviet Union has sent official observers to the annual meetings of ADB. These observers have faithfully attended the sessions, have been assiduous in contacting delegates from member countries, and have sounded out delegates and ADB officials on the possibilities of admitting the Soviet Union to full membership. No formal application for admission has been received from Moscow, and will probably not be submitted until and unless there is assurance that the Soviet Union will be admitted. This is still rather unlikely, unless Japan and the United States, which together, as the major donors, control 30 percent of the votes on the Board of Governors (a 75 percent vote is required for admission), drop their publicly expressed reservations regarding Soviet membership.[32]

The World Bank, the Bank's soft-loan affiliate, the International Development Association, the International Monetary Fund, and the Asian Development Bank provide the bulk of the multilateral development assistance extended to the poorer countries of Asia and the Pacific. While it carries on a wide variety of programs, the main thrust of ADB has been increasingly on the provision of concessional loans for hundreds of projects in the least developed countries of the Asia–Pacific region. "ADB has become a major catalyst in promoting the development of the most populous and fastest growing region in the world today. . . . The Bank's operations cover the entire spectrum of economic development, with particular emphasis placed on agriculture, rural development, energy and social infrastructure."[33]

For many reasons the twenty-second annual meeting of the board of governors of ADB was an especially noteworthy one.[34] More than two thousand persons attended—official delegates from the forty-seven member countries, representatives of several interregional and international organizations, bankers and financiers from many countries that were not members of official delegations, other observers, and journalists and other media representatives from many countries. It was the first meeting of the Bank to be held in a Communist country; it convened when conditions in Beijing were quite uncertain because of the massive demonstrations that filled Tiananmen Square; it marked the return of Taiwan to the annual meetings, still protesting its changed designation of "Taipei, China", and, as has been noted, the first visit of an official Taiwanese delegation since the Communist government took control of the Chinese mainland in 1949 (the fact that the leader of the ROC delegation, the finance minister, was a woman was an added distinction); the large delegation from South Korea, led by the finance minister, was the first high-level delegation from South Korea to visit China officially. For the first time South Korea attended an annual meeting of the Board of Governors as a donor, not as a beneficiary, thus showing that it had "graduated" from the borrower class and intended to take a more active role in the Asia–Pacific region.

At the Beijing meeting the longtime President of the ADB, Masoa Fujioka of Japan, announced that he would retire at the expiration of his term of office on 31 October 1989, and another Japanese financier, Kimimasa Tarumizu, was named as his successor.

An AFP report from Beijing presented a concise summary of the proceedings and results of the ADB meeting:

> The member nations of the Asian Development Bank (ADB) agreed in principle at their meeting here [Beijing] to pursue new directions in the next decade despite serious differences on how the moves should be implemented.

> The 47-member bank gave unanimous support at their annual meeting . . . for a report outlining the course the ADB will take into the next century. . . .

All agreed to the principle of an ADB-led multilateral dialog to boost economic policies in developing member countries. Members called for stepped up environmental protection, echoing similar calls in other international forums. . . .

The new ADB directives reinforce the agency's support of a strong role for the private sector. The creation of the Asian Finance and Investment Corporation (AFIC), a proposed body where the ADB is affiliated with commercial banks, received a lukewarm response. The AFIC is to boost participation in private enterprises in developing countries.[35]

While the ADB is not quite as comprehensive in its mandate and programs as ESCAP, it is about as comprehensive in its membership, and it provides much more substantial assistance than ESCAP for the economic development of the poorer countries of the Asia–Pacific region. Like ESCAP, it has a number of nonregional members, which provide much of the financial support and have a major role in decision making.

In many respects ADB is probably more influential in the region than ESCAP, and could therefore be described as the most important official all-Asia–Pacific organization that now exists. Like ESCAP it works closely with national governments of the region, with member states outside of the region, with major subregional organizations, notably ASEAN, SAARC, and the South Pacific Forum, and with international organizations. It is thus an outstanding example of the new regionalism in Asia and the Pacific, even though, like ESCAP, it was established during the period of the old regionalism.

The Colombo Plan

One other all-regional official organization which, like ECAFE/ESCAP, is of long standing and is perhaps more associated with the old regionalism than the new, should also be mentioned. This the Colombo Plan, originally called the Colombo Plan for Cooperative Economic Development in South and Southeast Asia.

The decision to embark on this Plan was made at a meeting of the foreign ministers of the member states of the Commonwealth of Nations in Colombo, the capital of Ceylon (now Sri Lanka) in January 1950. It was formally inaugurated on 1 July 1951. Its original members were the United Kingdom and other Commonwealth countries, plus Malaya and British Borneo.[36] It now has twenty-seven members. Most are countries in South and Southeast Asia, many of which are members of the Commonwealth; but there are four other members from the other two subregions of Asia and the Pacific—Australia, New Zealand, Japan, and South Korea—and three nonregional members—Canada, the United Kingdom, and the United States. Most of the economic assistance is provided by the nonregional members and by Japan.

Originally the Colombo Plan was designed to assist developing countries in South and Southeast Asia, most of which, as has been noted, were members of the Commonwealth; but gradually it broadened its membership and its functions, to the extent that today it provides assistance for the economic and social advancement of most of the nations of the Asia–Pacific region. "It was extended to the member countries of the Asia–Pacific region after the name of the organization was changed to 'The Colombo Plan for Cooperative Economic and Social Development in Asia and the Pacific' in 1977."[37]

While the Colombo Plan is less well known than ESCAP and ADB, it is not less effective and hardly less comprehensive in its membership and programs. It lacks the degree of institutionalization of the other two all-regional organizations, which some observers view as an advantage. It has modest headquarters in Colombo. It is not as prominently identified with the new regionalism as are ESCAP and ADB; but this may be due more to its deliberately limited public relations program than to its seemingly less central role in the new regionalism in Asia and the Pacific. It deserves more study and recognition.

Future Directions for Pacific Cooperation

In addition to the evolution of all-regional official and unofficial organizations for Pacific economic cooperation—and to a lesser extent for other forms of cooperation—there has been a burgeoning of official and unofficial studies, seminars, conferences, reports, books, articles, and other types of publications, to the extent that work in this field has become something of a growth industry. And in spite of the reluctance of most Pacific governments to move boldly in the direction of Pacific cooperation, many of these governments, notably those in Japan, the United States, and Australia, have set up special committees or groups to study, monitor, and suggest possible initiatives and policy directions in this field. Many "think tanks" in most of the nations of Asia and the Pacific, some of an official or semi-official nature, have undertaken special research and other projects relating to Asia–Pacific cooperation. This subject is often discussed by official delegates to regional or international conferences.

One major forum for such discussions is the post-ministerial dialogues that are now held after each annual meeting of the foreign ministers of the ASEAN countries between these ministers and their "dialogue partners" from the United States, Japan, Canada, Australia, New Zealand, and the Economic Community. Continuing opportunities for the exchange of views on Pacific cooperation among official representatives from virtually all of the countries of Asia and the Pacific, and in fact from most of the nations of the world, are provided through the vast United Nations system, especially at the lengthy annual sessions of the United Nations General Assembly, the frequent meetings sponsored by the specialized agencies of the U.N., and a large number of international conferences convened under U.N. auspices. Here again we have a reminder of the growing necessity of dealing with many problems on national, regional, and international levels.

In their essay, "Pacific Economic Cooperation and an Overview of the Canberra Process," published as one of the PBEC Papers in 1985, two veterans of the Pacific cooperation movement, M. Mark Earle, Jr., the International Director General of PBEC, and Eric A. Trigg, then chairman of both the Canadian National Committee on Pacific Economic Cooperation and the Standing Committee of PECC, identified three phases in the evolution of the Pacific cooperation concept. "During its first phase (1960–66), the concept began its evolution with individual contributions such as Kiyoshi Kojima's proposal for a Pacific Free Trade Area (PAFTA). During the second phase (1967–79), separate groups of businessmen and academics established organizations to examine elements of the idea on a continuing basis." For example, PBEC was established in 1967, and the first Pacific Trade and Development Conference was held a year later. The third phase, in the 1980s, was inaugurated by the Pacific Community Seminar in Canberra in September 1980, and took institutional form in PECC.

"The new objective was to establish an evolutionary process." This process, as Earl and Trigg point out,

> has followed many channels. Business efforts are maturing steadily with continuing practical attention to short-term matters, and increasing visionary concern about more fundamental long-term opportunities. Academics continue to expand their individual and collective research efforts, so the basic information needed for the discussion of Pacific issues is expanding. Governments in bilateral channels and tentatively in a few multilateral channels, have begun discussions of regional cooperation and development matters. Finally, the gradual "maturing" of the Pacific Economic Cooperation Conferences (PECC) tripartite process which began at Canberra, represents the last and most embracing of the four major channels in which Pacific Economic Cooperation is being discussed. Increasingly the correct issues are being addressed and mechanisms are being examined to strengthen means of consultation and communication.[38]

In speculating on "possible future directions for the cooperation process," these two champions of greater Pacific cooperation mentioned six possible options. It is significant that they found major obstacles in the way of each option. The six options, and the obstacles they see to each, are as follows:

1. "Create an EC organization for the Pacific similar to the EEC"—but "almost all agree that the diversity of cultures and economies of the Region make this outcome one of very, very low probability, even in the long run."

2. "Establish an OECD-type organization based on government consultation and communication"—but "it seems premature to establish such an organization while still trying to understand which regional issues need attention and what priority should be given to each."

3. "Strengthen the PECC (Canberra) process." This option has some promise, but many issues remain. Among these are issues of membership, finding an appropriate balance "between dialogue and the development of 'action' recommendations," "integrating the views of both the developing and the developed countries," and relationships with governments. The nonofficial status of PECC was more a source of strength than of weakness in the early stages, but it is still a question whether a nonofficial comprehensive regional economic organization can ever be a focus for the kind of cooperation a truly comprehensive and effective all-Asia–Pacific organization would require.

4. Establish a Pacific Commission—but this option "has not yet been fully articulated" and "would only be established with explicit involvement of governments."

5. "Expand the ASEAN dialogue"—but "there are clearly major problems with regard to membership." Moreover, "it is difficult to view the dialogue as the optimum means to examine and discuss broader problems of Pacific Cooperation."

6. "Enhance existing Pacific institutions," but before the activities of these institutions "become too fragmented and attract criticism for their 'overlapping' nature, some moves to achieve greater cohesion seem to be needed."[39]

All of these options, and innumerable other suggestions for more effective regional cooperation in Asia and the Pacific, merit careful examination. So too does the experience of PACTAD, PBEC, and PECC in the area of Pacific economic cooperation. But the conclusion that has to be reached after such an examination is that, for all the impressive advances of the past two decades, Pacific cooperation is still in an early stage of development, and is still far short of generating the kind of momentum for and implementation of such cooperation that the "new tides in the Pacific" would seem to require. Psychological and institutional breakthroughs seem to have been achieved, but these have not yet provided the basis for the next major steps in Asia–Pacific cooperation.

It should be remembered, however, that while the development of major regional and interregional organizations in Asia and the Pacific has been surprisingly extensive, far more linkages and associations among the states and peoples of the region exist and are proliferating at less than comprehensive regional levels. It is in this area that large numbers of international regimes, centering around issue areas and mostly without extensive institutionalization can be found. These regimes, which are of a regional, interregional, and international character, help to provide some order and coherence in this important dimension of Asia–Pacific regionalism.

It may be encouraging that at this stage advocates of Pacific cooperation have tended to shy away from the term "Pacific Community," which enjoyed a considerable vogue in the 1960s and 1970s and is still used freely—and loosely—by those who wax ecstatic about "the coming Pacific era." The tendency of those who have been most centrally involved is to favor the term "cooperation" instead of "community."

The circumstances that led the peoples and governments of Western Europe to embrace the term "community" and to develop an institutional form of "European community"—still well short of political integration—do not exist in the vast and diverse region of Asia and the Pacific. In short, there are psychological and other blocks to the acceptance of the term "community," except in a rhetorical or symbolic sense. The ultimate goal may be what Dr. Thanat Khoman described in 1982 as "the establishment of a monumental enterprise which will serve over two-thirds of humanity;" but, as he pointed out in the same address, a great deal of ground work must be done before any kind or form of "monumental enterprise" can have any hope of success.[40]

For the foreseeable future a more realistic and pragmatic course must be followed. This is the view of almost all of those who have been most closely associated, in leading roles, with the various steps and movements toward greater Asia–Pacific cooperation. In his closing remarks at the historic Canberra Conference in 1980, Sir John Crawford declared quite realistically: "Advance must be step-by-step. The first goal is to build arrangements that are loosely structured but purposeful arrangements which are worthwhile in themselves and encourage the practice of substantive cooperation on a regional basis."[41]

9
The Superpowers and Asia–Pacific Regionalism

I n various ways the United States and Russia have been involved in the Asia–Pacific region for many decades—Russia since the seventeenth century and the United States since the latter part of the eighteenth. Both Russian and American involvement became really significant in the late nineteenth century—Russia after its territorial expansion into eastern Siberia and to the Pacific Ocean, the United States after the Spanish–American War and the annexation of the Philippines. Russian activity in Asia was retarded by its defeat in the Russo–Japanese War of 1904–1905 and by the unsettling effects of the Bolshevik revolution of 1917 and its aftermath.

The immediate cause of the American entry into the Second World War was the Japanese attack on Pearl Harbor on 7 December 1941. The Western Pacific, China, and Southeast Asia were the second major theater of American military operations. The Soviet Union entered the war in the Far East only a few days before Japan surrendered, but by so doing it had a major voice in the postwar order in East Asia and the entire Asia–Pacific area.

Since the end of World War II these two countries—which came to be recognized as superpowers—have been the major external actors in the Asia–Pacific region, usually in competitive roles.[1] Their conflicting policies and actions in this region have obviously been shaped by their global rivalries. In fact, East Asia has been the second most important theater of these rivalries, second only to Western Europe and the North Atlantic region. Their relations with the countries of Asia and the Pacific must always be considered in this light.

This has been a source of great alarm and criticism on the part of the Asia–Pacific nations, as well as a complicating factor in overall U.S.–Soviet relations. The countries of Asia and the Pacific have often complained that the superpowers have been so preoccupied with the global conflict that they have not given adequate attention to the interests of other countries with which they have diplomatic relations. Moreover, these weaker countries have been apprehensive that they might be dragged into superpower disputes as pawns in the superpower game. The superpowers, in turn, have found their commitments to weaker nations to be a heavy burden—financially and militarily, at least; and, since most of the armed conflicts in the post–World War II years have taken place in or between Third World countries, the superpowers have an understandable fear of involvement in a major military conflict with each other as a result of the escalation of regional conflicts.

At present, when regional cooperation in Asia and the Pacific is assuming unprecedented dimensions, the United States and the Soviet Union are taking a much more positive attitude toward the burgeoning "new regionalism." No doubt, however, each superpower has rather ambivalent views regarding this new regionalism and its implications, just as the countries of the Asia–Pacific region still have ambivalent views regarding the genuine position of the superpowers toward their efforts to develop greater regional cooperation.

Superpower-Led Alliance Systems in Asia and the Pacific

Before considering recent patterns of regionalism in Asia and the Pacific, and the changing and more positive attitude of the superpowers toward these emerging patterns, a brief reminder and comment should be recorded about an older approach to regionalism in Asia and the Pacific that must be regarded, on the whole, as a barrier to effective and constructive regionalism. The regional structure that emerged, as a result of the conflictual state of Soviet–American relations, was a system of rival alliances. That system sharply divided the Asia–Pacific region along Communist–non-Communist lines and greatly added to the tensions and divisions in a region where these conditions already existed to an alarming degree. In each set of alliances the initiative was taken not by indigenous powers but by the contending superpowers. Thus many of the Asia–Pacific countries became a part of a worldwide system of alliances pitting the superpowers and their allies on opposite sides of the "protracted conflict," or the "cold war."[2] Presumably participation in these rival alliances gave them some assurance that in their conflicts with unfriendly neighbors they would have the support of a major power and that if one of the superpowers took military action against them, the other— their ally—would come to their rescue.

These alliance systems were regional only in the sense that they involved countries in all of the four subregions of Asia and the Pacific. In fact, most of these alliance relationships were bilateral in nature. Thus the United States, at various times, had bilateral security arrangements with Japan—by far its most important security relationship in the entire Asia–Pacific region—South Korea, the Republic of China on Taiwan, the Philippines, Thailand, and Pakistan. Only the relationships with Japan and South Korea, dating from the early or mid-1950s, have endured in a generally healthy state, and even these are becoming somewhat uncertain.

The security ties with the Philippines have endured, but they are jeopardized by political uncertainties in the Philippines and by the profoundly sensitive issue of the future of the U.S. bases in that country. Pakistan, which its leader, Ayub Khan, described as "America's most allied ally in Asia" in an address to both houses of the U.S. Congress in the summer of 1961, became disillusioned with its great ally, as suggested by the title of a book by Ayub, *Friends Not Masters*.³ Under Zufilkar Ali Bhutto, Pakistan in effect pulled out of the alliance, declared itself to be nonaligned, and was eventually admitted to the nonaligned movement. But after the Soviet invasion of Afghanistan in December 1979 the United States and Pakistan revived their alliance.

The alliance with Thailand became moribund, especially after the end of the Vietnam War and Thailand's request that all U.S. troops be withdrawn from its soil; but this alliance too was resurrected, in spirit if not completely in a formal way, after Vietnamese troops moved into Cambodia/Kampuchea in December 1978, thus posing an aggravated threat to Thailand and making Thailand a "front line state" in American eyes, just as Pakistan became a "front line state" after Soviet troops moved into Afghanistan.

The security relationship with the Nationalist Chinese regime on Taiwan, under which the United States became deeply involved in the defense of that island and in the tensions between Taiwan and mainland China (the People's Republic of China), was ended by the United States in the 1970s, as the price for its establishment of diplomatic relations with the PRC. The United States continues to take a special interest in the security of Taiwan, as expressed in the Taiwan Relations Act of 1979,⁴ to which the PRC continues to object most strongly, and it still maintains extensive relations with Taiwan; but the formal alliance relationship has ended.

The Soviet Union has security agreements with Mongolia, North Korea, and Vietnam and other agreements of the "treaty of peace, friendship, and cooperation" variety with Laos, Cambodia, and a few non-Communist states, notably India, that despite some provisions regarding security are not generally regarded as security arrangements. The most conspicuous alliance that the Soviet Union entered into with any Asian state was that with the People's Republic of China in the 1950s. Initiated by the treaty signed by Stalin and Mao Tse-tung (Mao Zedong) in 1950, this alliance seemed to consolidate the monolithic front presented by the two largest and most powerful Communist states and accentuated the conviction and apprehension of a massive Communist threat throughout the non-Communist world. But the alliance abruptly ended in effect with the Sino–Soviet split that became evident by the late 1950s and early 1960s, although it was not formally terminated until after China, in April 1979, announced its refusal to agree to a further extension of the treaty.

In 1969 then Soviet General Secretary and leader of the Soviet Union, Leonid Brezhnev, advocated "a system of collective security in Asia," presumably to include both Communist and non-Communist nations. This proposal attracted a great deal of attention but not much support, for many Asian nations perceived it to be, probably quite rightly, directed against China. The proposal has been repeated and revised many times since 1969, but it has never been specifically spelled out. It is significant primarily as one of the major Soviet propaganda initiatives directed toward Asia. More recently a similar proposal has been advanced by Mikhail Gorbachev as a part of his overall efforts to develop a new Soviet approach to Asia; but he and other Soviet spokesmen insist that this is a different and broader proposal than the one associated with Brezhnev's demarche in 1969.

The Soviet Union has made no successful attempts to form multilateral security relationships in Asia and the Pacific. Apparently it has decided to eschew the multilateral approach in its coordination of security planning in the Asia–Pacific region among Communist and Communist-oriented states and concentrate on developing a pattern of bilateral security agreements, under its supervision. Mikhail Gorbachev is the first Soviet leader who has been able to convince large numbers of people and leaders in non-Communist Asia that he means what he says and is really prepared to move from confrontation to cooperation in the Asia–Pacific region.

The United States has been far more assiduous and successful in promoting and participating in multilateral security arrangements in the Asia–Pacific region than the Soviet Union has been. The two outstanding examples are SEATO and ANZUS. Both of these were once flourishing and influential multilateral alliances; but eventually both were disrupted by changing circumstances and the gradual alienation of one or more of their members.

The Southeast Asia Treaty Organization (SEATO) was established in 1954. From the U.S. point of view it was a part of the worldwide system of alliances to deter Communist aggression and expansionism. From the point of view of its Asian members it was an arrangement that seemed to ensure that they would receive support from major outside powers in dealing with any military threat to their security, or even survival, from the Soviet Union or China or both, and also receive other benefits from their military association with the non-Asian members.

For some time SEATO seemed to be an effective multilateral security relationship, a less powerful but still significant Asian NATO. But while its focus was on Southeast Asia and its well-staffed headquarters were in the region (in Bangkok), it was never really a "Southeast Asia Treaty Organization." Only two of its eight members—Thailand and the Philippines—were Southeast Asian states, and only one other—Pakistan—was located in Asia. In the 1970s SEATO fell apart. France ceased to be a fully cooperative member, and Pakistan, disillusioned by its relations with the United States and by its experience in SEATO, withdrew from the alliance. After the United States reversed its policy toward the People's Republic of China, one of the main reasons for the existence of SEATO, at least from the viewpoint of the Southeast Asian members, was no longer valid. SEATO relapsed into a state of reduced activity and effectiveness. "The alliance remains on paper but in fact is defunct."[5] It was largely phased out in 1977.

In 1951 the United States entered into a trilateral alliance with Australia and New Zealand (known as ANZUS) for mutual cooperation in the defense of the Southwest Pacific region.[6] "[U]ntil the mid-1980s [this security pact] seemed to be one of the most stable security relationships in the world. . . . In the 1980s, however, ANZUS became an alliance in crisis because of New Zealand's refusal to allow any warships to enter its ports, even ships of ANZUS alliances, unless it was assured that these warships were not carrying nuclear weapons. The United States reacted strongly to this new policy, and when no compromise could be reached officially notified both Australia and New Zealand, in April 1986, that it was scrapping the ANZUS treaty. Two months later the U.S. secretary of state, George Shultz, told New Zealand's prime minister, David Lange, that the United States no longer considered itself bound to come to New Zealand's defense under the terms of the AN-ZUS treaty. With Australia, however, the United States is continuing its alliance commitments, under bilateral agreements and arrangements."[7]

Technically ANZUS is still in force, in spite of the impasse between the United States and New Zealand. Neither nation has formally withdrawn from the pact, although, as has been stated, the United States has notified New Zealand that it no longer regards its commitments under ANZUS to apply to New Zealand. As has been noted in another chapter, in an unofficial visit to the United States in the spring of 1989, when he was not invited to meet any high-ranking American officials, Prime Minister Lange told a *Time* interviewer that he regarded ANZUS as in fact dead, and that New Zealand might soon announce its formal withdrawal from the treaty.[8]

Through their bilateral and multilateral security arrangements with many of the nations of Asia and the Pacific, the United States and the Soviet Union have long participated in a form of regionalism and regional organization. But it must be admitted that this is a peculiar form of regional cooperation that perhaps should be considered as a part of superpower security systems rather than as examples of regional cooperation. Neither in their regional nor international manifestations can these security "systems" be accurately described as international security regimes. In any event, while the superpowers still have bilateral alliance relationships with several Asia–Pacific states, these relationships were more characteristic of the older, more limited, and unbalanced regionalism in this region and elsewhere than of the new regionalism that is emerging so significantly in this most dynamic of the world's regions. In terms of security relationships in Asia and the Pacific the more recent trend, as Robert A. Scalapino has often pointed out, is toward alignments, not alliances.[9]

Superpower Roles in Asia–Pacific Regionalism

Throughout the post–World War II years both superpowers have been deeply involved in regional conflicts in Asia and the Pacific as well as in other parts of the world. Examples that come readily to mind are conflicts in South Asia, especially between India and Pakistan, between India and China, and between Pakistan and Afghanistan; conflicts in Southeast Asia, including those between Indonesia and Malaysia, between Malaysia and the Philippines, and most notably between Thailand and Cambodia (backed by Vietnam), and more generally between ASEAN nations and the Communist states of Indochina; conflicts in East Asia, notably those between North and South Korea, between the People's Republic of China and the Soviet Union after the Sino–Soviet split, between mainland China and Taiwan, and between China and Vietnam; and conflicts or tensions in the Southwest Pacific and Oceania, such as those between the countries of this region and France over nuclear testing, nuclear waste disposal, and French colonial policies in New Caledonia and French Polynesia.

Since most of these conflict situations are still unresolved, although most of them seem to be assuming less dangerous forms, it would be difficult to evaluate the nature and consequences of superpower involvement. In some of these conflicts it could be argued that the superpowers helped prevent serious conflict escalation and eventually assisted in reducing the seriousness of the conflicts even without their actual resolution. However, in some cases that involvement has served more to exacerbate than to mitigate regional conflicts. In almost all, superpower involvement has raised apprehensions in the Asia–Pacific nations that superpower intervention would embroil them in larger world conflicts and in the superpowers that their involvement in regional conflicts might lead to direct military confrontation with each other.

In the period of the new regionalism in Asia and the Pacific there are encouraging examples of cooperation between the superpowers in keeping regional conflicts from erupting into armed conflict and even for working out tolerable compromise arrangements in situations that have only known long years of bitter hostility.[10] Both the United States and the Soviet Union seem genuinely to desire to restrain their Korean allies from further military conflict and to help them work out arrangements for peaceful coexistence, if not for peaceful reunification of the Korean Peninsula. In Southeast Asia the Soviet Union seems to be exercising a restraining effect on its Vietnamese ally and on the Communist regime in Phnom Penh, and perhaps also on China to cease its military and political support of the Khmer Rouge; and the United States is working with the ASEAN countries and with the United Nations in an attempt to defuse the Cambodian issue and work out some mutually acceptable and feasible arrangement for the political future of Cambodia.

Even in the confused situation in Afghanistan following the withdrawal of Soviet troops in 1988, the Soviet Union is showing some willingness to cooperate with Pakistan, the United States, the United Nations, Iran, and the Communist government that is still in shaky control in Kabul in working out some tolerable order in that country. It is not yet willing to cooperate with the still warring factions among the *mujahedin,* in Pakistan, Iran, or Afghanistan, and it is more critical than cooperative in its dealings with the United States and Pakistan, and even the United Nations, on issues relating to Afghanistan.

Another—and less well known—form of superpower cooperation in Asia–Pacific regionalism is through membership and participation in various regional, interregional, and all-regional organizations.[11] The United States is a member of a large number of these organizations. As yet, both because of its own orientation and the unwillingness of most Asian countries to admit the Communist superpower to essentially non-Communist associations, the Soviet Union participates in very few.

Of the all-regional groupings that have been specifically singled out for special attention—ESCAP, the ADB, the Colombo Plan, PAFTAD, PBEC, and PECC—the Soviet Union is a member of only one, ESCAP.[12] Since Gorbachev's rise to power, and especially since his historic statement of a new Asian policy in his speech in Vladivostok in July 1986, in which he announced that the Soviet Union was interested in establishing closer, more cordial relations with every nation in Asia and in participating actively in Asian regional organizations, the Soviet Union has taken a more positive approach toward Asian regionalism. It has been permitted to send official observers to the general meetings of the ADB, PECC, and PAFTAD, and has expressed an interest in becoming a regular and full member of the first two—thus far without success, because of the opposition, or at least the reservations, of some of the members of these organizations, notably the United States and Japan.[13]

The Soviet Union does, however, participate in some of the more specialized regional organizations in Asia and the Pacific, and it has developed some ties with all three of the comprehensive organizations that have been formed in three of the four regions, or subregions, of Asia and the Pacific— SAARC, the South Pacific Forum, and even ASEAN (of which it was sharply critical for many years). And of course, like the United States and most of the nations of the world, it is frequently in touch with representatives of Asia–Pacific nations in various international organizations, including the galaxy of organs, agencies, commissions, programs, committees, etc. in the United Nations system, and also at innumerable international conferences.

The United States is a much more active participant in Asia–Pacific organizations and conferences than is the Soviet Union. Through its official and/or unofficial representatives it plays a major role in all six of the all-regional organizations featured in chapter 8, in many more specialized and/ or more geographically limited organizations focusing on the Asia–Pacific area, including scores of unofficial organizations in professional or technical fields, and in almost daily international conferences that deal primarily with Asian affairs. The United States also has special ties with ASEAN, SAARC, and the South Pacific Forum. It is a regular participant in the post-ministerial meetings that top representatives of ASEAN countries (usually the foreign ministers but occasionally the heads of state or government) hold with their "dialogue partners" after the formal sessions of ASEAN have been concluded. These post-ministerial meetings provide an innovative and increasingly important forum for continuing high-level contacts between the members of the most important comprehensive regional—or subregional—organization that has emerged in Asia and the Pacific and the United States and other "dialogue partners."[14]

Regional Perspectives on Superpower Roles

It is obviously important to assess the role of the superpowers in Asia and the Pacific from the viewpoint of the people and leaders of the region, as well as from the perspectives of the superpowers themselves. While the attitudes have varied greatly at particular times, in particular countries and among particular groups, an overall generalization that would seem to be generally valid is that these attitudes have invariably been ambivalent, full of nuance and contradiction. Often they reflect more the frustrations of people with their own government and their own life conditions, on the one hand, or their hopes for improved political, economic, and social conditions, on the other, than any basic antagonism toward or faith in the major external powers. Certainly there is a great deal of suspicion of the superpowers— of both their specific actions and their basic motivations and intentions—in virtually all of the countries of the Asia–Pacific region.

Fears of military, political, or cultural intervention by a superpower, and convictions that only by banding together to promote common interests can the weaker nations of Asia and the Pacific hope to escape excessive influence or even domination, have been strong factors motivating the Asia– Pacific nations to develop an unprecedented degree of regional cooperation and institutionalization in the face of great obstacles and continuing differences. On the other hand, many regional organizations, like many countries of the region, would have even greater difficulty than they are now experiencing in developing, or even surviving, if they did not receive substantial help and cooperation, intangible as well as tangible, from the very powers of which they are the most suspicious. They want to avoid becoming the victims of superpower pressures and rivalries, but at the same time they want to receive greater assistance and cooperation from these same powerful external actors. In some, perhaps most, respects they would like to have a lowered superpower presence in their part of the world; but they realize that the superpowers will not, and probably cannot, go away, and that these powers are needed in many ways, for political, economic, and even security support.

One of the great dilemmas facing new and relatively weak states in a world of power is that they cannot avoid an unhealthy degree of dependence on stronger states. This creates the kind of asymmetric relationships that are so prevalent in the contemporary world—as they have been throughout history—relationships that can only be made less unequal (but never completely so) by enlightened actions and policies on the part of both weak and powerful nations.

The dilemma of dependence is particularly obvious on security and economic fronts. The Asia–Pacific states would certainly like to see a greatly reduced military presence of the superpowers in their region, and elsewhere; but few of them would like to see that presence completely removed.[15] The non-Communist countries of Asia and the Pacific would be alarmed if the United States did not maintain a formidable military presence in the region, at least as long as the even more formidable Soviet military presence is there. The Communist countries of the region—other than the People's Republic of China—might have the same concern about any substantial reduction of Soviet military power.

The PRC provides an example of the changing views of many Asian countries on this delicate security problem. While it has generally condemned both superpowers for their heavy military buildup in the Asia–Pacific area, during the height of Sino–Soviet tensions it reversed this position to the extent of modifying its frequent demand for a withdrawal of American forces from the Western Pacific. It obviously wanted a counterpoise to the escalating military presence of the Soviet Union along its borders and its offshore waters.

On the economic front the paradox and ambivalence are even more obvious. Most non-Communist Asia–Pacific countries, large and small, are heavily dependent on the United States for markets for their exports, for sources of needed imports, and for economic and technical assistance. At the same time they are fearful of the consequences of such heavy dependence.

During the two decades of strained relations with the Soviet Union, the PRC was forced to turn to the non-Communist developed countries of the West, especially the United States and the countries of the European Community, and to Japan, for trade, investment, and technology transfer. Even today, when the Sino–Soviet rift has officially ended, and when relations with the United States have become cooler than they have been since they were restored in the 1970s, the PRC has much more extensive economic relations with the United States than it has with the Soviet Union. But this fact does not inhibit its leaders in their continuing barrage of criticism of the United States and U.S. policies, which reached new heights after the tragic events in Tiananmen Square in early June 1989 and the U.S. reactions to these acts of brutality.[16]

Undoubtedly both superpowers, especially the United States, have had some direct involvement in and some influence on the development of Asia–Pacific regionalism, especially in the era of the new regionalism. The attitude of the Asia–Pacific nations toward superpower involvement and influence in their developing regionalism, like that toward the role of the superpowers in the region generally, is, as has been indicated, quite ambivalent. It would be difficult to determine whether these countries regard superpower involvement in Asia–Pacific regionalism as, on the whole, primarily helpful or primarily harmful. Certainly there are evidences of both reactions.

New Superpower Approaches to the New Asia–Pacific Regionalism

There are encouraging signs that both superpowers have embarked on new approaches to Asia–Pacific regionalism, and toward the region generally. This is primarily a consequence of the improvement in their overall relations in the era that is sometimes characterized as Detente II. It is also a consequence of a realization on the part of the United States that the need for "new thinking" and for a recognition of "new realities" is not confined to the Soviet Union, and on the part of the Soviet Union that its past policies in the Asia–Pacific region, which have been largely based on a military power approach, have been increasingly counterproductive. Both superpowers have had to adjust to the changing political, security, and economic environment in this dynamic region and to the new regionalism that is developing in this part of the world. They have also had to adjust to two other main trends that in this study have been linked with the new regionalism, namely the trends toward a more assertive nationalism, on the one hand, and toward a growing interdependence and internationalism, on the other.

On the Soviet side, the new approach can be dated from Gorbachev's accession to power in 1985, and particularly from his speech in Vladivostok in July 1986, in which he outlined a new Asian policy in a broad and challenging way. Later, in Krasnoyarsk in September 1988, he reaffirmed this new policy in more concrete, if less inspirational, terms.[17] A major result of this new approach is the Soviet rapprochement with the People's Republic of China, dramatized and formalized by Gorbachev's official visit to Beijing in May 1989 (even though it was overshadowed and embarrassingly interfered with by the student demonstrations against their government and leaders and for democracy). Other evidences are a more positive attitude toward ASEAN; some evidences of Soviet restraint on allies in the region, thereby possibly contributing to the withdrawal of Vietnamese troops from Cambodia and to a lessening of tensions on the Korean Peninsula; and the gradual establishment of trade and other links with South Korea following the twenty-fourth Olympiad in Seoul in September and early October 1988. There are even some indications that the Soviet Union is at long last willing to make at least minimal concessions on the Northern Territories and other issues in dispute with Japan and thereby inaugurate a new era in Soviet–Japanese relations.

Soviet interest in playing a larger and more constructive role in Asia–Pacific affairs was again evidenced by an extraordinary "international meeting" that was held in Vladivostok from 30 September to 3 October 1988, under the sponsorship of the USSR Academy of Sciences. Specially invited persons from thirty-five countries attended this conference. A leading role was taken by Academician Evgeny M. Primakov, who, in addition to his other high positions, is the chairman of the Soviet National Committee on Asian–Pacific Ocean Economic Cooperation. The overall theme of the conference was "Asia–Pacific Region: Dialogue, Peace, Cooperation." "Free and informal discussions," in three sections, concentrated on the following topics: (1) "political problems of the region and their relation with global dynamics of international relations;" (2) "economic and scientific cooperation in Asia and the Pacific;" and (3) "role of culture and mass media in the process of international interaction in Asia and Pacific."[18]

Judging by the amount of attention given to it by the Soviet media, the Soviet Union attached great importance to this conference. It must have been disappointed by the limited coverage and rather cool reception in the nations of Asia and the Pacific and the almost complete neglect of the meeting elsewhere. Soviet spokesmen expressed annoyance at an article in the *New York Times* while the conference was in session, by two prominent officials of the Reagan administration who were especially concerned with East Asian affairs, Gaston Sigur, Assistant Secretary of State for Asian and Pacific Affairs, and Richard Armitage, Assistant Secretary of Defense for International Security. In this article the authors questioned "the claim of the Soviet Union to be a full-fledged member of the Asian–Pacific community."[19]

In Asia and the Pacific, as elsewhere, the basic relations between the United States and the Soviet Union, even in the Gorbachev era, are more conflictual than cooperative, and this limits their capacity to contribute positively to the creation of the kind of environment that is conducive to greater cooperation and institutionalization in the region. To the extent that they are genuinely seeking to improve their overall relations in all the regions of the world, they may be said to be making a positive contribution to Asia–Pacific regionalism. And conversely, to the extent that they continue to project their longstanding rivalry to all parts of the world, they tend to deter rather than promote regional cooperation, especially cooperation between Communist and non-Communist states and among their respective allies. Hence, as has been stated, it is difficult to determine whether on balance the superpowers are contributing to or hindering Asia–Pacific regionalism. This is a conclusion that spokesmen of both superpowers would indignantly reject, and that the sharpest critics of one superpower or the other, or both, would all too enthusiastically endorse. Obviously a case could be made for either point of view; but a more objective assessment would undoubtedly lie somewhere in between.

The nature and reasons for the rivalry of the United States and the Soviet Union in Asia and the Pacific, and the problems that this rivalry poses for the countries of the region, are generally well known and are frequently well documented. Less well known and documented are the compulsions toward cooperation in the region, created by common interests and concerns. Nevertheless, both superpowers share a common interest in reducing their military confrontation and rivalry, and their military establishments, in what is now perhaps the most highly militarized region in the world, and in helping to defuse regional conflicts and especially in preventing these conflicts from escalating into direct military confrontations with each other.[20] In the past they shared what might be called a reverse common interest, which was to counter and reduce the power and influence of the other in the region. In recent years both superpowers have been less open in emphasizing this objective, but there can be little doubt that it is still a priority objective in their overall Asia–Pacific policy.

By improving their overall relations and their relations with the countries of the Asia–Pacific region, by showing an unprecedented interest in regional cooperation and institutionalization, and by seeking to reduce regional tensions and conflicts, the superpowers are helping to create conditions conducive to more effective and extensive regionalism. By continuing to follow policies that stemmed from an essentially conflictual and confrontational frame of reference, they are still open to charges that they are carrying their cold war mentality into the Asia–Pacific region, thereby complicating the search of the peoples and countries of the region for peace, stability, and development. There are, therefore, still doubts in the region about the credibility of the new policies and approaches that spokesmen of both superpowers profess to be following. To Asians, it seems, there is still a great gap between superpower rhetoric and superpower reality.

Both the United States and the Soviet Union face the challenge of adopting and implementing broader, more positive policies and approaches to the changing scene in the Asia–Pacific region. In the past the United States has worked more closely with the countries of the region than has the Soviet Union; but in more recent years the latter, under the stimulus of Gorbachev's call for a new Asian policy, has appeared, and has to some extent translated appearance into tentative reality, to be making a greater effort to understand the "new realities" in Asia and the Pacific than has the United States. In this region, as elsewhere, there is a widespread feeling that the United States has yielded the initiative to the Soviet Union and has been more reactive than positive in its basic approach.

There are many signs that the Soviet Union is indeed adopting a more flexible, more cooperative, and apparently less militaristic approach to the Asia–Pacific region. Hence there are solid grounds for hope that the Communist superpower will become a more constructive force for and supporter of the developing new regionalism in Asia and the Pacific. There are also solid grounds for hope that the non-Communist superpower will continue to encourage and, to the extent that it would seem desirable and welcome by the Asian–Pacific nations, actively participate in the various movements and organizations for regional cooperation. As three of the wisest leaders of the three greatest centers of economic power in the world—East Asia, Western Europe, and North America—stated in a report to the Trilateral Commission in 1989, "There should be no obstacle to the Soviet Union eventually becoming a good partner in the Asia–Pacific community if Soviet military forces in the region are reduced, pending issues are resolved one by one, and the Soviet Union removes the barriers that now prevent its Asian territories from truly cooperating with their neighbors."[21]

Even if these conditions are not fully met, the prospects for a more cooperative and constructive role by the Soviet Union in Asia and the Pacific are probably brighter than they have ever been. Obviously this does not mean that they are very bright, or that the Soviet Union will not revert to its militaristically-oriented hard-line approach to Asia, in spite of Gorbachev's inspiring words and promises. But if Gorbachev can demonstrate by concrete acts that he really means what he says and can retain control of the troubled Soviet juggernaut, the promised new Soviet approach to Asia may contribute greatly to the further development of Asia–Pacific regional cooperation. The United States has not yet formulated a comparable new approach; but, as has been noted, it has cooperated with the non-Communist nations of the region—the vast majority—much more closely than has the Soviet Union.

The Superpowers and All-Asia–Pacific Institutionalization

A major aspect of the role of the United States and the Soviet Union in the developing new regionalism in Asia and the Pacific is their position regarding and their contributions to the creation of an official all-Asia–Pacific organization or organizations more comprehensive than any that have thus far been established. Mikhail Gorbachev has made a number of proposals along these lines;[22] but he has not yet shown much interest in any of the other proposals (except one or two Mongolian proposals), especially those which have been advanced by other nations since the beginning of 1988. His proposals have been more specific and more promising than any earlier Soviet proposals, including the idea of "a system of collective security for Asia"; but there is little evidence that any of them is moving toward the stage of implementation, that the Soviet Union is pushing any of them vigorously, except in words, or that the nations of Asia and the Pacific, let alone the United States, have shown much interest in Gorbachev's many demarches along the avenue of all-Asia–Pacific cooperation.

In keeping with its overall policy, to the extent that one exists, the United States has tended to react, usually negatively, to the Soviet proposals for all-regional institutionalization and cooperation, rather than to take any leading role in initiating proposals of its own. Official American spokesmen reject this interpretation and insist that the United States favors and supports any proposal for comprehensive regional institutionalization on which the nations of the region can reach a consensus. They argue that greater initiative on the part of the United States would be counterproductive. Moreover, they would point out that the United States has been supportive of many regional organizations of various kinds that have emerged in Asia and the Pacific, and that American businessmen, academics, and officials in a "private capacity" have been leaders in the efforts to establish unofficial all-regional organizations, of which the three featured in this study, PAFTAD, PBEC, and PECC, are leading examples.[23] It is also significant that the Bush administration has shown more positive and concrete interest in creating a comprehensive, official all-regional organization than any previous American administration.

Perhaps this is an indication not so much of a major change in America's previously reactive policy as of the fact that, as Secretary of State James Baker declared in a major address to the Asia Society in New York in June 1989, "the need for a new mechanism for multilateral cooperation among the nations of the Pacific rim is an idea whose time has come." In this address, as has been noted, Mr. Baker stated that "The United States will not offer a definitive blueprint," but instead would be looking "for a consensus, drawing on the best elements from various plans."[24] Although he did not even suggest such a thought, there can be little doubt that he did not give a high priority to any of Mr. Gorbachev's proposals when he referred to "various plans."

It is difficult to determine how serious Gorbachev was when in his two historic addresses in which he laid down a new Asian policy—at Vladivostok in July 1986 and at Krasnoyarsk in September 1988—he stressed the interest of the Soviet Union in playing a constructive role in Asia–Pacific cooperation. In each address he made several specific proposals for the achievement of this objective.

A few examples will be taken from his Vladivostok address, in the order in which they were presented. "Our interest," he affirmed, "is in the pooling of efforts and in cooperation, with full respect for the right of each nation to live as it chooses and resolve its problems on its own in conditions of peace." "How, then," he asked, "should one envisage the process of establishing international security and peaceful cooperation in this vast region?" He was apparently more concerned with this kind of cooperation than with any other, but he also stated that "economic cooperation is of mutual interest." In order to advance these common objectives, he declared, "we would like to propose a conference, in the mold of the Helsinki conference, to be attended by all countries gravitating towards the [Pacific] Ocean." And then he added: "I would like to emphasize that we stand for integrating the Asian–Pacific region into the general process of establishing a comprehensive system of international security proposed at the twenty-seventh Congress of the CPSU." He outlined six "concrete views on this issue," dealing with "regional settlement," "blocking the proliferation and buildup of nuclear weapons in Asia and the Pacific Ocean," the initiation of talks "on the reduction of the activity of naval forces in the Pacific, in particular, nuclear-armed ships," the resumption of "talks on establishing the Indian Ocean as a peace zone," "the radical reduction of armed forces and conventional armaments in Asia," and "practical discussions on confidence-building measures and on the non-use of force in this region." And in his closing remarks Gorbachev declared: "The Soviet state calls upon all Asian and Pacific nations to cooperate for the sake of peace and security. Everyone who strives towards these goals and who hopes for a better future for one's people, will find that we are willing to talk and are honest partners."[25]

In this address Gorbachev recognized that the United States too, like the Soviet Union, was an Asia–Pacific power and must be included in any joint efforts toward regional cooperation and institutionalization. "We recognize clearly," he said, "that the United States is a great Pacific power. Primarily because a considerable part of the country's population lives on the shores of this ocean, the western part of America, gravitating towards this area, is playing a growing part in the country's development and is a dynamic force. Furthermore, the United States, undoubtedly, has important and legitimate economic and political interests in the region. No doubt, without the United States and its participation, it is not possible to resolve the problem of security and cooperation in the Pacific Ocean to the satisfaction of all nations in the region." And then, as would be expected, Gorbachev reverted to a longstanding Soviet complaint: "Regrettably, Washington has thus far shown no interest in this issue. . . . If the issue is taken up, it inevitably leads to the trodden path of the 'Soviet threat' and to saber-rattling corroborating this myth."[26]

The United States would obviously repudiate this final barb; but it should welcome the new evidence that the Soviet Union is at long last taking a more positive, less militaristic approach to cooperation in Asia and the Pacific; and it probably would be wise to acknowledge publicly the obvious fact that the Soviet Union too "has important and legitimate economic and political interests in the region."

In his Krasnoyarsk address Gorbachev concentrated even more heavily than he did at Vladivostok on "strengthening security in the Asia–Pacific region," to cite the title of his address. Among a variety of proposals, one resurrected a longstanding proposal for "an international conference . . . on making the Indian Ocean a zone of peace," to be held "not later than 1990," and another envisioned that "a mechanism will be created to negotiate the proposals of the Soviet Union and other nations dealing with the security of the Asia–Pacific region."[27]

Both the United States and the Soviet Union, therefore, seem to be embarking on more constructive approaches to the need for greater all-Asia–Pacific institutionalization. Both seem to agree that this should be more comprehensive in nature than any existing organizations. Each, however, seems to be particularly concerned with only one major dimension of comprehensive institutionalized cooperation—the United States with economic cooperation, and the Soviet Union with cooperation in the field of security.

Two reactions to Gorbachev's speech at Krasnoyarsk suggest the ambivalence of non-Communist views of his proposals and the continuing suspicions that linger regarding basic Soviet motivations and objectives, even in the era of *glasnost* and *perestroika*. "True," wrote the editorial page editor of the *Asian Wall Street Journal* (published in Hong Kong), "these may be the days of *glasnost* and missile treaties, but behind Mr. Gorbachev's talk of disarmament for Asia is a record that suggests the ultimate result of any U.S. withdrawal would be a Soviet advance. . . . Above all, the Soviets want access to a region that combines some of the world's most dynamic economies with some of the West's most vulnerable allies." But, she admitted, "A new approach is visible."[28] A more favorable view was expressed by the *New York Times*. In an editorial on "Mr. Gorbachev's Asian Serenade," the *Times* presented this interpretation: "The Gorbachev speech gives further evidence of a distinctly different Soviet diplomacy. Coalition-building, persuasion and diplomacy are beginning to overtake pure might in importance. . . . Gorbachev seeks fresh opportunities and shows a talent for providing them." In contrast, the *Times* opined, "new departures in American diplomacy await a new President."[29]

There is encouraging evidence that the "new President" is taking a greater and more informed interest in Asia–Pacific affairs than any of his predecessors. The Asia Society address and other statements by Secretary of State Baker and other administration spokesmen certainly place the Bush administration, like the new leadership in Moscow, on record as committed to positive support for what both Gorbachev and Secretary Baker have referred to as some kind of "mechanism" or "mechanisms" for more comprehensive multilateral cooperation in Asia and the Pacific. It remains to be seen whether their deeds will match their words.

A Concluding Note

Whatever their future policies and approaches in Asia and the Pacific may be, the superpowers will be regarded with ambivalence by most, and indeed probably all, of the nations of the region. These nations will look to the superpowers for major support and assistance, even while they fear the consequences of dependency and involvement in larger quarrels as a result of their needs.

In the last analysis the nature and extent, the success or failure, of all the many efforts at regional cooperation and institutionalization in Asia and the Pacific will depend upon the nations of the region, and not upon outside powers. But a high degree of understanding and support, and of concrete assistance and perhaps leadership in many areas, on the part of outside countries and international institutions, especially on the part of the superpowers, will be necessary if the present encouraging trends that make Asia and the Pacific perhaps the leading laboratory of the new regionalism that is developing in all parts of the world are to predominate over the formidable barriers to their effective development.

10
The New Asia–Pacific Regionalism in Perspective

As has been pointed out many times in this volume, the simultaneous upsurge of nationalism, international regionalism, and internationalism is one of the most significant developments in the contemporary world. These three trends, especially the first and the third, are apparent in virtually all parts of the world. The trend toward regionalism, which has developed a new momentum, is perhaps less obvious on a universal scale, but it may be able to play an important mediatory role between a growing and more assertive nationalism and a pervasive but still rather inchoate internationalism.

Intermediary Role of the New Regionalism

The nature of the modern world is such that nationalism can no longer meet basic human political needs. Since so many problems now facing humankind are truly global, they cannot be dealt with adequately on a national level. They require an unprecedented degree of international cooperation. But since in many instances international cooperation on a "macro" scale is difficult, some intervening level of cooperation, probably of a regional nature, may be essential to serve in a role intermediary between a nationalism that is too narrow for problems that cross national boundaries and an internationalism that is too broad, vague, and undeveloped to provide more than a supplement to efforts on national and regional levels.

There is, furthermore, a growing realization that all efforts to deal with the world's problems, at all levels, are still far from adequate or satisfactory. While the acceptance of the need for greater cooperation and institutionalization at all levels to deal with pressing global problems seems to be almost universal, the scope and seriousness of the problems are escalating much more rapidly than the capacity and willingness, in real terms, to deal with them.

This is a familiar dilemma in human existence—the capacity to handle common problems decreases even as the need to do so increases. This is particularly serious in the contemporary world, for many of the problems that call for national, regional, and international action and management clearly are life-threatening unless they can be handled more adequately, even if they cannot be really solved.

The New Regionalism in Western Europe and North America

Western Europe was the main laboratory for what has been called the old regionalism—hardly old in historical terms. This was the regionalism that developed in the 1950s and 1960s, and that assumed its most comprehensive and far-reaching institutional form in the institutions of the European Community—first the European Coal and Steel Community, then the European Economic Community and the European Atomic Community, and finally the umbrella European Community. It was this regionalism that seemed to provide a unique and ingenious solution for bridging the federal-functional divide through a "community" approach with both federal and functional features, and that stimulated an unprecedented degree of scholarly interest and innovative thinking (more than has as yet been prompted by the new regionalism). Some of this innovative thinking was related to the new forms of regionalism emerging in Western Europe, and resulted in some new contributions to regional analysis, as represented in studies of such concepts as transaction flows, integrated and nonintegrated and amalgamated and non-amalgamated security communities, and neofunctionalism.[1]

Many of the studies focused on the theme of integration at a time when some of the more farseeing founders of the West European communities were openly proclaiming that their ultimate objective was a European Political Community (and some added a European Security Community as well).[2] Whether they believed this would lead to a United States of Western Europe or even to a United States of Europe was less clear, but there was no doubt that some of these statesmen harbored such grandiose dreams and aims. The European Community movement, while a major new departure in regional institutionalization, obviously fell far short of this goal.

Similarly, many of the regional theorists who were stimulated by the progress in community building in Western Europe to add new dimensions to the study of international regionalism became absorbed with the concept of "integration." This term that had many meanings, ranging from the kind of special associations that were developing in the West European communities to integration in a truly supranational sense, involving the genuine surrender of sovereignty on the part of the participating nations and the establishment of some form of regional government as envisioned by advocates of a European Political Community. This broader objective motivated some of the proponents of regional or world government and led many of them to rally behind the interpretation of integration in the broadest sense.

While integration was a favorite theme of scholars of regionalism, the fact that it had so many different meanings and that in its broadest sense it was out of touch with reality, even in Western Europe, has led many students of regionalism to shy away from using it as a central theme for analyzing the developing new regionalism. The term is still used quite frequently—in fact its use seems to be growing again—but it is usually used more cautiously, and many other terms, such as "community," or simply "regional cooperation," are used with equal or greater frequency and greater accuracy.

Neither North America, except in relation to the Atlantic Community concept, quite different from the European Community concept, nor the Asia–Pacific region, a region that seemed to be notable for its lack of regionalism and to be on the periphery of the world that mattered, received much attention from students of the old regionalism. Their focus was clearly on Western Europe, where exciting and often novel things were happening on the regional front.

In the period of the new regionalism Western Europe is still a major focus of attention and interest, mainly because it is familiar ground for students of regionalism (most of whom are still Western scholars), and, more importantly, because of the resumption of the momentum of the European Community movement, to take concrete form in the establishment of a single common market among the members of the European Community in December 1992.[3] This opens up exciting possibilities of even greater associational ties (perhaps even real integration) among the nations of Western Europe, and perhaps in due course even among most of the European states.

North America, like the Asia–Pacific region, is a new focus for students of regionalism. The main reason, of course, is the conclusion of a free trade agreement between the United States and Canada,[4] which created the largest free trade area in the world (at least until the formation of the West European single market). The U.S.–Canada free trade agreement was reached after many months of negotiations, and in the face of strong opposition in both countries, especially in Canada, where nationalists won wide support by playing up the danger of being even more overwhelmed by the American colossus. Its conclusion, and its generally satisfactory operation to date[5] (not all Canadians and Americans would agree with this evaluation), marked a new era in U.S.–Canadian relations, made North America a more genuinely cooperative region, and gave it additional "clout" on the international stage.

The Asia–Pacific Region: A Laboratory for the New Regionalism

The phenomenon of the new regionalism is one of three dominant trends in Asia and the Pacific that should be given much more attention and analysis than they have received to date. The other two trends are a growing and more abrasive nationalism and a growing internationalism. The first of these tends to exacerbate the internal divisions among the many disparate and widely separated Asia–Pacific nations, whereas the second tends to link them with the larger international community and compels them to consider their regional as well as national interests from a broader perspective.

The new regionalism gives the Asia–Pacific states meaningful and increasingly important mediatory linkages and institutions between their own countries and the outside world. This is particularly important at a time when many of the problems concerning national development and human survival require cooperation at the regional and international levels, and when, at the same time, the practice of working at the latter level through international diplomacy and international channels and institutions has not yet been well developed or generally accepted. The new regionalism provides intermediary agencies and opportunities that, though often rather unfamiliar and viewed with some suspicions and reservations, offer more understandable and more available channels for necessary cooperation.

This is one of the many aspects of the new regionalism that is still little understood and inadequately utilized, but which offers great promise for the future. It is but one aspect, although a major one, that makes the new regionalism a phenomenon of great potential utility and importance in the increasingly interdependent world and that calls for more extensive research by students of international relations.

Probably the three most important laboratories for a study of the new regionalism are Western Europe, certainly the main focus of development and analysis in the era of the old regionalism in the 1950s and 1960s, North America, where two of the nations that share this continent have had long experience in cooperation with one another and with the countries of Western Europe, and Asia and the Pacific, where the old regionalism had relatively little impact or development, but where the new regionalism has had a surprising growth.

It would seem that the main laboratories for the study of the new regionalism would be in the Western world, especially in Western Europe, the main center of the institutionalization, development, and study of regionalism in all previous periods. It can be argued, however, that Asia and the Pacific, with its four major subregions, is an even more important and also an even more exciting laboratory for the study of the new regionalism, partly because it provides rather convincing evidence that regionalism can emerge and develop at an unexpectedly rapid pace in parts of the world where the obstacles seem to be unusually great, and where there has previously been little experience in integrative regionalism. An added reason is that since the Asia–Pacific region has become a center of world economic strength and since, as many predict, the twenty-first century, which is fast approaching, may be a "Pacific Century," or at least a Pacific as well as an Atlantic century, greater attention must be given to this rapidly emerging part of the world by all other countries and peoples. And one of the phenomena that should be given far greater attention than it has received is that of the new regionalism, Asia–Pacific version.

Characteristics of Asia–Pacific Regionalism

One of the miracles of the new regionalism is that, in spite of the impressive upsurge of regionalism in the Western world, where regionalism was already well developed, a—perhaps *the*—main laboratory for the new regionalism has become the Asia–Pacific region. This is a vast region, or mega-region, where regionalism was conspicuously underdeveloped in the past, for various historical, cultural, economic, and other reasons. This is a truly remarkable development, one that gives a clear signal that this increasingly dynamic region has become a major actor on the international stage.[6] It is a powerful reminder that an exclusively Western-oriented approach to international affairs is now very much out of touch with reality.

It is difficult to evaluate the extent and significance of this emerging new regionalism in Asia and the Pacific. There has been so little regional cooperation in this region in the past and what little there has been was not widely recognized or even identified. But because the new regionalism has led to a much more variegated and extensive pattern of cooperation in Asia and the Pacific and to the emergence of a comprehensive regional organization in each of three of these four subregions (in all but East Asia), and because so much attention is now being given to the Asia–Pacific region, there is a natural tendency to move beyond the analysis of the new regionalism in this region to an almost euphoric assessment of the exciting developments in regional cooperation in this part of the world.

The extent of this cooperation merits special attention and comparative analysis. It may revolutionize and alter, generally for the better, the relations among the many nations in this vast region; and it may be the region where the new regionalism will have its most dramatic, if not most complete, development. This will stimulate further interest throughout the world in regionalism as a phenomenon that seems to be having a new birth in recent years. But it should always be borne in mind that this new regionalism in Asia and the Pacific is still limited, especially in comparison with the much older, if episodic, patterns that have developed in the Western world, and that there are still many obstacles to its further development.

In spite of all the obstacles, a surprising amount of regionalism has developed in Asia and the Pacific. There is an extensive network of regional contacts and cooperation through scores of professional, scientific and technical associations[7] and through the increasing movement of people, goods, and services in and between various subregions. More broadly based regional organizations have emerged, notably the three comprehensive regional organizations in Southeast Asia (ASEAN), South Asia (SAARC), and the Southwest Pacific and Oceania (the South Pacific Forum), the three most comprehensive official all-regional organizations, all with international membership and links (ESCAP, the ADB, and the Colombo Plan), and at least as many all-regional unofficial organizations, of which the PECC, the PBEC, and PAFTAD are leading examples.[8]

All these organizations have important international linkages. Indeed, this has become one of the most notable features of the new regional institutionalization in the Asia–Pacific area. It is also worth noting that only three of the comprehensive regional organizations that have been singled out for special analysis are intraregional, whereas the other six are interregional or all-regional in character and operation. Both intraregional and interregional contacts are growing at many other levels and in many other forms, ranging from personal contacts on both official and unofficial levels to various forms of institutionalization.

Another striking feature of Asia–Pacific regionalism is that at long last the Communist–non-Communist divide has been extensively breached, especially since the prolonged Sino–Soviet rift has been largely repaired and since the United States and the Soviet Union have entered a new period of worldwide detente. The Soviet Union under Gorbachev has taken a less militant and more cooperative approach to the entire Asia–Pacific region. Tensions between Taiwan and mainland China have ebbed and contacts between the two Chinas—one Communist, the other non-Communist—have increased. South Korea and other non-Communist states in all of the four subregions have developed increasing contacts and trade and other economic relations with the "socialist" countries, notably with China, the Soviet Union, and the East European nations.

In many cases these increasing contacts have developed without the establishment of formal diplomatic relations. Even in Southeast Asia, the only one of the four subregions where the Communist—non-Communist divide is still a major barrier to regional cooperation, some developments are occurring which may lead to more extensive and cooperative relations between the member states of ASEAN and the Communist states of Indochina.

Another important feature of the Asia–Pacific scene is that the countries of the region are members of an astonishing number of international organizations. These range from hundreds in the case of the most internationally active countries of the region, notably Japan and Australia, to scores, even in the case of countries that are generally regarded as virtual nonparticipants in international life, notably Mongolia, North Korea, and in recent years Burma.[9]

This pattern of participation in international organizations would seem to indicate that the nations of Asia and the Pacific are more active in international than in regional or subregional affairs. A more accurate observation would be that they are more active in both regional and international affairs than is generally recognized, and that this largely unrecognized degree of involvement seems to be much more complementary than contradictory. Indeed, it seems to promote rather than interfere with greater regional cooperation. Its relation to the growing and more assertive nationalism that characterizes most of the nations of the Asia–Pacific region is less clear.

This international participation also provides further evidence of another important dimension of the new regionalism in Asia and the Pacific, namely its outward-looking character. This is a particularly noteworthy aspect, which seems to characterize the new regionalism worldwide. It is especially impressive in the Asia–Pacific region because of the less than outward-looking behavior in the past, the existing doubts, apprehensions, and inhibitions of the Asia–Pacific states regarding the desirability and consequences of greater involvement beyond their region or subregion, and the conflicting trends toward "international mercantilism" rather than "international liberalism" that are still so strong in the region.[10] It may be, of course, that the outward-looking character of Asia–Pacific regionalism is more apparent than real, and that trends toward inward-turning nationalism and protectionism will prevail; but in professions and to a large degree in practice the trend has been toward a more open regionalism, propelled by the kind of "new thinking" and the more pragmatic facing of the "new realities" that seem to prevail in most of the world.

Trading Blocs and the New Regionalism

In at least one major respect there are widespread apprehensions that the new regionalism will lead to the formation of protectionist "trading blocs" characterized by freer intraregional markets isolated by restrictive policies toward countries of other regions. These apprehensions have been frequently voiced with respect to the coming single market in Western Europe. The fear is that this largest of the world's free market areas will turn into a "Fortress Europe," and will not be open on an equal basis to trade and other relations with other countries—in other words, that it will follow free, or freer, trade policies within and protectionist policies without. The same fear has been expressed with respect to the free trade arrangement between the United States and Canada and any similar "trading bloc" that may emerge in the Asia–Pacific region.[11]

In this latter region there seems to be little prospect that a "trading bloc" will emerge in the near future. Much more progress in regional cooperation and institutionalization must occur before anything comparable to the U.S.– Canadian free trade arrangement or the single market of the European Community members can emerge in East Asia. In the other three subregions of Asia and the Pacific greater progress has been made in comprehensive regional institutionalization, but in none of these subregions do the indigenous countries have sufficient economic strength, political cohesion, and experience in mutual cooperation to establish a "trading bloc" or any other grouping that could hold its own with the giant free trade areas emerging in North America and Western Europe. The real center of economic power in Asia and the Pacific is in East Asia, with Japan as the towering economic giant and China the towering demographic giant; and this happens to be the subregion where regional institutionalization is least developed. Hence the talk of a trading bloc or trading blocs emerging in East Asia or among two or more subregions in Asia and the Pacific is premature.

It is to be hoped that any comprehensive regional groupings that develop anywhere in the world will be quite different from "trading blocs," and will be more open to the rest of the world than the invidious term "trading bloc" suggests. Fortunately, the regional trends in Asia and the Pacific seem to be developing in another and more hopeful direction. The task ahead is to develop these trends still further, and to resist any countertrends, however powerful, in other and less cooperative directions. This will be no easy task.

Here we have a crucial test for the future course of the new regionalism. Will it move in an outward-looking direction, as virtually all of those involved in the creation of larger free trade areas in the three major centers of economic power insist is their intention and objective, or will it increasingly move in the opposite direction, developing into "trading blocs" and succumbing to the inward-looking trends that are also strong in the world today? In other words, are we on the verge of a freer and more open global economy, and perhaps even a freer and more open global political system, or will the 1990s witness a "Fortress Europe," a "Fortress North America," and perhaps before the end of the decade and the century a "Fortress East Asia"? Will there be a reversion to the kind of bitter and dangerous economic, political, and military confrontation that seemed to be giving way in the late 1980s to greater openness and greater political freedom—in other words, to a kind of nascent global *glasnost* and *perestroike*? This seemed to be an almost worldwide trend until the tragedy in Tiananmen Square in June 1989 and signs that *glasnost* and *perestroika,* and Gorbachev along with them, were in serious trouble in the Soviet Union.

Asia–Pacific Interactions with Other Regions

Since Western Europe, North America, and East Asia are the centers of economic power in today's world and the major centers of the new regionalism, the interactions and interrelations of these three regions are of special importance. These interactions and interrelationships are growing rapidly, as are relationships between all three regions and the developing countries of the world. For obvious reasons more attention is being given to the new dimensions and the changing nature of the relationships between the two main regions of the Western world than to the tripartite relationships involving also the third major region of Asia and the Pacific, centered on East Asia and particularly on Japan. But, as Richard Solomon, a leading American specialist on Asia, a longtime senior scholar at the Rand Corporation who serves as assistant secretary of state for Asian and Pacific Affairs in the Bush administration, has emphasized, "a transition to new relationships among the major players in the world economy is clearly under way."[12]

In this transition the major players are no longer confined to the Western world. The Asia–Pacific region must be included, for, as Solomon has described it, it is "a dynamic region that increasingly rivals Europe for influence in world affairs."[13]

In any event, the relationships of the Asia–Pacific countries with the rest of the world, and particularly with Western Europe and North America, will doubtless continue to grow in many directions, both cooperative and conflictual. These countries will have continuing difficulties in "getting their own act together," and in laying the basis for greater cooperation among themselves. If they succeed, they will be in a better position to develop positive relations with other countries and regions. However they evolve, they will have to deal increasingly with the rest of the world. Therein lie many opportunities and many dangers.

Many of the leaders of the new regionalism in Asia and the Pacific are inclined to concentrate on the opportunities, although they will be compelled to follow a cautious course because of their relative inexperience and lack of cohesion, internally and regionally. Those Asia–Pacific leaders who are more resistant to the idea of changes that are required to enable their countries and regions to adjust to and take advantage of the opportunities provided by the "new realities," including the new regionalism, will doubtless be more fearful than confident as they try to adapt to the novel, complex structure of a world based on relationships and alignments very different from anything in their past or in their traditions.

A distinguished Japanese scholar lists the "strains between the Pacific Asia region and other parts of the world, particularly North America and Western Europe," as one of the "three major features of Pacific dynamism." He argues that the countries of Asia and the Pacific, even including Japan and the NICs, are not well oriented or organized to meet these external pressures, and that this inability to agree on common approaches and to develop sufficiently powerful responses to external challenges will also complicate the already difficult task of finding common grounds for regional cooperation as well as of establishing satisfactory outside relationships. "[T]he increasing intraregional transactions," he writes, "when accompanied by the relative weakening of superpower dominance and confrontation, mean the potential divergence among Pacific Asians on how to give order to a still fluid Pacific dynamism. . . . Pacific Asians might find it somewhat more difficult to organize themselves while coping with counteractions from the rest of the world to the very Pacific dynamism it has been creating."[14]

Forms of Asia–Pacific Regional Cooperation

As in Western Europe and North America, the new regionalism in Asia and the Pacific is most obvious and most advanced in the area of economic cooperation. All of the three comprehensive regional organizations in three of the four subregions, and all of the six major examples of comprehensive all-regional organizations, official and unofficial, that have been singled out for special treatment were established primarily as agencies for promoting economic cooperation among their members, with considerable emphasis also on social and human development. All professed to eschew political and security issues, on the ground that these issues are too sensitive and too divisive; but, as has been demonstrated in previous chapters, political issues have inevitably arisen in all of the nine organizations referred to above (such issues can hardly be avoided in any official organizations, or even in organizations of an unofficial character), and security issues intrude in the deliberations of the leaders of these regional organizations, even though they may be kept off the formal agenda.

Political cooperation may be more difficult than economic cooperation, but it is difficult—indeed, impossible—to separate the two approaches in any comprehensive regional organizations. Security issues may be kept in the background, unless compelling circumstances make this impossible—as happened in the case of ASEAN after the end of the Vietnam War, the dispatch of Vietnamese military forces to Cambodia/Kampuchea, where they remained for more than a decade, and the consequent tensions between the Communist states of Indochina and the ASEAN nations.

During the period of the old regionalism the most conspicuous examples of regional cooperation in all four subregions seemed to be security arrangements or military alliances; but these were hardly good examples of true regional institutionalization. To be sure, all of these alliances required some degree of military—and also political—cooperation among the Asia–Pacific member countries; but in all of the major examples of such alliances the initiators and dominant members were one or the other of the superpowers, and most of them were bilateral in nature, involving little real regional cooperation. In any event, most of these alliances are either now defunct, as in the case of SEATO, or are faced with increasing opposition and an uncertain future. This applies to the alliances which the Soviet Union has with Vietnam, Mongolia, and North Korea, and the United States with Japan and South Korea. And ANZUS, once seemingly one of the most stable of military alliances, is now virtually in abeyance, although technically it is still in existence.

Perhaps the main reasons for the decline of alliance relationships in Asia and the Pacific, and in other parts of the world, are to be found in the basic changes in the entire global *problematique*—to use a favorite term of the Club of Rome. For some time the trend in the security field has been away from alliances and toward alignment.[15]

Some of the general conclusions that emerge from any analysis of the Asia–Pacific experience with regionalism in recent years are that really significant breakthroughs in regional cooperation have been made primarily in the economic domain, that political cooperation, while growing and ever-present, lags well behind, and that security cooperation, which seemed to flourish in the era of the old regionalism, in the form of alliances between regional and external powers, is now much less conspicuous.

Many other forms of regional cooperation are assuming new dimensions and significance, especially in a period when some of the major barriers to such cooperation have been largely broken down. This applies to the growing contacts among the nations and peoples of the entire Asia–Pacific area, and especially within the four subregions. The mounting tide of contacts among officials, businessmen, professional people, scholars, students, tourists, and others is reaching new heights with every passing year. It is sometimes partially and temporarily diminished by such tragic and sobering reminders that the openness and humaneness of countries of the area cannot be taken for granted as the crackdown and brutalities in Tiananmen Square in Beijing in June 1989 and the reversal of the more encouraging trends in China since the late 1970s.

These extensive contacts among peoples and groups have undoubtedly helped to develop a more favorable environment for regional cooperation, in and between regions of Asia and the Pacific, and between these regions and the outside world, and to create the kind of open-mindedness and receptivity and regional consciousness that makes significant progress in regional cooperation possible. Clearly this is a less well known and more intangible factor in promoting the new regionalism than the growth of cooperation among the nations of the region on official levels or the emergence of comprehensive regional institutions. It is also a logical development and expansion of trends that have been under way for some time, on a reduced scale, and therefore appears to be less innovative and dramatic than the kinds of new departures and new institutions that have been given special treatment in this volume. But in the long run the cumulative impact of the growing personal interactions and contacts in the Asia–Pacific area may prove to be one of the major stimuli to the regional as well as national dynamism that is often described as the leading characteristic of the contemporary Asia–Pacific scene.

Many of the generalizations about the new regionalism in Asia and the Pacific can be applied to the entire region; but obviously, in each of the four subregions regionalism has appeared in many distinctive forms and has had varying degrees of successful implementation. In terms of comprehensive institutionalization it would appear that the greatest progress has been made in Southeast Asia, with ASEAN as the most visible and impressive evidence, with the Southwest Pacific and Oceania next in line, with the South Pacific Forum and at least two other official organizations, the South Pacific Commission and the South Pacific Conference, as the most impressive evidences of significant progress, with South Asia next in order of progress, with SAARC showing considerable growth and survival capacity, and with East Asia in the rear, because of the absence of a comprehensive regional organization.

If one considers the extent of intraregional contacts and especially the significance and influence of such contacts, East Asia would have to be given first place, followed by a considerable margin by the other three subregions, in none of which intraregional contacts have developed as impressively and extensively as in East Asia. It would therefore be difficult to compare, contrast, and evaluate the relative impact and significance of what Robert Scalapino has aptly called the "soft regionalism" in East Asia[16] with the regionalism that is developing in the other three subregions.

East Asia lags behind in comprehensive institutionalization, probably exceeds the other three subregions in the extent of intraregional interactions and contacts, and certainly is in a class by itself in terms of its power, influence, and impact, extending throughout the entire Asia–Pacific and into the world arena. Japan is the economic giant and China is the demographic giant of the entire region. No other country in the region comes close to Japan in terms of economic power, a fact that is hardly surprising since Japan has become the second most important economic power in the entire world. And only one other country in Asia and the Pacific, namely India, comes even close to China in demographic terms, which again is not surprising since China is the homeland of nearly one-fifth of the human race.

Progress in Asia–Pacific Regional Economic Cooperation

Primary emphasis on economic cooperation and development has been a logical focus for the regional organizations in Asia and the Pacific, for economic cooperation is obviously a matter of mutual concern to all countries, both economically advanced and developing, and is presumably a major area for possible agreements among regional neighbors, in spite of differences and divisions on political and security issues.

The extent of regional institutionalization in economic fields in Asia and the Pacific has been truly remarkable, and it will become even more remarkable if the current efforts to establish an all-regional official economic organization are successful. But even if these efforts are successful, any organization that will be created will be relative primitive, probably not even comparable to the early stages of the European Community movement. It certainly will lag far behind the kind of European Community that has developed over the past four decades and that will gain further momentum, cohesion, and integration in the 1990s.

One must conclude that the great progress in institutionalized economic cooperation that has been one of the most marked and impressive features of the new regionalism in Asia and the Pacific is still a long way from the kind of regional institutionalization that will be required if it is to meet the needs of the countries of the region in the new era. Hence, as a distinguished Japanese scholar has advised, "the paradigm for Pacific economic cooperation must be one involving 'the art of having an affair,' which may (or may not) lead to a marriage."[17]

The Canberra Recommendations: Then and Now

One way to assess the progress of Asia–Pacific regionalism during the era of the new regionalism is to take the statement of the items that were identified at the famous Canberra seminar in 1980 as important to the Pacific Community (a term that was in wider use then than now) and to consider the progress, if any, that has been made over the ensuing decade. These items, which may be regarded as goals for the Pacific Community, were concisely summarized in twelve points by Peter Drysdale in 1983:[18]

the need to avoid military/security issues in order to create a sense of community without creating a sense of threat;

[the need to avoid] EEC-style discriminatory trading arrangements [as] inappropriate in the Pacific;

the need to "hasten slowly," to see the full blooming of the Pacific Community idea as a longer time objective and to proceed toward long-time goals step by step, with each intermediate step being useful in itself and not dependent for success on further steps being taken;

the need to ensure that existing bilateral, regional, and global mechanisms for cooperation are not undermined by any new wider arrangements and that it be complementary to them;

the need to ensure that it is an outward-looking arrangement;

the need for an "organic approach" building up private arrangements already in existence in the Pacific, including such bodies as the Pacific Basin Economic Council and the Pacific Trade and Development Conferences and other privately based activities;

the need to involve academics, businessmen, and governments jointly in this cooperative enterprise;

the need to avoid unnecessarily bureaucratic structures;

the need for a fairly loose and so far as possible noninstitutionalized structure recognizing that, while settlement of disputes may prove difficult in sensitive areas, the discussion of problems may contribute towards ameliorating them;

the need for all members to be placed on an equal footing (that is, no EEC-style associate membership);

the need to concentrate attention on areas of mutual regional interest;

the need to make substantive progress in improving upon the benefits emanating from existing bilateral, global, and regional arrangements.

On the whole, these are quite modest objectives. Some of the participants at the Canberra seminar in 1980 criticized them on precisely these grounds. While they agreed that the idea of a Pacific Community was a longtime objective and that efforts at regional cooperation should concentrate on more immediate and practical goals and aim to "hasten slowly," they also argued that the longer-term goals should not be lost sight of in the concentration on more immediate steps.

A decade later the step-by-step approach is still favored, as more realistic and less divisive than grander enterprises. The concerns that "existing bilateral, regional, and global mechanisms for cooperation are not undermined by any new wider arrangements"—a concern that the ASEAN countries often voiced in subsequent years—and that special efforts should be made "to make substantive progress in improving upon the benefits emanating from existing bilateral, global, and regional arrangements," are still quite prevalent, although there has been a noticeable ebbing of these apprehensions and concerns and a growing recognition of the need for greater progress in regional institutionalization. There is also a rather general, but not universal, acceptance of the view that neither an EEC-type nor a NATO-type organization would be suitable or desirable for the Asia–Pacific region.

Regional organizations in Asia and the Pacific have generally heeded the advice of the Canberra seminar "to avoid unnecessarily bureaucratic structures." In fact, all three comprehensive intraregional organizations—ASEAN, the South Pacific Forum, and SAARC—were hesitant about establishing any adequate institutional base whatever. All have now moved beyond this point, perhaps because of the sheer necessity to provide some continuity and support base for their organizations. ASEAN is the only one of the three that seems to have at least a minimally adequate "bureaucratic structure;" but its member countries are still wary of bureaucratic proliferation—as they have good reason to be. Some of the other comprehensive regional organizations in the Asia–Pacific area may already have passed the excessively bureaucratic stage. This may be the case, in particular, of one of the most effective regional organizations in Asia and the Pacific, namely the Asian Development Bank, whose headquarters staff in Manila already numbers over fifteen hundred persons.

There is also general agreement on "the need to concentrate attention on areas of mutual regional interest," and "to avoid military/security issues in order to create a new sense of community without creating a sense of threat;" but since the Canberra seminar it has been increasingly difficult to keep military/security and other controversial issues out of the growing number of regional organizations. These issues are also "areas of mutual regional interest" that constantly intrude into deliberations of leaders of the Asia–Pacific countries whenever they get together, whether in bilateral meetings or in summit or near-summit meetings of regional organizations. The formula that has been worked out so far has been to keep such issues off the formal agenda of high-level regional meetings but for the leaders attending such meetings to discuss their mutual concerns, even the divisive ones, with each other and, in the case of ASEAN, and more recently the South Pacific Forum, also with their "dialogue partners." This latter arrangement has been formalized in the "post-ministerial meetings" held immediately after ASEAN high-level meetings. The arrangement may prove to be one of the truly innovative contributions of the new regionalism in Asia and the Pacific to the international relations of the future, on a global as well as an Asia–Pacific scale.

There is general agreement, at least in principle, that the regional arrangements in Asia and the Pacific should be outward-oriented. As has been pointed out, this is a dominant characteristic of the new regionalism in that part of the world. But there is also a recognition that there are many trends in the opposite direction, in the region and throughout the world. Hence, as Robert Scalapino has observed,

[W]e witness a series of seeming paradoxes. While interdependence, even integration, is moving swiftly ahead, economic nationalism is running strong. . . . Democratization, far from providing solutions, is likely to compound the problem. . . . We have not yet seen the flood-tide of nationalism, economic or otherwise. Although economic internationalization is rapidly advancing, we are witnessing a psychological retreat, a strong reluctance to adopt innovative policies and create interstate institutions. . . . To a considerable extent . . . this inward-looking trend encompasses each of the major Pacific Asian states—the United States, the USSR, China, and even Japan.[19]

Regionalism and International Regimes Reviewed

The existence of regional organizations is one of the most conspicuous signs of regionalism. These organizations develop at various levels, ranging from specialized and limited to comprehensive all-regional associations and institutions. But there are many other less institutionalized kinds of agreements, arrangements, norms, and rules in international regions. Here, as has been noted, the concept of international regimes can be helpful, as a supplement to—but not a substitute for—the study of regional organizations.

The meaning and possible utility of this concept were discussed in the introductory chapter of this study, and the nature and role of international regimes were noted in all subsequent chapters. In this concluding chapter further observations on regionalism and international regimes, based on the most recent literature and its applicability to the Asia–Pacific region, will be presented.

Some students of international regimes draw a sharp distinction between institutions and organizations (although most dictionaries do not). International regimes, as Donald Puchala and Raymond Hopkins point out, "are formalized in varying degrees. . . . [T]he degrees of formality tend to have relatively little to do with the effectiveness of regimes measured in terms of the probabilities of participants' compliance."[20] While "regimes tend to become more formal over time," they do not necessarily include formal organizations. Regimes, explains Arthur A. Stein, "can be noninstitutionalized as well as institutionalized, and international organizations need not be regimes, although they certainly can be. . . . [T]here are many regimes, they vary in character, they exist in some issue areas and not in others. States will form regimes with one another in one dominion while they are in conflict in another."[21] Most students of international regimes would agree with Puchala and Hopkins that "a regime exists in every substantive issue area in international relations where there is a discernibly patterned behavior," although many might not go so far as these authors in asserting that "For every political system . . . there is a corresponding regime" (if they did, they would probably speak of regimes rather than "a corresponding regime").[22]

International regimes may be regarded as important intervening variables in a study of regionalism and regional organizations, just as regionalism, in what has been characterized in this study as one of its most important and largely neglected aspects, can be considered as an important intervening variable in the study of the relations between nationalism and interdependence. Using this approach, the study of international regimes becomes as integral part of the study of regionalism, for it provides a conceptual framework for an analysis of many forms of "discernibly patterned behavior" in a variety of issue areas of great regional significance which otherwise might be included in a haphazard fashion.

It should be noted, however, that international regimes could be considered as a very different kind of approach, and a much more comprehensive one, than that of regionalism, and that, while the existence of regimes may be considered as an important aspect of regionalism, usually but not always tending to promote cooperation, regional organizations and other forms of association and cooperation in various world regions could also be considered as indices of the prevalence and importance of international regimes. Thus the two phenomena—regional institutionalization and international regimes—should be viewed as largely supplementary, but rather distinct, aspects of the contemporary international system.

All of these observations have been found to be relevant to the new regionalism in Asia and the Pacific. The role of international regimes in this region should certainly be noted. These regimes are important dimensions of Asia–Pacific regionalism.

Regionalism and Community

Many Asian leaders seem to believe that effective institutionalization in their part of the world cannot be hoped for until and unless a greater sense of community develops. Some even seem to be wary of too much emphasis on institutionalization, not only because their area is not yet ready for much of this but also because this is a Western approach antithetical to the Eastern belief in consensus and community. A frank proponent of this view is Prime Minister Mahathir of Malaysia. "[A] sense of community," he has said, "is the primary requisite. This approach . . . is foreign to westerners who are intent on setting up organizations, deciding modalities, and delineating responsibilities. The Western instinct to organize has led many proponents of the Pacific Basin Community to assume that it must be an intergovernmental organization."[23]

A thoughtful article in the *Far Eastern Economic Review* at the beginning of the era of the new regionalism discussed "the difficult and abstract notion of Community itself," and suggested that the many views of the idea of PEC [Pacific Economic Cooperation] can be classified into two major streams, which reflect two classes of conceptions of community. The first derives the concept primarily from ideas of structure, a geographic area, a system of interrelated economic activities and institutions, and a politically self-governing unit. The second, which is a newer conception of community, is devised principally from the idea of process. . . . In this sense, a community is any process of social interaction that gives rise to a more intensive or more extensive attitude and practice of interdependence, cooperation, collaboration, and unification.[24]

Most of the discussions of community, in the regional and global sense, even in the Asia–Pacific area, seemed to be based on the first concept. The "newer conception" is also a useful one. It is in fact not so new, as any examination of sociological and other social science literature will reveal. It is nevertheless a concept to bear in mind in any treatment of the relation between regionalism and community. It is worth noting that on the basis of either conception of community, regionalism in Asia and the Pacific has made impressive progress, far greater than most observers would have dared to expect not so many years ago, but that it still falls far short of either definition of community, for it has led neither to "a politically self governing unit" nor to real "unification."

New Horizons for International Relations Research

This study has revealed that Asia–Pacific regionalism has many similarities with regionalism in other parts of the world, as well as many distinctive aspects. Its distinctive and innovative features, as well as some of its special difficulties, deserve special attention.

After a period of decline international regionalism is experiencing a major revival, and is taking new and significant forms in the era of the new regionalism. Hence it deserves to be given again a central place in the study and practice of international relations.

Some students of regionalism in Asia and the Pacific have argued that the new regionalism in that part of the world has already opened up new horizons for international relations research. Michael Haas, for instance, has suggested that the concept of "the Pacific Way" introduces "a new theory of international integration." "A new form of international statecraft," he writes, "has developed in the region. This innovation, known as the Pacific Way, goes beyond previous theories of international integration." Haas is impressed with what he calls "the new relevance of integration theory for contemporary world affairs."[25]

Haas's approach is challenging, but it would be even more promising if it were not based so heavily on the nebulous concept of "the Pacific Way," which seems to be another version of a "Pacific Community," and on integration theory, which was a central area of theoretical concern for students of regionalism in Western Europe in the 1950s and 1960s. The term "integration" is less commonly employed in studies of the new regionalism, because it suggests—like the term "Pacific Way"—a degree of regional cohesion that has not in fact yet developed and that seems unlikely to develop in the foreseeable future. Most students of Asia–Pacific regionalism use such terms as "Pacific cooperation," or "Asia–Pacific cooperation," or "Pacific Asia cooperation," or even the more limited term "Asia–Pacific economic cooperation" more frequently and more accurately than such vague terms as "Pacific Community" or "Pacific Way." The advantage of the latter two terms is that they do call attention to the need for developing a greater sense of Asia–Pacific community, without which regionalism in the area can never realize its full potential.

However its nature and progress are assessed, the new regionalism should be considered from a comparative viewpoint; and the comparative perspective should be intraregional, interregional, and international in character. In the September 1989 issue of *The Annals* of the American Academy of Political and Social Science—a particularly useful issue for students of the new regionalism in Asia and the Pacific, entitled "The Pacific Region: Challenges to Policy and Theory"—Peter A. Gourevitch, the special editor, presents some arresting and relevant comments on the importance and difficulties of comparative analysis in the study of regionalism:

> Comparisons across regions and country are both imperative and difficult. They require new ways of putting together traditional variables—culture, institutions, economics, geopolitics, micro components and macro influences, leadership, ideology. . . . The micro variables of economic organization, individual motives, on one side, and the macro variables of the international economic system and national and international decision making—these relationships are rather more complex perhaps than either policymakers or theorists realized several decades ago. They require more interaction across area studies, disciplines, and professional schools than used to be the case—and fortunately, some of that is taking place.[26]

These observations are a reminder that the study of the new regionalism is a challenging and difficult task, one calling for a higher level of analysis than has yet been given to this important phenomenon. From a theoretical and analytical point of view the contributions of students of the old regionalism were more impressive than those of students who are focusing on the new regionalism; but in practice the new phenomenon is taking on dimensions—geographic and institutional, for example—and is developing linkages on both regional and international levels that have given it a new role and significance in the contemporary world.

In Asia and the Pacific, in what seemed to be an unpropitious environment, the new regionalism has developed to an extraordinary degree. It may prove to be one of the most convincing evidences that the vast area of Asia and the Pacific is challenging the West on increasingly equal terms, and not just responding to the Western impact and Western initiatives. Perhaps the era of internationalism has truly dawned; and in this new era, in the coming century, the Asia–Pacific region will play an increasingly important role.

Notes

Chapter 1 Regionalism in International Relations: Old and New

1. See Ernst Haas, "The Challenge of Regionalism," *International Organization* 12 (Autumn 1958); R. J. Yalem, *Regionalism and World Order* (Washington, D.C.: Public Affairs Press, 1965); Bruce M. Russett, *International Regions and the International System: A Study in Political Ecology* (Chicago: Rand McNally, 1967); Joseph S. Nye, Jr., comp., *International Regionalism: Readings* (Boston: Little Brown, 1968); Roger D. Hansen, "Regional Integration: Reflections on a Decade of Theoretical Efforts," *World Politics* 20, no. 2 (January 1969); Louis J. Cantori and Steven L. Spiegel, *The International Politics of Regions: A Comparative Approach* (Englewood Cliffs, N.J.: Prentice-Hall, 1970).

2. See Gordon Mace, "Regional Integration," *World Encyclopedia of Peace* (Oxford: Pergamon Press, 1986), 2:323–25; Karl W. Deutsch, *Political Community at the International Level—Problems of Definition and Measurement* (New York: Doubleday, 1954); Philip E. Jacob and Joseph V. Toscano, eds., *The Integration of Political Communities* (Philadelphia: Lippincott, 1964); Ernst Haas, "The Study of Regional Organization," *International Organization* 24, no. 4 (Autumn 1970); Joseph S. Nye, Jr., *Peace in Parts: Integration and Conflict in Regional Organization* (Lanham, Maryland: University Press of America, 1971); Leon N. Lindbergh and Stuart A. Scheingold, eds., *Regional Integration: Theory and Research* (Cambridge, Mass.: Harvard University Press, 1971).

3. Cal Clark, review of 1987 reprint of Nye, *Peace in Parts*, in *The American Political Science Review* 82, no. 4 (December 1988):1424–25.

4. Donald Lampert, "Patterns of Transregional Relations," chap. 13 in Werner Feld and Gavin Boyd, eds., *Comparative Regional Systems* (Oxford: Pergamon Press, 1979), 472.

5. Cantori and Spiegel, *The International Politics of Regions*, 1.

6. Lampert, "Patterns of Transregional Relations," 472.

7. Joseph S. Nye, Jr., Introduction to Nye, comp., *International Regionalism: Readings*, v.

8. "Pacific Development and the New Internationalism," address by Richard

H. Solomon before the Pacific Future Conference, Los Angeles, 15 March 1988; *Current Policy* No. 1060, Bureau of Public Affairs, U.S. Department of State.

9. See Karl W. Deutsch, et. al., *Political Community in the North Atlantic Area* (Princeton: Princeton University Press, 1957); and Deutsch, *Political Community at the International Level.*

10. See Ernst Haas, *The Uniting of Europe* (Stanford: Stanford University Press, 1958); and Ernst Haas, *The Obsolescence of Regional Integration Theory* (Berkeley: Institute of International Studies, University of California, 1975), Research Series No. 25.

11. Nye, Introduction to Nye, comp., *International Regionalism: Readings,* vi.

12. See Cantori and Spiegel, *The International Politics of Regions,* especially 22–25; and Michael Haas, "International Subsystems: Stability and Polarity," *The American Political Science Review* 64 (March 1970).

13. Leonard Binder, "The Middle East as a Subordinate International System," *World Politics* 15 (1963).

14. See William P. Thompson, "The Regional Subsystem: A Conceptual Explanation and a Propositional Inventory," *International Studies Quarterly* 17, no. 1 (March 1973).

15. Bruce M. Russett, "International Regimes and the Study of Regions," *International Studies Quarterly* 13, no. 4 (December 1969):338.

16. Cantori and Spiegel, "The International Politics of Regions," 22–25.

17. Karl Kaiser, "The Interaction of Regional Subsystems: Some Preliminary Notes on Recurrent Patterns and the Role of Superpowers," *World Politics* 21, no. 1 (October 1968):84, 85.

18. See Haas, *The Uniting of Europe;* and Leon N. Lindberg and Stuart A. Scheingold, *Europe's Would-Be Polity—Patterns of Change in the European Community* (Englewood Cliffs, N.J.: Prentice-Hall, 1976).

19. "For a number of years, we have talked about 'Eurosclerosis—that hardening of the economic arteries in the 1970s and 1980s that seemed to indicate that the EC nations were entering their twilight years. And there is a strong case that the EC nations have become burdened with the weight of too much regulation and have paid too little attention to the importance of dynamics and change." ("U.S. Views on the EC Single Market Exercise," address by Eugene J. McAllister, assistant secretary of state for Economic and Business affairs, before the American Association of Exporters and Importers, New York, 18 May 1989; *Current Policy* No. 1193, Bureau of Public Affairs, U.S. Department of State).

20. Charles A. Duffy and Werner J. Feld, "Whither Regional Integration Theory?," chap. 13 in Werner J. Feld and Gavin Boyd, eds., *Comparative Regional Systems* (New York: Pergamon Press, 1980), 497.

21. Haas, *The Obsolescence of Regional Integration Theory,* 6.

22. Ibid., 1, 9, 17.

23. Ibid., 9.

24. Ibid., 23.

25. Stephan Haggard and Beth A. Simmons, "Theories of International Regimes," *International Organization* 41, no. 3 (Summer 1987):491–92.

26. Robert O. Keohane and Joseph S. Nye, Jr., "Power and Interdependence Revisited," *International Organization* 41, no. 4 (Autumn 1987): 740.

27. Stephen D. Krasner, "Structural Causes and Regime Consequences: Regimes as Intervening Variables," in Stephen D. Krasner, ed., *International Regimes* (Ithaca, N.Y.: Cornell University Press, 1983), 2.

28. Bruce Russett and Harvey Starr, *World Politics: The Menu for Choice* (San Francisco: W. H. Freeman and Company, 1981), 430.

29. Donald J. Puchala and Raymond F. Hopkins, "International Regimes: Lessons from Inductive Analysis," in Krasner, ed., *International Regimes,* 63.

30. Haggard and Simmons, "Theories of International Regimes," 508.

31. Oran R. Young, *International Cooperation: Building Regimes for Natural Resources and the Environment* (Ithaca, N.Y.: Cornell University Press, 1989).

32. Haggard and Simmons, "Theories of International Regimes," 509.

33. Keohane and Nye, "Power and Interdependence Revisited," 742.

34. Friedrich Kratochwil, "The Force of Prescriptions," *International Organization* 38, no. 4 (Autumn 1984):685.

35. Susan Strange, "Cave! Hic Dragones: A Critique of Regime Analysis," in Krasner, ed., *International Regimes,* 343.

36. "National Success and International Stability in a Time of Change," address by Secretary of State George Shultz before the World Affairs Council of Washington, D.C., 4 December 1987: *Current Policy* No. 1029, Bureau of Public Affairs, U.S. Department of State.

37. Haas, *The Obsolescence of Regional Integration Theory,* 9, 17.

38. Sally Shelton-Colby, "Latin America: Political Progress, Economic Stagnation," chap. 7 in Barry M. Blechman and Edward N. Luttwak, eds., *Global Security: A Review of Strategic and Economic Issues* (Boulder, Colorado: Westview Press, 1987), 187.

39. Lester H. Brown, "Regional Collaboration in Resolving Third-World Conflicts," *Survival* 28, no. 3 (May–June 1986):218.

40. See Jeffrey E. Garten, "Trading Blocs and the Evolving World Economy," *Current History* 88, no. 534 (January 1989); and John Yemma, "Trade Blocs Push to the Fore," *Christian Science Monitor,* 4 January 1989.

41. For a good statement of the ambivalent views of the United States government regarding the emerging single market in Western Europe, see McAllister, "U.S. Views on the EC Single Market Exercise." In this address Mr. McAllister declared: "[T]he United States is supportive, indeed, enthusiastic about EC integration—both from a foreign policy and economic perspective. But there is a caveat: The promise of 1992 will only be fulfilled if the European Community becomes more open, more outward oriented."

Chapter 2 Asia–Pacific Regionalism: An Overview

1. "National Success and International Stability in a Time of Change," address by Secretary of State George Shultz before the World Affairs Council of Washington,

D.C., 4 December 1987; *Current Policy* No. 1029, Bureau of Public Affairs, U.S. Department of State.

2. Glenn D. Hook, "The Asia–Pacific Region," *Journal of Peace Research* 25, no. 4 (December 1988):335.

3. Robert A. Scalapino, "Regionalism in the Pacific: Prospects and Problems for the Pacific Basin," *The Atlantic Community Quarterly* 26, no. 2 (Summer 1988):178.

4. "Combined Average Ratings: Independent Countries," *Freedom at Issue*, no. 106 (January/February 1990):24.

5. Scalapino, "Regionalism in the Pacific," 178.

6. "Pacific Development and the New Internationalism," address by Richard H. Solomon, director of the Policy Planning Staff, U.S. Department of State, before the Pacific Future Conference, Los Angeles, California, 15 March 1988; *Current Policy* No. 1060, Bureau of Public Affairs, U.S. Department of State.

7. Walt W. Rostow, *The United States and the Regional Organization of Asia and the Pacific, 1965–1985* (Austin, Texas: University of Texas Press, 1986), 18.

8. Richard C. Holbrooke, Roderick MacFarquhar, and Kazuo Nakazawa, *East Asia in Transition: Challenges for the Trilateral Countries,* a task force report to the Trilateral Commission, The Triangle Papers 35 (New York: The Trilateral Commission, 1988), 77.

9. For information on all of these all-regional technical and professional organizations, and many others of similar kind, see *Yearbook of International Organizations 1988/89,* compiled by the Union of International Associations, Brussels (Munich: K. G. Saur, 1988), vol. 2.

10. John Yemma, "Trade Blocs Push to the Fore," *Christian Science Monitor,* 4 January 1989.

11. Ibid.

12. Huan Xiang, "Relative Detente Befalls the World," *Beijing Review* 32, no. 1 (2–8 January 1989):17, 18.

13. Solomon, "Pacific Development and the New Internationalism," 3.

14. K. S. Nathan and M. Rathmantham, eds., *Trilateralism in Asia: Problems and Prospects in U.S.–Japan–ASEAN Relations* (Kuala Lumpur: Antani Book Company, 1986), vii.

15. "An American Agenda for Pacific Basin Issues," address of Senator Alan Cranston at the annual meeting of the United States Committee of PBEC, Washington, D.C., 27–28 February 1989; in *PBEC Bulletin* (Washington, D.C.: United States Committee of PBEC, n.d.).

16. Walter S. Mossberg and Robert S. Greenberger, "Baker Calls for 'Pan-Pacific' Alliance Linking U.S., Japan and Other Nations," *The Wall Street Journal,* 27 June 1989.

17. "A New Pacific Partnership: Framework for the Future," address of Secretary of State James Baker to the Asia Society, New York, 20 June 1980; *Current Policy* No. 1185, Bureau of Public Affairs, U.S. Department of State. Secretary Baker repeated his endorsement of a new all-Pacific organization in two statements made at the post-ministerial conference of ASEAN foreign ministers with their counterparts from their "dialogue partners" in Bandar Seri Begawan, Brunei, on 6 and 7 July

1989. "Pacific rim economic cooperation," he said on 6 July, "is an idea whose time has come. Building a consensus to turn these ideas into reality is a top item on our agenda. We do not bring a definitive blueprint. Rather, through dialogue with ASEAN and other market-oriented countries, we seek accord on the guiding principles and structure of such a mechanism." And in his closing remarks at the conference he returned to the same theme: "A ministerial meeting toward the end of this year could possibly assist in developing or securing a consensus. Through one means or another, we need to maintain forward movement on this important initiative. . . . We want to broaden and deepen the network of our public and private ties with Asia—and this cooperation mechanism could assist to that end. I hope, therefore, your governments give it thorough consideration." "ASEAN: Challenges and Opportunities," prepared statements by Secretary of State James Baker to the post-ministerial conference of the Association of Southeast Asian Nations (ASEAN), Bandar Seri Begawan, Brunei, 6 and 7 July 1989; *Current Policy* no. 1190, Bureau of Public Affairs, U.S. Department of State.

18. Norman D. Palmer, "Organizing the Pacific Community: From Another Round of Proposals to a Larger World Role," *Peace Forum* 4, no. 10 (May 1989): 8.

19. Daniel Sneider, "Pacific Rim Nations Strengthen Economic Ties," *Christian Science Monitor,* 6 November 1989.

20. Ibid.

21. Ibid.

22. Ibid.

23. Ruth Leger Sivard, *World Military and Social Expenditures 1987–88,* 12th ed. (Washington, D.C.: World Priorities, 1987), 7.

24. Young Seek Choue, "The Role of Korea, Japan and China in the Era of East Asia during the 21st Century," keynote address at the international seminar, "The Northeast Asian Era and the Role of Korea, China and Japan in the 21st Century," organized by the Institute for Northeast Asia Studies, Kyung Hee University, Seoul, South Korea, 24–25 August 1988.

Chapter 3 Regionalism in East Asia

1. Roy Kim and Hilary Conroy, "Introduction," in Roy Kim and Hilary Conroy, eds., *New Tides in the Pacific: Pacific Basin Cooperation and the Big Four (Japan, PRC, USA, USSR)* (New York: Greenwood Press, 1987), 3–4.

2. See Norman D. Palmer and Howard C. Perkins, *International Relations: The World Community in Transition,* 3d ed. (Boston: Houghton MIfflin Company, 1969), 593.

3. W. W. Rostow, *The United States and the Regional Organization of Asia and the Pacific, 1965–1985* (Austin, Texas: University of Texas Press, 1986), 23–24.

4. Ibid., 23.

5. Quoted in Palmer and Perkins, *International Relations,* 593.

6. Bernard K. Gordon, "A U.S. Policy for Asia in the 1980s," chap. 15 in

Charles E. Morrison, ed., *Threats to Security in East Asia–Pacific: National and Regional Perspectives* (Lexington, Mass.: Lexington Books, 1983), 204.

7. Robert A. Scalapino, *Major Power Relations in Northeast Asia* (Lanham, Maryland: University Press of America, for the Asia Society, 1987), 7.

8. For more information on the PECC and the Trilateral Commission, see chapter 8.

9. *The Report of the Advisory Group on Economic and Structural Adjustment for International Harmony* (the Maekawa Report), submitted to Prime Minister Yasuhiro Nakasone on 7 April 1986.

10. See Byung-Joon Ahn, "South Korea's New Nordpolitik," *Korea in World Affairs* 12, no. 4 (Winter 1988).

11. Valéry Giscard d'Estaing, Yasuhiro Nakasone, Henry A. Kissinger, "East–West Relations," *Foreign Affairs* 68, no. 3 (Summer 1989):15. This article is adapted from a report to the Trilateral Commission (Triangle Paper No. 36, 1989).

12. "Mr. Gorbachev's Asian Serenade," Editorial, *The New York Times*, 24 September 1988. See also She Duanzhi, "Soviet Diplomatic Harvest in 1988," *Beijing Review* 32, no. 5 (30 June–5 February 1989):19.

13. See chapter 2.

14. See Ishizaki Teruhiko, "Trade Blocs: A Disturbing Development," *Japan Echo* 15, no. 4 (Winter 1988).

15. There are relatively few East Asian technical and professional associations, but citizens of the countries of this subregion are members of a very large number of interregional and international associations of this kind. See chapter 2 and the *Yearbook of International Organizations 1988/89*, compiled by the Union of International Associations, Brussels (Munich: K. B. Saur, 1988), vol. 2, table 3, "Country Participation in International Organizations."

16. Donald S. Zagoria, "Soviet Policy in East Asia; A New Beginning," *Foreign Affairs* 68, no. 1 (1989):134–35. This is a special issue on "America and the World 1988/89."

17. Ibid., 135.

Chapter 4 Regionalism in Southeast Asia: Focus on ASEAN

1. "The best and perhaps the last best hope for peace, stability and economic development in Southeast Asia is regionalism, which may well prove to be the most important force shaping relations within the region and between the region and the superpowers. Even if it does not prove to be decisive, it is a phenomenon to be watched, for in its dynamism it is a weathervane." (Douglas Pike, "Southeast Asia and the Superpowers: The Dust Settles," *Current History* 82, no. 483 (April 1983):179.)

2. See D. G. E. Hall, *A History of South East Asia*, 2d ed. (London: Mac-Millan; New York: St. Martin's Press, 1963).

3. Ibid.

4. For the texts of the Manila Treaty and the Pacific Charter, see *The New York Times*, 9 September 1954.

5. John Sterling, "ASEAN: The Anti-Domino Factor," *Asian Affairs* 7, no. 5 (May/June 1980):274.

6. Michael Haas, "Alliance," in Ervin Laszlo and Jong Youl Yoo, eds., *World Encyclopedia of Peace* (Oxford: Pergamon Press, 1986), 1:10.

7. See above, chapter 2, 26. See also Norman D. Palmer and Howard C. Perkins, *International Relations: The World Community in Transition*, 3d ed. (Boston: Houghton Mfflin, 1969), 593.

8. Stirling, "ASEAN: The Anti-Domino Factor," 276.

9. Ibid., 275–76.

10. Palmer and Perkins, *International Relations*, 590.

11. For the text of the Bangkok Declaration, see Michael Haas, ed., *Basic Documents of Asian Regional Organizations* (Dobbs Ferry, N.Y.: Oceana Publications, 1974), 1269–71.

12. Palmer and Perkins, *International Relations*, 593–94.

13. Stirling, "ASEAN: The Anti-Domino Factor," 277.

14. Francis J. Galbraith, "ASEAN Today: Feeling the Heat," *Asian Affairs* 8, no. 1 (September/October 1980):34.

15. Ibid.

16. Linda G. Martin, ed., *The ASEAN Success Story: Social, Economic, and Political Dimensions* (Honolulu: East–West Center, 1987).

17. See Galbraith, "ASEAN Today: Feeling the Heat"; and James Clad, "Rising Sense of Drift," *Far Eastern Economic Review*, 10 July 1986, 15.

18. Quoted in Galbraith, "ASEAN Today: Feeling the Heat."

19. Clad, "Rising Sense of Drift," 15.

20. J. Soedjati Djiwandono, "The Strategic Significance of ASEAN," unpublished paper (Jakarta: Centre for Strategic and International Studies, n.d.), 2.

21. Quoted in ibid.

22. See Robert O. Tilman, *Southeast Asia and the Enemy Beyond: ASEAN Perceptions of External Threats* (Boulder, Colorado: Westview Press, 1987). This is a revised and expanded version of a monograph entitled *The Enemy Beyond: External Threat Perceptions in the ASEAN Region*.

23. Quoted in Djiwandono, "The Strategic Significance of ASEAN," 3.

24. See Djiwandono, "The Strategic Significance of ASEAN"; Sheldon W. Simon, "The ASEAN States: Obstacles to Security Cooperation," *ORBIS* 22, no. 2 (Summer 1978); Robert L. Rau, "Southeast Asian Security in the 1980s: An Intraregional Perspective," chap. 4 in William T. Tow and William R. Feeney, eds., *U.S. Foreign Policy and Asian–Pacific Security: A Transregional Approach* (Boulder, Colorado: Westview Press, 1982); Sheldon W. Simon, *The ASEAN States and Regional Security* (Stanford, Calif.: The Hoover Institution Press, 1982); J. Soedjati Djiwandono, "The Political and Security Aspects of ASEAN: Its Principal Achievements," *The Indonesian Quarterly* 11, no. 3 (July 1983); and Sheldon W. Simon, "ASEAN's Strategic Situation in the 1980s," *Pacific Affairs* 60, no. 1 (Spring 1987).

25. For a description and evaluation of the role of ASEAN countries, and of ASEAN, in the Cambodia/Kampuchea crisis, see Simon, *The ASEAN States and Regional Security;* Sukhumbhand Paribatra, "Irreversible History? ASEAN, Vietnam, and the Polarization of Southeast Asia," chap. 14 in Karl D. Jackson, Sukhumbhand

Paribatra, and J. Soedjati Djiwandono, eds., *ASEAN in Regional and Global Context* (Berkeley, Calif.: Institute of East Asian Studies, University of California, 1986); Leszek Buszynski, "ASEAN: A Changing Regional Role," *Asian Survey* 27, no. 7 (July 1987); and Clayton Jones, "Paris Talks Open: Is Peace at Hand for Cambodia?," *Christian Science Monitor*, 24 July 1989.

26. There has been considerable ambivalence within ASEAN concerning its proper relations with the major Pacific powers. "Many fear that the more advanced Pacific partners would probably overwhelm ASEAN and that Pacific cooperation will dilute the unity of ASEAN" (Lee Jay Cho, "ASEAN; The Challenges Ahead," in Martin, ed., *The ASEAN Success Story*, 216).

27. The Soviet Union has expressed an interest in becoming one of ASEAN's "dialogue partners." This is an unlikely possibility in the foreseeable future; but it is an intriguing one. See Donald S. Zagoria, "Soviet Policy in East Asia: A New Beginning," *Foreign Affairs* 68, no. 1 (1989), "America and the World 1988/89," 130.

28. For further information on the relations of ASEAN countries, and ASEAN, with ASEAN's "dialogue partners," and on the roles of the major external powers in Southeast Asia, see Jun Nishikawa, *ASEAN and the United Nations System* (New York: United Nations Institute for Training and Research, 1983), Regional Study No. 9; Simon, *The ASEAN States and Regional Security;* Jackson, Paribatra, and Djiwandono, eds., *ASEAN in Regional and Global Context;* Martin, ed., *The ASEAN Success Story;* Simon, "ASEAN's Strategic Situation in the 1980s"; and K. S. Nathan and M. Pathmanathan, ed., *Trilateralism in Asia: Problems and Prospects in U.S.–Japan–ASEAN Relations* (Honolulu: University of Hawaii Press, 1987). For details regarding the relations of ASEAN countries, and ASEAN, with the European Community, see Robert Hull, "European Community–ASEAN Relations: A Model for International Partnership?" *Asian Affairs* 15, part 1 (February 1984); Malcolm Subhan, "U.S., E.C. Compete for Markets in ASEAN Countries," *Europe*, no. 252 (November/December 1985); and Hu Yongzhen, "EC–ASEAN: Blocs Pledge to Strengthen Ties," *Beijing Review*, 16–22 May 1988.

29. See chapter 2, 41–43. See also David Sneider, "Pacific Rim Nations Strengthen Economic Ties," *Christian Science Monitor*, 6 November 1989, 10–11.

30. See Donald C. McLoud, *System and Process in Southeast Asia: the Evolution of a Region* (Boulder, Colorado: Westview Press, 1986); and Charles E. Morrison, "Progress and Prospects in Foreign Policy Cooperation among the ASEAN Countries," and Agerico O. Lacanlale, "Community Formation in ASEAN's External Relations," in R. P. Anand and Purificacion V. Quisumbing, eds., *ASEAN: Identity, Development & Culture* (Honolulu: East–West Center Press, 1981).

31. "Ironically . . . the security challenges of the 1970s have provided the impetus necessary to transform a moribund economic group into the most dynamic political association in the region's history. . . . ASEAN in the 1980s has become a much more formidable international actor than those who observed it a decade earlier ever predicted." Simon, *The ASEAN States and Regional Security*, 134.

32. See Chan Heng Chee, "ASEAN: Subregional Resilience," chap. 5 in James W. Morley, ed., *Security Interdependence in the Asia–Pacific Region* (Lexington, Mass.: Lexington Books, 1986).

Chapter 5 Regionalism in South Asia: Focus on SAARC

1. "India's population is three times more than the combined population of all the regional states and it is nearly eight times bigger than Bangladesh, the second most populous state. In area, India occupies 72 percent of the total area and is four times larger than Pakistan, the second largest State in the region. In economic development too, especially in industrialization, India is far ahead of other countries. It is known to have virtually 100 percent of the total resources in the region in respect of uranium, iron ore, bauxite, copper, gold, lead, manganese, silver, tungsten, zinc, asbestos and diamonds, and more than 90 percent of the resources in coal, crude petroleum, chromium, magnesite and salt. India's GNP is 78 percent of the total of South Asia" (Ali T. Sheikh, "South Asian Regional Cooperation for Peace and Stability," unpublished paper presented at the International Conference on "South Asian Regional Cooperation: A Socio-Economic Approach to Peace and Stability in South Asia," Dhaka, 14–16 January 1985, 8.)

2. See Eugene Black, "The Indus: A Moral for Nations," *New York Times Magazine,* 11 December 1960.

3. See Linda Feldman, "Bangladesh Asks How to End Floods," *Christian Science Monitor,* 9 September 1988; and Sheila Tefft, "South Asian Tempers Rise as Flood Waters Fall," *Christian Science Monitor,* 28 September 1988.

4. S. D. Muni, "South Asian Association for Regional Cooperation: Evaluation and Prospects," *Internationales Asienforum* 18, nos. 3–4 (November 1987): 239.

5. W. W. Rostow, *The United States and the Regional Organization of Asia and the Pacific, 1965–1985* (Austin, Texas: University of Texas Press, 1986), 131.

6. Muni, "South Asian Association for Regional Cooperation," 242.

7. See Sheikh, "South Asian Regional Cooperation for Peace and Stability," 4–5.

8. Lt. Col. Shah Salahuddin, "Problems and Prospects of SARC as an Organization for Regional Cooperation," unpublished paper presented at the International Conference on "South Asian Regional Cooperation: A Socio-Economic Approach to Peace and Stability in South Asia," Dhaka, 14–16 January 1985, 4.

9. Mizanur Rahman Khan, "SARC and Regionalism in South Asia," unpublished paper presented at the International Conference on "South Asian Regional Cooperation: A Socio-Economic Approach to Peace and Stability in South Asia," Dhaka, 14–16 January 1985, 18.

10. S. D. Muni, "South Asian Association for Regional Cooperation," 242.

11. S. D. Muni, "SAARC as an Approach to Mutual Confidence Building," *SAARC Perspective* 2, no. 4:20 (Kathmandu: SAARC Secretariat, n.d.).

12. Ibid.

13. Tefft, "South Asian Tempers Rise as Flood Waters Fall."

14. Lawrence Ziring, ed., *The Subcontinent in World Politics: India, Its Neighbors, and the Great Powers,* revised edition (New York: Praeger Publishers, 1982), especially chap. 1 (Lawrence Ziring, "South Asian Tangles and Triangles") and chap. 2 (Leo E. Rose, "India and Its Neighbors: Regional Foreign and Security Policies").

15. Mohammed Ayoob, "The Primacy of the Political: South Asian Regional

Cooperation (SARC) in Comparative Perspective," unpublished paper presented at the International Conference on "South Asian Regional Cooperation: A Socio-Economic Approach to Peace and Stability in South Asia," Dhaka, 14–16 January 1985, 13, 14.

16. S. D. Muni, "Geo-Strategic Implications of SARC," in Sridhar Khatri, ed., *Regional Security in South Asia* (Kathmandu: Centre for Nepal and Asian Studies, Tribhuvan University, 1986), 246.

17. Ibid., 250, 252, 257.

18. Quoted in S. D. Muni, "SAARC as an Approach to Mutual Confidence Building," 16.

19. Quoted in Muni, "South Asian Association for Regional Cooperation," 247.

20. *The Times of India*, 1 December 1985.

21. Muni, "South Asian Association for Regional Cooperation," 246.

22. See chapter 4.

23. Muni, "SAARC as an Approach to Mutual Confidence Building," 18, 23–24.

24. Muni, "India and the SAARC," 26.

25. Ibid., 26–27.

26. See "Son and Daughter of Slain Leaders Now in Command," *The Seattle Times,* 29 December 1988.

27. S. D. Muni, "India and the SAARC," *The Journal,* Souvenir Issue (Kathmandu: Nepal Council of World Affairs, December 1987):29.

28. Khan, "SARC and Regionalism in South Asia," 25.

29. Ibid.

30. Quoted in Muni, "South Asian Association for Regional Cooperation," 245. Apparently India had more reservations about this practice than the other South Asian states. These reservations were reflected by Dr. Muni: "There is, however, a risk in taking such consensus positions, that the strong 'north' connections of some of the South Asian countries may influence them and manipulate adoption of such positions which may be in the larger interests of the developed countries and not of the South Asian countries." Ibid.

31. Ibid., 249, 251.

32. W. W. Rostow, *The United States and the Regional Organization of Asia and the Pacific, 1965–1985* (Austin, Texas: University of Texas Press, 1986), 139.

33. Muni, "SAARC as an Approach to Mutual Confidence Building," 22.

34. Ibid., 22, 23.

35. Muni, "South Asian Association for Regional Cooperation," 237.

Chapter 6 Regionalism in the Southwest Pacific and Oceania: Focus on the South Pacific Forum

1. This paper is reprinted as Appendix 7 in "Developments in the South Pacific Region," Hearings before the Subcommittee on Asian and Pacific Affairs of the Committee on Foreign Affairs, U.S. House of Representatives, 99th Cong., 2d sess., 10

September 1986 (Washington, D.C.: U.S. Government Printing Office, 1987), 250–73. Hereafter cited as "Developments in the South Pacific."

2. Ibid., 255.

3. These figures are taken from *The 1988 Information Please Almanac* (Boston: Houghton Mifflin Company, 1988). See also the latest issues of *Pacific Islands Yearbook* (Sydney: Pacific Publications).

4. Frederica M. Bunge and Melinda W. Cooke, eds., *Oceania: A Regional Study*, 2d ed. (Washington, D.C.: The American University, 1984), 470. The United States "conducted numerous aboveground, underground, and underseas test explosions in the Central Pacific after World War II, but all such tests were suspended in 1962."

5. David Clark Scott, "Increasingly Volatile S. Pacific Troubled by Nationalism and Unfulfilled Hopes," *Christian Science Monitor*, 2 August 1988.

6. Peter O'Loughlin, "Fiji Still Sailing Troubled Waters," *The Seattle Times*, 15 May 1988.

7. David Clark Scott, "French to Vote on New Caledonia Peace Plan," *Christian Science Monitor*, 5 November 1988. For a summary of the results of the vote in France on 6 November 1988, see *The Americana Annual 1989* (Danbury, Conn.: Grolier Incorporated, 1989), 241.

8. *Pacific Islands* (January 1988), 13–15; David Clark Scott, "Coup Attempt in S. Pacific Nation," *Christian Science Monitor*, 12 December 1988.

9. See section on "Second Wave of Leadership" in paper by Robert Kiste, "Economic Security Issues in the South Pacific," in "Developments in the South Pacific," 269–70.

10. See "Approving the Compact of Free Association Between the U.S., the Marshall Islands, and the Federated States of Micronesia," Hearings before the Subcommittee on Human Rights and International Organizations, Committee on Foreign Affairs, U.S. House of Representatives, 98th Cong., 1st sess., 23–24 April, 2, 14, and 15 May 1985 (Washington, D.C.: U.S. Government Printing Office, 1985).

11. See Shelby Scates, "Trouble in Palau Paradise, Nuclear Arms Not Welcome," *The Seattle Times*, 5 April 1988.

12. See Norman MacQueen, "Papua New Guinea's Relations with Indonesia and Australia: Diplomacy on the Asia–Pacific Interface," *Asian Survey* 29, no. 5 (May 1989).

13. See table 4, "1986 Trade Flows of Selected Pacific Island Nations," in prepared statement of Charles W. Greenleaf, Jr., in "Developments in the South Pacific," 117.

14. "The ANZUS Alliance," *Gist*, April 1987 (Bureau of Public Affairs, U.S. Department of State).

15. See Norman D. Palmer, *Westward Watch: The United States and the Changing Western Pacific* (Washington, D.C.: Pergamon-Brassey's International Defense Publishers, 1987), 138–43.

16. Colin James, "Adrift from Anzus," *Far Eastern Economic Review*, 28 August 1986. See also Henry S. Albinski, *ANZUS, the United States and Pacific Security*, Asian Agenda Report 17 (Lanham, Maryland: University Press of America, 1987).

17. Quoted in "New Zealand Takes on the United States," *Time*, 8 May 1989, 45.

18. For basic information about these organizations, see *South Pacific Handbook*, 3d ed. (Chico, Calif.: Moon Publications, 1986); *South Pacific Bulletin* (published by the South Pacific Commission); Bunge and Cooke, eds., *Oceania;* and Michael Haas, *The Pacific Way: Regional Cooperation in the South Pacific* (New York: Praeger Publications, 1989).

19. Bunge and Cooke, eds., *Oceania*, 503. See also T. R. Smith, *The South Pacific Commission: an Analysis after Twenty-Five Years* (Wellington, N.Z.: Price Milburn, for the New Zealand Institute of International Affairs, 1972).

20. *Fodor's Australia, New Zealand and the South Pacific 1988* (New York: Fodor's Travel Publications, 1987), 556.

21. Bunge and Cooke, eds., *Oceania*, 48.

22. Ibid., 46.

23. For an excellent explanation and analysis of "the Pacific Way" see Haas, *The Pacific Way.*

24. Chapter 8 in *The Pacific Way* is a particularly informative discussion of the South Pacific Forum.

25. See Peter Van Ness and Carolyn M. Stephenson, "A Nuclear-Free South Pacific," *The Nation*, 23 Nov. 1985.

26. Kiste, "Economic Security Issues in the South Pacific," appendix 7 in "Developments in the South Pacific," 266.

27. David Clark Scott, "Shoring up Regional Interests in South Pacific," *Christian Science Monitor*, 22 September 1988.

28. Statement of Peter Watson, in "Developments in the South Pacific," 12.

29. See statement by James P. Walsh, Counsel, American Tunaboat Association, in "Developments in the South Pacific," 43–57.

30. Scott, "Shoring up Regional Interests in South Pacific."

31. David Clark Scott, "Ban on 'Walls of Death' Gaining," *Christian Science Monitor*, 21 July 1989.

32. "The low-lying atolls scattered over the Pacific would be among the first to disappear if, as scientists predict, the world's oceans rise as a result of a warming trend caused by gases in the atmosphere trapping heat at the Earth's surface" (David Stamp, "Kiribati, Pacific Nation, Is Doomed If Sea Rises," *The Seattle Times*, 30 July 1989). "As many as 500,000 'greenhouse' refugees could result from the Pacific and Indian Ocean islands made uninhabitable" (Scott, "Shoring up Regional Interests in South Pacific").

33. See David Clark Scott, "South Pacific Expanding Ties: Region Attracts Global Interest," *Christian Science Monitor*, 28 July 1989.

34. Haas, *The Pacific Way*, 128.

35. For a list of other South Pacific regional organizations, see *The Pacific Way*, table 1.2, 14.

36. Ibid., 126.

37. An example of the surprising amount of international involvement of the nations of Oceania is provided by the following summary of Vanuatu's "international cooperation": "A member of the Commonwealth of Nations, Vanuatu joined the

UN on 15 September 1981 and participates in FAO, IBRD, ICAO, IDA, IFC, IMF, and WHO. It also belongs to the Asian Development Bank (which opened a regional office in Port-Vila in 1984), the French Community, G-77, and various regional Pacific bodies. Vanuatu has taken an active role in Pacific affairs, campaigning for a nuclear-free zone and advocating independence for New Caledonia. Vanuatu has established diplomatic relations with a number of OECD countries, as well as China, Cuba, Viet-Nam, Libya, and the USSR." *Worldmark Encyclopedia of the Nations,* 7th ed. (New York: Worldmark Press, 1988), 3:406.

38. Possibly Fiji should no longer be listed as a member of the Commonwealth. The military coup in May 1987 and the proclamation of the Republic of Fiji in October 1987 led Queen Elizabeth to issue a statement of the ending of Fiji's tie with the British Crown, and the Commonwealth Summit in Vancouver a few weeks later released an announcement that Fiji's membership in the Commonwealth had "lapsed."

39. "A key ASEAN member, Indonesia, is likely to be added to the dialogue meeting guest list next year" (Scott, "South Pacific Expanding Ties").

Chapter 7 Interregional and International Cooperation: A Growing Trend

1. "When Ideology Bows to Economics," *U.S. News & World Report,* 6 February 1989, 30.

2. See the discussion of ASEAN in chapter 5.

3. Peter Drysdale, "The Pacific Basin and Its Economic Vitality," in James W. Morley, ed., *The Pacific Basin: New Challenges for the United States* (New York: The Academy of Political Science, 1986), 12.

4. "When Ideology Bows to Economics," 31.

5. These figures are from the International Monetary Fund, *Direction of Trade Statistics Yearbook 1987,* table A–7, "Bilateral Trade Balances of Trilateral Countries with East Asian Developing Countries, 1980, 1983, and 1986," in Richard C. Holbrooke, Roderick Mac Farquhar, and Kazuo Nukazawa, *East Asia in Transition: Challenges for the Trilateral Countries,* a report to the Trilateral Commission (New York: The Trilateral Commission, 1988), The Triangle Papers: 35, 69.

6. "When Ideology Bows to Economics," 31.

7. Ibid.

8. These figures are taken from table A–8, "Direct Foreign Investment in Developing East Asia, 1986," in Holbrooke, MacFarquhar, and Nukazawa, *East Asia in Transition,* 70. The sources for the data in this table are JETRO, *Sekai to Nihon no Kaigai Chokusetsu Toshi* (Direct Foreign Investment of the World and Japan), 1987 and 1988; Taiwan Kenkyu-jo, *Taiwan Soran* (Taiwan Survey), 1987.

9. "When Ideology Bows to Economics," 30–31.

10. Based on table A–9, "Total Net ODA from Trilateral Countries and Australia to East Asian Developing Countries, 1980 and 1986," in Holbrooke, MacFarquhar, and Nukazawa, *East Asia in Transition,* 71. The figures in this table were taken from OECD, *Geographical Distribution of Financial Flows to Developing Countries, 1983–86* (Paris, 1988).

11. "When Ideology Bows to Economics," 31.

12. Evelyn Colbert, "Regional Cooperation and the Tilt to the West," in Morley, ed., *The Pacific Basin,* 53.

13. Professor Scalapino used the term "East Asia" to embrace Southeast Asia as well as Northeast Asia. His observations could also be extended to the other two subregions of Asia and the Pacific, although "the process of Asianization" is less apparent and less extensive in these subregions than in East and Southeast Asia.

14. Robert A. Scalapino, "Key Strategic Issues in Northeast Asia," a paper prepared for a workshop on "Opportunities and Constraints in Asian Regional Cooperation," held in Tokyo in August 1987; quoted in Colbert, "Regional Cooperation and the Tilt to the West," 46–47.

15. Robert A. Scalapino, "The Uncertain Future: Asian Pacific Relations in Trouble," chap. 1 in Charles E. Morrison, ed., *Threats to Security in East Asia–Pacific: National and Regional Perspectives* (Lexington, Mass.: Lexington Books, 1983), 3–4.

16. Holbrooke, MacFarquhar, and Nukazawa, *East Asia in Transition,* 36.

17. See "Participation of Countries of Asia and the Pacific in International Organizations (1960–1982)," in *Yearbook of International Organizations 1988/89* (Brussels: Union of International Associations, 1988), vol. 2, table 3.

18. Walter S. Mossberg and Robert S. Greenberger, "Baker Calls for 'Pan-Pacific' Alliance Linking U.S., Japan and Other Nations," *Wall Street Journal,* 27 June 1989.

19. These figures are taken from table A–14, "University Students Abroad in Trilateral Countries and Australia," in Holbrooke, MacFarquhar, and Nukazawa, *East Asia in Transition,* 76.

20. Institute of International Education, *Open Doors 1989.* These figures are reported in "52% of Foreign Students Enrolled in U.S. Colleges Are Asians," *International Herald Tribune,* 16 November 1989.

21. See chapter 2.

22. Saburo Okita, "Pacific Development and Its Implications for the World Economy," in Morley, ed., *The Pacific Basin,* 33–34.

23. Ibid., 33.

Chapter 8 Interregional Organizations: Six Major Examples, with Focus on PECC

1. See James W. Morley, "The Genesis of the Pacific Basin Movement and Japan," chap. 1 in Roy Kim and HIlary Conroy, eds., *New Tides in the Pacific: Pacific Basin Cooperation and the Big Four (Japan, PRC, USA, USSR)* (New York: Greenwood Press, 1987), 13; and Kiyoshi Kojima, "A Pacific Free Trade Area Proposed," *Pacific Community* 2, no. 4 (July 1971).

2. "Brief History of PECC—From Canberra to Osaka," a report to the sixth International General Meeting of the Pacific Economic Cooperation Conference (PECC), held in Osaka in 1988, 1.

3. Peter Drysdale, *The Pacific Trade and Development Conference: A Brief*

History (Canberra: Australia–Japan Research Centre, Research School of Pacific Studies, Australian National University, 1984), Research Paper No. 112, Appendix C, 12–13; and *Pacific Trade and Development Conference Newsletter,* no. 1 (August 1985), no. 2 (March 1986), no. 3 (July 1987), and no. 4 (May 1988).

4. Drysdale, *The Pacific Trade and Development Conference: A Brief History.*

5. Ibid., 3, 6.

6. Ibid., 5.

7. Congressional Research Service, Library of Congress, *An Asian–Pacific Regional Economic Organization: An Exploratory Concept Paper,* prepared for Committee on Foreign Relations, United States Senate (Washington, D.C.: U.S. Government Printing Office, 1979).

8. Morley, "The Genesis of the Pacific Basin Movement and Japan," 18.

9. Letter to the author, dtd. 25 July 1989.

10. "The conference theme . . . reflected both Australia's achievements in the bicentennial year and the challenge facing the Pacific in the coming century." "Beyond 200—Towards 2000: Succeeding in a Changing World," Pacific Basin Economic Council, Twenty-first Annual International General Meeting, Sydney, Australia, 23–25 May 1988, Executive Summary, 1.

11. "Conference Agenda," ibid., 2–3.

12. "Conference Statement," ibid., 4–5.

13. Summary of a report of the Special Committee on Pacific Economic Cooperation, presented at the Sydney general meeting, in ibid., 7.

14. "Policy Issue Positions Directed to the U.S. Government," United States Member Committee Position Paper, Pacific Basin Economic Council, 21 May 1989, 6.

15. Morley, "The Genesis of the Pacific Basin Movement and Japan," 17.

16. Letter to the author, dtd. 25 July 1989.

17. Daniel Sneider, "Thriving Pacific Rim Nations Organize for Economic Cooperation," *Christian Science Monitor,* 23 May 1988.

18. Morley, "The Genesis of the Pacific Basin Movement and Japan," 20.

19. "PECC: History and Institutional Arrangements," in Report of PECC–V, held in Vancouver in 1986, 154.

20. Ibid.

21. "Highlights: Pacific Cooperation Conference, Bangkok," *Pacific Community Newsletter* 2, no. 2 (Summer 1982): 5–6.

22. Quoted in ibid., 5.

23. Quoted in ibid., 5.

24. "Highlights: Pacific Cooperation Conference, Bali," *Pacific Community Newsletter* 3, no. 4 (Winter 1983/1984):3.

25. "PECC: History and Institutional Arrangements," 156.

26. "Vancouver Statement on Pacific Economic Cooperation," in report of the PECC–V, Vancouver, 1986, 30.

27. "Osaka Conference Debates GATT Round, Sets New Initiatives," *Pacific Economic Cooperation* (a newsletter of the United States National Committee for Pacific Economic Cooperation) 4, no. 2 (Summer 1988):1–2.

28. For detailed information on the organization and activities of ESCAP, see

the issues of the main publication of this organization, the *Economic and Social Survey of Asia and the Pacific*. Also useful are the issues of *ESCAP: Social Development Newsletter*.

29. See *Economic and Social Survey of Asia and the Pacific*, 1986, part 2: "Human Resources Development."

30. See Asian Development Bank, Annual Report 1988; and "Asian Development Bank," a special supplement, *The Korea Times*, 30 April 1989.

31. For accounts of the ADB meeting, see *The Korea Times*, 2, 3, 4, 7, and 9 May 1989.

32. Claudia Rosett, "Soviets Bank on Asian Development," *Wall Street Journal*, 9 May 1989.

33. "Asian Development Bank," a special supplement, *The Korea Times*, 30 April 1989.

34. See *The Korea Times*, 2, 3, 4, 7, and 9 May 1989.

35. "ADB to Pursue New Directions in Next Decade," *The Korea Times*, 9 May 1989.

36. See Sir Percy Spender, *Exercises in Diplomacy* (New York: New York University Press, 1969), part 2:193–282. This is a detailed account of the origins and early days of the Colombo Plan. See also Norman D. Palmer and Howard C. Perkins, *International Relations: The World Community in Transition*, 3d ed. (Boston: Houghton Mifflin Company, 1969), 590–91.

37. "Presidentship of Colombo Plan Council," *India News* 28, no. 7 (July 1989):8.

38. M. Mark Earle, Jr., and Eric A. Trigg, "Pacific Economic Cooperation and an Overview of the Canberra Process," *PBEC Papers 1985*, 3–4.

39. Ibid., 12–14.

40. Thanat Khoman, "Pacific Interdependence: Development of the Pacific Economic Cooperation Concept," address delivered to the Fifteenth General Meeting of the Pacific Basin Economic Council, Nagoya, 11 May 1982. Quoted in "Highlights: Pacific Cooperation Conference, Bangkok," 7.

41. Earle and Trigg, "Pacific Economic Cooperation and an Overview of the Canberra Process," 15.

Chapter 9 The Superpowers and Asia–Pacific Security

1. See Norman D. Palmer, *Westward Watch: The United States and the Changing Western Pacific* (Washington, D.C.: Pergamon-Brassey's International Defense Publishers, 1987), chap. 3, "The United States and the Soviet Union in the Western Pacific."

2. "As the U.S. Joint Chiefs of Staff asserted in their FY82 *Military Posture Statement*, 'the Asia–Pacific region constitutes part of an interlocking system of strategic zones ranging from North America and Western Europe to Southeast Asia and Northeast Asia. . . . [I]t is no longer practical to design autonomous regional strategies, for a threat to one strategic zone will almost certainly have a serious impact

on the security of others." William T. Tow and William R. Feeney, eds., *U.S. Foreign Policy and Asian–Pacific Security: A Transregional Approach* (Boulder, Colorado: Westview Press, 1982), 3.

3. Mohammad Ayub Khan, *Friends Not Masters: A Political Biography* (London: Oxford University Press, 1967).

4. The text of the Taiwan Relations Act may be found in Richard H. Solomon, ed., *The China Factor: Sino–American Relations and the Global Scene* (Englewood Cliffs, N.J.: Prentice-Hall, 1981), Appendix 4, 304–14.

5. Michael Haas, "Alliance," in Erwin Laszlo and Jong Youl Yoo, eds., *World Encyclopedia of Peace* (Oxford: Pergamon Press, 1986), 1:10.

6. See Henry S. Albinski, *ANZUS, the United States & Pacific Security* (New York: The Asia Society, 1987), Asian Agenda Reports No. 17; and Alan Burnett, *The ANZUS Triangle* (Canberra: Strategic and Defence Studies Centre, Australian National University, 1988).

7. Palmer, *Westward Watch,* 134, 139.

8. See "New Zealand Takes on the United States," *Time,* 8 May 1989, 45.

9. Robert A. Scalapino, *Major Power Reltaions in Northeast Asia* (Lanham, MD: University Press of America, 1987), xiv, 68.

10. See John J. Stephan and V. P. Chichkanov, eds., *Soviet–American Horizons on the Pacific* (Honolulu: University of Hawaii Press, 1986).

11. See chapter 7.

12. See chapter 8.

13. Ibid.

14. See chapter 4.

15. This generalization would seem to be valid for the governments of most Asia–Pacific countries, although it would not be difficult to find many statements by official spokesmen that suggest a different position. Opposition to foreign military bases seems to be growing, even in official circles. In October 1989, for example, representatives of the member nations of ASEAN called for "the early removal of foreign military bases from the Asia–Pacific region." They are obviously particularly concerned about the U.S. bases in the Philippines and the Soviet bases in Vietnam. "The Philippines is the lone member of the six-nation ASEAN that hosts foreign bases, regarded as an obstacle to the ASEAN goal of eventually making the region a so-called Zone of Peace, Freedom and Neutrality. . . . Vietnam is not a member of ASEAN." "Asians Seek Removel of Foreign Bases," dispatch from Manila, *The Seattle Times,* 24 August 1989. All of the governments of the Southwest Pacific and Oceania are on record, through the South Pacific Forum, in support of a nuclear free zone in their region. In unofficial circles in most Asia–Pacific countries, including all of the countries allied with the United States, demands for the complete withdrawal of foreign military forces are frequently voiced.

16. "China Resents U.S. Sanctions, American Told," dispatch from Beijing, *The Seattle Times,* 24 August 1989. This complaint was made by Wang Zhen, vice president of the People's Republic of China, to Anna Chennault, widow of General Chennault of World War II fame, "a prominent Republican" who went to Beijing "on what some believe to be a mission for President Bush."

17. See this chapter, 172.

18. A good summary of this conference was given in *World Affairs Report* 19, no. 1 (the journal of the California Institute of International Studies, Stanford, California).

19. Gaston Sigur and Richard Armitage, "To Play in Asia, Moscow Has to Pay," *New York Times,* 2 October 1988.

20. See Stephan and Chichkanov, eds., *Soviet–American Horizons on the Pacific.*

21. Valéry Giscard d'Estaing, Yasuhiro Nakasone, and Henry A. Kissinger, "East–West Relations," *Foreign Affairs* 68, no. 3 (Summer 1989):16. "This article is adapted from a report to the Trilateral Commission, to be published as Triangle Paper No. 36." Ibid., 1.

22. Many of these proposals were advanced in his speeches in Vladivostok in July 1986 and in Krasnoyarsk in September 1988. See this chapter, 170–172.

23. See chapter 8.

24. "A New Pacific Partnership: Framework for the Future," address by Secretary of State James Baker to the Asia Society, New York, June 26, 1989; *Current Policy* No. 1185, Bureau of Public Affairs, U.S. Department of State.

25. The text of this address was made available by the Novosti Press Agency in Moscow, immediately after it was delivered. The three topics that were listed on the front cover of the Novosti pamphlet were "Vladivostok Is Awarded the Order of Merit," "A New Stage in the Development of the Soviet Far East," and "Peace and Security for the Asian Pacific Region."

26. Ibid.

27. Official Tass news agency report; quoted in Duan Pin, "Soviet Union: Gorbachev in the Limelight Again," *Beijing Review* 3, no. 41, 10–16 October, 1988, 14.

28. Claudia Rosett, "Mr. Gorbachev Can't Fool Asia, Even Some of the Time," *The Wall Street Journal,* 21 September 1988.

29. "Mr. Gorbachev's Asian Serenade," editorial, *New York Times,* 24 September 1988.

Chapter 10 The New Asia–Pacific Regionalism in Perspective

1. See Karl W. Deutsch, et al., *Political Community in the North Atlantic Area* (Princeton: Princeton University Press, 1957); Karl W. Deutsch, *Political Community at the International Level—Problems of Definition and Measurement* (New York: Doubleday, 1954); and Ernst Haas, *The Uniting of Europe* (Stanford: Stanford University Press, 1958).

2. See Philip E. Jacob and Joseph V. Toscano, eds., *The Integration of Political Communities* (Philadelphia: Lippincott, 1964).

3. See "Toward Real Community?," *Time,* 18 April 1988; Stanley Hoffmann, "The European Community," and Giovanni Agnelli, "The Europe of 1992," *Foreign Affairs* 68, no. 4 (Fall 1989). The steps leading to the formation of a single market in the European Community in December 1992 are chronicled in some detail in the

issues of *Europe: A Magazine of the European Community,* published by the Delegation of the Commission of the European Communities, Washington, D.C.

4. The U.S.–Canada Free Trade Agreement was signed by President Reagan and Prime Minister Mulroney on 2 January 1988. It entered into effect on 1 January 1989. For a summary of its provisions, see "U.S.–Canada Free Trade Agreement" (Washington, D.C.: Bureau of Public Affairs, U.S. Department of State, June 1988).

5. "Trade Pact with Canada Not the Boom or Bust Predicted," *The Seattle Times,* 9 June 1989.

6. In March 1988 Richard H. Solomon, then director of the Policy Planning Staff in the U.S. Department of State, and later assistant secretary of state for Asian and Pacific Affairs in the Bush administration, described the Pacific area as "a dynamic region that increasingly rivals Europe in world affairs." "Pacific Development and the New Internationalism," address by Richard H. Solomon before the Pacific Future Conference, Los Angeles, 15 March 1988; *Current Policy* No. 1060, Bureau of Public Affairs, U.S. Department of State (March 1988), 1.

7. For brief descriptions of scores of these associations, see *Yearbook of International Organizations 1988/89* (Brussels: Union of International Associations, 1988).

8. See chapters 4, 5, 6, and 8.

9. See *Yearbook of International Organizations 1988/89,* vol. 2, table 3, "Country Participation in International Organizations (1960–1982). See above, p. 128, table entitled "Participation of Countries of Asia and the Pacific in International Organizations (1960–1982)."

10. In regard to the international economy, the East Asian states are adherents not of international liberalism but of international mercantilism." James R. Kurth, "The Pacific Basin Versus the Atlantic Alliance: Two Pardigms of International Relations," *The Annals* of the American Academy of Political and Social Science 505 (September 1989):34.

11. See Jeffrey Garten, "Trading Blocs and the Evolving World Economy," *Current History* 88, no. 534 (January 1989); and John Yemma, "Trade Blocs Push to the Fore," *Christian Science Monitor,* 4 January 1989.

12. Solomon, "Pacific Development and the New Internationalism," 2.

13. Ibid., 1.

14. Takashi Inoguchi, "Shaping and Sharing Pacific Dynamism," *The Annals* of the American Academy of Political and Social Science 505 (September 1989):48, 49–50.

15. Robert A. Scalapino, *Major Power Relations in Northeast Asia* (Lanham, Maryland: University Press of America, 1987), xiv, 68.

16. Robert A. Scalapino, "Regionalism in the Pacific: Prospects and Problems for the Pacific Basin," *The Atlantic Community Quarterly* 26, no. 2 (Summer 1988):172.

17. Hadi Soesastro, "ASEAN and the Political Economy of Pacific Cooperation," *Asian Survey* 23, no. 12 (December 1983):1269.

18. Peter Drysdale, "The Proposal for an Organization for Pacific Trade and Development Revisited," *Asian Survey* 23, no. 12 (December 1983):1298–99.

19. Scalapino, "Regionalism in the Pacific," 177–78.

20. Donald J. Puchala and Raymond F. Hopkins, "International Regimes: Lessons from Inductive Analysis," in Stephen D. Krasner, ed., *International Regimes* (Ithaca, N.Y.: Cornell University Press, 1983), 88.

21. Arthur A. Stein, "Coordination and Collaboration: Regimes in an Anarchic World," in Krasner, *International Regimes,* 133, 134–35.

22. Puchala and Hopkins, "International Regimes: Lessons from Inductive Analysis," 62, 63.

23. Quoted in "Exploiting the Pacific Tide," *Far Eastern Economic Review,* 21 December 1979.

24. "The Pacific Community: Hands Across the Sea," *Far Eastern Economic Review,* 29 February 1980.

25. Michael Haas, *The Pacific Way: Regional Cooperation in the South Pacific* (New York: Praeger Publishers, 1989), 167, 169. See also Michael Haas, *The Asian Way to Peace: A Story of Regional Cooperation* (New York: Praeger Publishers, 1989).

26. Peter A. Gourevitch, "The Pacific Rim: Current Debates," *The Annals* of the American Academy of Political and Social Science 505 (September 1989):22–23.

Index

About the Author

Norman D. Palmer is professor emeritus of political science, University of Pennsylvania. A native of Maine, he has degrees from Colby College (B.A. and honorary L.H.D.) and Yale University (M.A. and Ph.D.). A member of the faculty of the University of Pennsylvania for thirty-five years, he served as chairman of the political science department and the international relations graduate program. He has taught at several other universities in the United States and abroad. He is a former national president of the International Studies Association. During World War II he was a naval air combat intelligence officer, with service in the Pacific combat theater. Since then he has visited Asia frequently, sometimes for extended periods. He is the author or co-author of more than twenty-five books, including *The United States and India: The Dimensions of Influence* (New York: Praeger Publications, 1984), and *Westward Watch: The United States and the Changing Western Pacific* (Washington, D.C.: Pergamon-Brassey's International Defense Publishers, 1987), and *New Tides in the Pacific: Pacific Basin Cooperation and the Big Four (Japan, PRC, USA, USSR)* (New York: Greenwood Press, 1987).